The Political Pulpit Revisited

The Political Pulpit Revisited

By Roderick P. Hart and John L. Pauley II

Purdue University Press / West Lafayette, Indiana

Printed in the United States of America

Library of Congress Cataloging-in-Publication Data

The political pulpit revisited / [edited by] Roderick P. Hart
and John L. Pauley II.
    p. cm.
 Rev. ed. of: Political pulpit. 1977.
 Previous edition entered under Hart, Roderick P.
Includes bibliographical references and index.
 ISBN 1-55753-365-2 (pbk.)
 1. Church and state--United States. 2. United States--Religion--1945-I. Hart,
Roderick P. Political pulpit. II. Hart, Roderick P. III. Pauley, John Lester, 1951- IV.
Hart, Roderick P. Political pulpit.
 BR517.H37 2004
 322'.1'0973--dc22
                                2004002502

Contents

Acknowledgments

The first edition of this book was dedicated to three extraordinary teachers who shaped the character of the first author's thoughts as well as the length of his horizon. James Clarke, Jay Savereid, and Carroll Arnold encouraged him to think and then did not jump back in horror when he attempted to do so.

Particularly helpful to the first author when writing the first edition of *The Political Pulpit* were Professors Richard Gregg of Pennsylvania State University, Professor Conrad Cherry of Indiana-Purdue University at Indianapolis, Professor Lawrence Rosenfield of the University of New Hampshire, Professor Charles Stewart of Purdue University, and Professor Kathleen Jamieson of the University of Pennsylvania, a former colleague of the first author and a mentor to the second author. What problems still persist in the book remain our fault, not theirs.

Also blameless are Professors Carol Jablonski, Michael Hyde, and James Walsh, who assisted the first author in matters both practical and theoretical. In addition, we are flattered that the eight scholars who contributed to Unit III of this edition did so with vigor and seriousness. Their love of ideas and their willingness to wrestle with complex—and consequential—issues is laudatory. We also thank Professor Edward Lamoureux for having encouraged their re-analysis of *The Political Pulpit* and the Executive Council of the Religious Communication Association for giving us reprint rights. Finally, we thank Diana Cable and Jan Terrell for clerical assistance provided many years ago and Melissa Huebsch and Kristie Kenney for help supplied more recently.

Roderick P. Hart—*Austin, Texas*
John L. Pauley II—*South Bend, Indiana*

Unit 1

The Issues at Hand

Chapter 1

American Politics and the Problem of Religion

The theme of this book is contained in the title of this chapter. No matter how consoling religion might be for individual Americans, no matter how reliably it soothes souls and comforts the afflicted, no matter how integral religious organizations are to the nation's small towns and inner cities, religion is also a problem in the United States. It has always been a problem in the United States. The nation was founded by persons who had been persecuted for their religion elsewhere or who had been made to feel devalued because of their faith. So they came to the United States and brought their religions with them. In addition, they brought their prejudices and intolerances and that caused problems too. But except for the earliest years of the Founding, they left something behind in Europe—the idea of a church-state. Americans have never really been secularists but they have generally resisted doing politics in church. Instead, they have worried constantly about religion and their worrying has been their salvation, perhaps even their glory, as a people.

Some Traditional Concerns

The United States is hardly an irreligious place. Recent studies show that 63% of Americans claim some sort of religious affiliation and that virtually all Americans profess belief in a higher power. By the dawn of the twenty-first century, Americans had arranged themselves into some 2,000 different religious denominations and some 300,000 individual congregations. 76.5% of American adults call themselves Christian (52% Protestant, 24.5% Catholic), but Buddhists, Hindus, and followers of Islam have also been part of a growth industry.[1] Americans are also intense about religious matters. According to one recent study, more than half of those surveyed in the U.S. (53 percent) said that religion was "very important" to them, a view expressed by only 16 percent of U.K. respondents and 13 percent of those interviewed in France and Germany.[1] Americans also act on their religious beliefs. Compared to Australians, for example, 38.4% of American men and 47.4% of American women attend church weekly (or more often), while the figures for Australia are only 22.1% for men and 29.4% for women.[2]

Despite this high level of religiosity—or perhaps because of it—Americans have also worried about mixing politics and religion. Even the staunchly devout Baptists, for example, have treasured the First Amendment because it insured that no *federal* religion would be established in the land, thereby leaving them and their sister denominations to their own devices. The meaning of Thomas Jefferson's famous metaphor—a wall of separation between church and state—has been variously interpreted over the years but its most popular meaning has been to keep religious things religious and political things political and to make them as separate as possible.

Mais non! shout a thousand activists. Entire libraries can be stocked with books and pamphlets decrying this so-called separation of church and state. Indeed, until the middle of the nineteenth century most states in the U.S. had a nominal state religion (some less nominal than others) and a great many of the most successful social movements (including temperance, pacifism, feminism, and civil rights) found their roots in church-related activity. That is, the theory of church-state separation has never really dovetailed with actual practice and that remains true today as well. Recently, for example, George W. Bush announced that he had heard the call. "I believe God wants me to run for president" Mr. Bush declared in the fall of 2000.[3] The Reverend Al Sharpton heard that same call, as had the Reverend Jesse Jackson twenty years before him. As the 2004 election year dawned, the mingling of religion and politics was rampant:

- An Office of Faith-based and Community Initiatives had been established in Washington to help religious charities qualify for federal funding.

- A split opened up between Democrats and Republicans, with heavy church attendees voting Republican by 63% to 37% and with low attendees voting in the opposite direction.[4]

- In 2003, Democratic front-runner Governor Howard Dean raised a ruckus when declaring he was tired of coming to the South and fighting elections on the basis of "race, guns, God and gays" instead of jobs, health insurance, and foreign policy.

- In September of 2003, Chief Justice Roy Moore defied the Alabama Supreme Court by insisting that his monument to the Ten Commandments remain in the judicial building's foyer (the judge ultimately lost the argument as well as his job).

- And even in the starchy environs of Connecticut, Governor John Rowland said he had been in direct contact with God when preparing to face federal charges of inappropriately awarding state contracts to his friends and associates.

God and country separate? In the United States? That has almost never been the case. But a more basic question—the question raised in this book—is a question of method: *How* do church and state relate in the U.S.? As it turns out, that is a complicated question, complicated enough to have launched the first edition of this book some twenty-five years ago. Much has changed since 1977 but this question of method, this question of the *propriety* of church-state relations, still abides.

When the first author wrote the original version of *The Political Pulpit*, the United States was ushering into office a young president from Georgia whose deep religious roots were the talk of the campaign. Mr. Carter was a lay minister, a Sunday school teacher, a rather decent biblical scholar, and one startlingly willing to open himself up to the American people (he once told them he had felt "lust in his heart" on occasion, a disclosure that set many tongues wagging). Southern Baptists, previously a poorly understood and often trivialized denomination, became part of the American mainstream during the Carter presidency.

The 1980s brought the Moral Majority to the fore, a loose collection of conservative Christians led by Jerry Falwell, who lobbied for prayer in the schools (as well as the teaching of creationism) and who opposed the Equal Rights Amendment, homosexual liberties, abortion, and even the SALT treaty. The Moral Majority came to think of Ronald Reagan as their champion, a divorced man who had been spiritually adrift for most of his life but whose politics matched their organizational goals nicely. This decade also saw the arrival of Reverend Pat Robertson, who ran for president, badly, in 1988 but who forced the eventual winner, George Bush, to discuss matters that few Yale Episcopalians feel comfortable discussing in public.

The 1990s brought Bill Clinton to the stage, a person who was eminently comfortable discussing matters of the soul. But Mr. Clinton was also secular enough to attract high-tech America and to broaden the base of the Democratic Party during a period of unprecedented economic growth. And yet it was Mr. Clinton's softer side that got him through a wild succession of special prosecutors, bimbo eruptions, real estate fraud, and an impeachment attempt. African-Americans, especially, responded to his soulful appeals. Magically, it sometimes seemed, Clinton used his spiritual strengths to explain away his spiritual weaknesses. From a God's eye perspective, Jimmy Carter was probably a better man than Bill Clinton, but Clinton made most Americans forget that for eight astonishing years.

This book is a meditation on these intertwinings of God and country. The first edition of *The Political Pulpit* was published in 1977 as Purdue University Press's contribution to the nation's bicentennial. The book offered a novel understanding of church-state relations, arguing that the U.S. had happened upon a unique solution to tensions in this arena. Church and state have signed a "contract," the book argued, a contract that regulates how they relate to one another. The contract specifies the duties of the signatories, outlines the benefits they will garner from the contract, and details what will happen if either party ignored its stipulations. These contractual relationships are played out, the book argued further, in the public square, where all can see what needs to be seen. The mechanism used to regulate these church-state relations is public discourse, rhetoric.

The Political Pulpit observed that politicians and church leaders are required to play out their roles on symbolic grounds and to relate to one another in highly constrained ways. The book specified the formulas to be followed when doing so and shows how faithfully the contract has been honored throughout the nation's history.

Reviewers were comparatively kind to *The Political Pulpit* even though it de-mythologized a highly mythologized set of institutional connections. The book offered a pragmatic, almost mercantile, model of church-state interfaces. As such, it ran counter to the views of many. Strict separationists, for example, decry any system that even tacitly promotes close relations between church and state. On the other end of the continuum, staunch believers can object to the passive, non-interventionistic role accorded religion in the book. Even middle-of-the-roaders can find fault with a rhetorical model that objectifies religion or that sometimes makes patriotism seem a canard.

The Political Pulpit dealt with each of these objections, arguing that the contractual model's great advantage is its efficacy. The book celebrates the fact that the United States has chosen to wage its church-state battles on symbolic grounds, a signal achievement since the casualties of rhetorical war always live to fight another day. The book admits that the contract is imperfect (because politics itself is imperfect) but it also stresses the flexibility afforded when human relationships are negotiated rhetorically. That is, the contract permits close, even intimate associations between church and state but also ensures that those associations will remain extra-legal. This latter codicil makes the contract repugnant to the religious Right but it makes the contract functional and, from a societal perspective, respectful, humane, and protective of the nation's religious diversity.

Subsequent to writing *The Political Pulpit*, the first author busied himself with other projects, one of which introduced him to the second author. The latter recently observed that twenty-five years had passed since the book's publication and that it was time to judge how the contract had fared in the intervening years. Accordingly, he asked eight scholars to do an autopsy of the book, ultimately producing a set of papers published as a special issue of the *Journal of Communication and Religion*. As might be expected, some of these scholars declared the book outmoded while others felt it retained a more rapid pulse. All of these scholars, though, add important insights to the discussion of religion and politics and so their essays are reprinted here as Unit III of this book. Unit II, on the other hand, presents the argument as originally made in 1977. Minor editing has removed the first author's youthful excesses but otherwise *The Political Pulpit* is reproduced here in its entirety. Unit IV of the current volume presents the first author's reactions to the perspectives offered in Unit III.

Some Recent Concerns

Before turning to the details of our argument, however, we must ask if it makes sense to revisit it at all. At the dawn of the new millennium, an age featuring cloned animals, miniaturized medical devices, the perfection of interplanetary travel, and the computerization of everything else, why should we bother ourselves with these hoary matters of God and country, especially when the worlds of pleasure and commerce beckon so enticingly? That is, why should a modern people reflect upon matters of church and state at all? Was not God declared quite dead on the nation's campuses in the 1960s? Did not the Watergate era adequately expose the dangers of facile patriotism? Did not Iran-Contra and Enron prove that conservatives cannot be trusted? Did not Whitewater and Monica Lewinsky do the same for liberals? Has not the rapaciousness of consumerism, the enmities of the Middle East, and the coarseness of popular culture made skeptics of an entire nation?

This is a sad history, but it is not all of American history. Between 1977 and the present, politics and religion have both vexed and delighted one another. Even an abbreviated timeline of the last twenty-five years proves that.

1976— Jimmy Carter is elected president of the United States

1979— Evangelist Jerry Falwell begins his "I Love America" tour; Pope John Paul II visits the U.S. and decries abortion

1980— The Reagan era gives birth to the New Christian Right; a Massachusetts law permitting prayer in public schools is struck down by the state supreme court

1981— "Creation science" goes on trial in Arkansas

1982— Roman Catholic bishops denounce nuclear weaponry; the City Hall crèche in Pawtucket, Rhode Island is outlawed

1983— An ecumenical assortment of clergy members petitions Congress to forbid genetic engineering; after a lapse of 117 years, the U.S. establishes full diplomatic relations with the Vatican

1984— A Constitutional amendment to permit prayer in public schools fails in the U.S. Senate; a New York judge orders medical treatment for a Jehovah Witness' child; Roman Catholic vice-presidential candidate Geraldine Ferraro is attacked by bishops for her pro-choice stance

1985— The U.S. Supreme Court voids a Connecticut law giving workers an absolute right to take their Sabbath day off; Arizona members of the Sanctuary Movement go on trial for illegally sheltering Central American refugees

1986— A survey estimates that 21% of the nation's TV households tune into Christian TV shows for at least six minutes a week

1987— U.S. District Judge Brevard W. Hand of Alabama bans textbooks that promote a "secular humanist" religion; the U.S. Supreme Court decrees that a Louisiana law requiring

> the teaching of creationism is unconstitutional; Reverend Pat Robertson declares his intention to run for president

1988— The Third Circuit Court of Appeals bans an 18-foot menorah in front of the City-Council building in Pittsburgh, Pennsylvania

1990— The U.S. Supreme Court weighs the constitutionality of letting student religious groups meet on public high schools campuses

1992— Americans United for Separation of Church and State file a brief against a New York church that engaged in blatant partisan politicking

1994— Freedom of Access to [Abortion] Clinic Entrances Act is signed into law by President Clinton

1995— Radical Islamic minister Louis Farrakhan hires 11,000 buses to bring attendees to the Million Man March in Washington, D.C.

1997— Ralph Reed leaves the Christian Coalition, an organization he built to include 1.9 million members and a $27 million annual budget; former football coach Bill McCartney oversees Promise Keepers' Rally in Washington, D.C.

1998— Sociologist Robert Wuthnow publishes an 875-page volume entitled *The Encyclopedia of Politics and Religion*; Wisconsin Supreme Court rules the State of Wisconsin can underwrite a school voucher program for private schools

1999— Mayor Rudolph Giuliani pledges to cut $7 million in city funds if the Brooklyn Museum of Art goes ahead with a show depicting the Virgin Mary alongside shellacked clumps of elephant dung

2000— George W. Bush is elected president of the United States

That two such different men as Jimmy Carter and George W. Bush bracket the last quarter of the twentieth century is significant. Both were men of the South and both were—by most reckonings—evangelical Christians. Politically, of course, they could not have been more different but they differed religiously as well, with Carter emphasizing Christianity's social mission (he helped build Habitat for Humanity homes, for example), and George W. Bush embracing a more confessional (and doctrinal) brand of religion. But they jointly serve as bookends for an era that has worried constantly about matters of church and state. Just a random sampling of articles in *Time* magazine, for example, shows how persistent those worries have been. The apocalyptic language used by *Time*'s writers is also noteworthy:

- "Aftershock from a Papal Visit"
- "Caroling Crisis: 1st Noel vs. 1st Amendment"
- "Catholics Take to the Ramparts"
- "Sanctuary without Safety"
- "Harsh Cacophony of Jingle Bells and Legal Jangles"
- "Thunder on the Right: The Growth of Fundamentalism"
- "A Courtroom Clash over Textbooks"
- "Threatening the Wall [of Separation]"
- "Is the Court Hostile to Religion?"
- "Bishops, Politicians, and the Abortion Crisis"
- "The Right Hand of God: Meet Ralph Reed"
- "The Promise Keepers: Should they be Cheered–or Feared?"[5]

Naturally, some of this language can be chalked up to the colorful style expected in any mass-circulation outlet. But Time's rhetoric is also a function of the knotty relationship church and state has had throughout American history. The Political Pulpit argued that that relationship survives, even thrives, because of this tension. To talk about such matters (loudly, brashly, concernedly) rather than to do anything about them is the United States' special solution to its church-state difficulties. The resulting hand-wringing lets politics and religion stay in touch with one another and the mass media's celebration of this hand-wringing keeps their relationship alive and flourishing. Hand-wringing, to be sure, is a distracted sort of action, movement without consequence, but it makes one feel better nonetheless.

The presidency of George W. Bush is a fitting example of all this. Although he led a comparatively dissolute life as a young adult, Mr. Bush credits a conversation with Billy Graham (and his decision to stop drinking alcohol) with turning his life around. More than most politicians, Bush felt comfortable speaking a language of faith. When asked during the 2000 presidential primary who his favorite philosopher was, for example, Bush declared "Christ, because he changed my heart."[6] On inauguration day of 2001, Bush went further than most new presidents when declaring that "Some needs and hurts are so deep they will only respond to a mentor's touch or a pastor's prayer. Church and charity, synagogue and mosque, lend our communities their humanity, and they will have an honored place in our plans and laws."[7] All presidents attend White House prayer breakfasts but few have been as disclosive as Mr. Bush when doing so: "Faith teaches humility. As Laura would say, I could use a dose occasionally. A recognition that we are small in God's universe, yet precious in His sight. It has sustained me in moments of success, and in moments of disappointment. Without it I would be a different person, and without it I doubt I'd be here today."[8]

Remarks like these, of course, are largely ceremonial. More notable were some of Mr. Bush's policy statements. One of the most worrisome was made by Bush ten days after the September 11, 2001 attack on the World Trade Center:

"This crusade, this war on terrorism is going to take a while."[9] A Christian country declaring war on a Muslim nation? On a group of Muslim nations? Was this to be a reprise of events transpiring nine centuries earlier? Mr. Bush's remarks concerned many in the United Sates and in the Middle East as well. At around that same time, he encouraged "employers to permit their workers time off during the lunch hour to attend the noontime services to pray for our land."[10] The line between church and state, between ritual and policy, seemed indistinct to Bush, especially after the extraordinary events of 9/11. And he muddied the waters further when criticizing Congress for not embracing his faith-based initiatives: "We waited for Congress to act. They could not act on the issue. So I just went ahead and signed an executive order which . . . says the federal agencies will not discriminate against faith-based programs. They ought to welcome the armies of compassion as opposed to turning them away."[11]

Many worried that Bush was ushering in a new theocracy. Some scribes even wondered if he intended to turn the federal government into a wholly owned subsidiary of the Religious Right:

> Is President Bush a religious zealot, or does he just pander to that crowd? That, crudely put, is probably the most persistent question I hear about Mr. Bush when I travel outside the country, and it comes up all the time in the less godly American precincts (universities, Bush-hater Web sites, Hollywood, the island of Manhattan). On issues from Saddam to sodomy, the assumption is that Mr. Bush is an evangelist for a moralistic agenda that grows from his born-again Christianity. Or else (the more cynical variation), regardless of what he believes in, he has handed over the presidential portfolio to the preacher polls of the religious right in exchange for their influence as campaign ward heelers."[12]

For other writers, Mr. Bush's religious remarks were permissible politically but wrong-headed hermeneutically:

> President Bush uses religious language more than any president in U.S. history, and some of his key speechwriters come right out of the evangelical community. Sometimes he draws on biblical language, other times old gospel hymns that cause deep resonance among the faithful in his own electoral base. The problem is that the quotes from the Bible and hymnals are too often either taken out of context or, worse yet, employed in ways quite different from their original meaning.[13]

Still other writers claimed that the Bush administration was willing to overturn the historic separation of church and state in the U.S.:

> "Over the past two years, President Bush and his faith-based initiative have repeatedly eroded 200 years of carefully pro-

tected separation between church and state," [Senator Richard] Durbin said, contending that providing government funding to religious groups not only subsidizes employment discrimination with federal dollars, but creates great potential for religious strife. "It appears that what the president wants to achieve with this initiative is to fundamentally change the historic balance in the relationship between government and religion that our founding fathers struck over 200 years ago."[14]

Were these worries justified? Was Mr. Bush the reincarnation of Billy Sunday and Aimee Semple McPherson? Could the nation survive four to eight years of biblical myopia cum political careerism? Should American Jews get themselves to Canada in light of Mr. Bush's second Great Awakening? Would the rapidly growing Islamic community in the U.S. be crushed under the weight of a Christocentric presidency? Could Roman Catholics survive without becoming washed in the blood of Jesus?

Questions like these have been asked—in one way or another—since the nation's founding. They will always be asked—in one way or another—in the nation's future. George W. Bush is only the most recent politician to find himself in the eye of the storm. His successors will find themselves there as well. The ship of state will continue to pitch and roll because religious issues have always confounded a nation expected to be both a shining city on a hill and a diverse, secular society on the cutting edge of modernity.

Religion is America's oldest problem but it is not its only problem. The nation also has too great a land mass to give its people an easy sense of community. The nation has too much economic inequality to make all its citizens feel equally supported. The nation is only one of many nations in the world and that puts both economic and military pressures on it. The nation has only a short history and that makes it harder to build a sense of destiny among its people. The nation is home to a thousand ethnicities, ten thousand professions, a hundred thousand lifestyles. Yes, religion is a problem in the United States but it is not its biggest problem. It has never reached that exalted, or benighted, status in the last several hundred years and it is unlikely to do so in the future.

Conclusion

The argument made in Unit II of this book—*The Political Pulpit*'s original argument—is that the American people are too pragmatic to let religion overwhelm them. They are bound together by a tissue of religion but it is a tissue they find supportive. Americans wishing to live in a completely secular society will object to even this tissue of religion, of course, but many more Americans will choose not to make an issue out of it, hoping that the rhetoric of God and country will bind them together and still keep separate what needs to be kept separate. It takes talent, charm, eloquence, and passion to make this rhetoric function properly but, after two hundred and thirty years, the rules have finally been written. George W. Bush follows them carefully. He, like all presidents, has his own style but the contract preceded him and it will succeed him as well. Mr. Bush is merely a variation on themes long since established. This book explains those themes and delights in their variations.

Unit 2

The Original Argument

Chapter 2

Varieties of Civic Piety in the U.S.

For the jealous viewers in the northern portions of the United States, it appeared to be an ideal evening for a football game. The lights of the stadium burned brightly, as had the southern sun just hours before. The teams, Penn State and L.S.U., were among the best in the nation, a fitting gladiatorial contest with which to terminate another season of college football. The year was just barely 1974, many of the sellout New Year's Day crowd still nursing the bacchanalian wounds suffered the night before. The half-time show was gang-busters.

Seemingly no expense had been spared to provide for home viewers and stadium crowd alike a stirring, emotional half-time extravaganza. The show was all of America on a small scale. The bands marched smartly; the "Stars and Stripes" production number was breathtaking; a clean-cut, young group of singers called the New Directions sang the national anthem with gusto; and the Reverend Bill Bright gave the invocation. The theme of the Reverend Bright's address was a familiar one—that of returning the nation to its proper Christian heritage. To all but the most wary observer, the Orange Bowl game of January 1, 1974, was a proper affirmation of what the then president would call "what's right with America."

The Orange Bowl, of course, is located in Miami, a city known, among other things, for its sizable Jewish population. Some might find it strange that the national head of the Campus Crusade for Christ was selected for such a rhetorical plum in a city known for its opulence and delicatessens. And yet to many there was something terribly appropriate about the affair, something traditional, something American. The fact that few eyebrows were raised at the religious curiosities seemed to attest to this. It was as if sectarian religious impulses had been set aside on this evening in Miami—set aside for football and the national anthem. It was as if, on New Year's Day at least, there was no Jewish or Christian God, only an American God.

In the pages to follow, we will attempt to explain why Reverend Bright's rhetoric was received as it was, why his sermon was viewed as being so typically American, and why such an invocation was opted for at all by the Orange Bowl promoters. We shall point out why, no matter what the radical theologians may contend, God is very much alive in the United States. God dead? In America? No! shouts every American Legion chaplain, every ward-heeler and back-room politico, every country and city parson, every U.S. ambassador to the Vatican, every *Pro Deo Pro Patria* scholarship winner, every star-spangled sermonette . . . and every Bill Bright in every Orange Bowl.

American Civic Piety: Its Prevalence

Presidential Piety

Ever since Robert Bellah directed attention to what he termed (in Rousseauian fashion) the "American civil religion," commentary about his analysis has not abated. While very few scholars have questioned the fact that Bellah isolated a significant phenomenon for analysis, many were antagonistic to (or nonplussed by) one of Bellah's conclusions: that the American civil religion has potentially salutary implications for the people of the United States. Michael Novak, for example, argues that this national faith is jingoistic, too culturally self-conscious, and not conscious enough of its own moral failings.[1] According to Conrad Cherry, other commentators have accused it of being theologically naive, sentimentally pious, and idolatrously chauvinistic.[2] Perhaps the most strident attack has been launched by those who see presidential piety and ecclesiastical fawning as evidence of the meanest sort of political bed-fellowing. As George Gordon notes: "A president is . . . free to take his oath of office *sans* Bible and not to mention of God if he so desires, but none has yet had the nerve, or inclination, or both. More significant, perhaps . . . is the fact that few politicians, no matter how cynical or skeptical of religion they personally are, will end a major political address without a prayer."[3]

Cavil though they might at this civil religion, few Americans have reason to doubt the significance of the phenomenon Bellah discovered. What Bellah saw in presidential inaugurals was noteworthy: every president since the time of Washington publicly requested or acknowledged help from God for the American people. Taken collectively, Bellah argues, such entreaties reflect what the people in the U.S. find to be most important, to be most right, to be most true. An American president thus becomes, according to Novak, "a priest, a prophet, and a king," a prelate who reveres the nation's "holy calendar, its sacred cities and monuments and pilgrimages, its consecrated mounds and fields."[4]

Thus, when an American president is inaugurated, he is also ordained. According to Robert Alley, Harry Truman carried out his duties as high priest of the American civil religion as competently as any other president:

> In all his actions Mr. Truman had a unique way of injecting religion into policy. From the earliest period of his administration he had requested prayer for his office. He was a member of the First Baptist Church of Washington which he attended on occasion, but it is probably stretching the point to say he at-

tended with "unfailing regularity." He did receive the praise of
the religious press when he attended Sunday school in 1947.
In a typical overstatement he was acclaimed for setting a good
example for all citizens to follow.[5]

Why, one might ask, does the press take pains to offer such "overstatements" and why are such overstatements "typical?" The answer to such questions
appears to be "deeply rooted in the American conscience," to borrow a phrase
from the scriptures of the American civil religion.

According to Herberg, there are three central components to the American
Way of life, and these beliefs intertwine to make religious pronouncements by
American presidents mandatory. Such tenets include belief in God, belief in religion, and belief in the three-faith system (Protestant, Catholic, and Jewish).[6] No
American president, it would seem, has the rhetorical option of refusing to pay
sufficient and regular homage to such fundamental aspects of the civil religion or
of not embellishing such themes. Especially in their public rhetoric, American
chief executives must, time and time again, remind themselves and the American
people of their obligations to God, to country, and to God-and-country. As Billy
Graham has remarked, every president has "left the presidency with a very deep
religious faith."[7] Indeed, with Thanksgiving proclamations, Christmas messages,
prayer breakfasts, congressional invocations, convention benedictions, and the
like, such a set of conditions may well have resulted from a rhetorical hangover.

National Piety

The president, of course, is only the central figure in the American civil religion.
All Americans have the possibility (according to some, the obligation) of participating regularly and vocally in the nation's religious ceremonies. During the
1976 bicentennial celebration, for example, Religion in American Life, a national
clearinghouse for religious advertising, spent $25 million on an advertising cam-
paign which focused largely on the First Amendment (which guarantees freedom
of religion).[8] The program resulted in the dissemination of some 4,000 roadside
posters, 3.25 million lines of newspaper print, 98,000 car cards on buses, trains,
and subways, and a campaign in the electronic media which reached (via repeated exposure) some 1.5 billion home viewers.[9] When such a campaign was
coupled with those launched by groups such as the Knights of Columbus, the
Volunteers of America, the Exchange Clubs of America, the American Legion,
the Catholic War Veterans, and literally thousands of similar groups, the 1976
bicentennial celebrations provided a veritable field day for renewed worship in
the American tabernacle of nationhood.

But we would miss the ubiquitous and far-reaching importance of this national
cult were we to focus solely on the grand and unabashedly public means by
which the American civil religion is preached. Take, for example, the case of
Mary Lou Kierswetter, a Munster, Indiana, housewife who possesses bountiful
nationalistic zeal. For a number of years, Ms. Kierswetter directed a campaign to
encourage every person living on U.S. 41 (a highway that traverses eight states and

runs for some three thousand miles) to fly the American flag regularly. When asked to explain the motivations which sustained her during her admittedly arduous campaign, Ms. Kierswetter remarked: "If we didn't keep this great nation free it would be sacrilegious. . . . God gave it to us; it's our responsibility to keep it free as He meant it to be."[10]

Organized religion, too, is an equal partner in the preservation and proclamation of the nation's religious self-understanding. Hardly a day goes by that some religious gathering does not explicitly and forthrightly acknowledge the religious intensity of the American people. In the mid-1970s, every "mainstream" religious denomination in the U.S. planned extensive bicentennial ceremonies in every urban, suburban, and rural nook and cranny. The Interchurch Center even established a separate, New York City-based national headquarters (Project F.O.R.W.A.R.D. '76) for the bicentennial celebration, funded it generously, and charged it with retelling the story of America's peculiar tolerance for religious testimony. As Herbert Schneider has said:

> Religion is a pervasive institution. It gets mixed up with education, medicine, politics, business, art—there is nothing free from its grasp and grasping. All efforts to fence off certain areas of life from which the churches must "keep out" have been as futile as similar efforts to curtail government or science. Anything can be done religiously, and nothing is safe from ecclesiastical concern. Gone are the days when the salvation of the soul was a distinct and separate business. The separation of church and state does not separate religion and politics, any more than the separation of school and theater separates education and art.[11]

Political Piety: Its Immutability

Such civil-religious goings-on are hardly twentieth-century inventions. The linking of God and Caesar is older than the United States itself. Even the novice student of American history is aware of the pains the American people have taken to surround themselves with things divine. Myriad examples of such interlacings abound:

- The Mayflower Compact, authored by forty-one solitary pilgrims in 1620, is replete with numerous references to the Deity.
- Election sermons, popular vehicles for promulgating American independence in the seventeenth century, are viewed by many historians as constituting one of our first attempts at fashioning a "civil religion."
- Fast and Thanksgiving sermons in the eighteenth century can be viewed as ranking "almost on a par with newspapers, pamphlets, and quasi-legal organizations as mainstays of the war of words which preceded and accompanied the American Revolution."[12]

- In the early years of the republic, "the anniversary of independence was a solemn, quasi-religious ceremonial . . . a prayer was spoken, a hymn or ode sung, the Declaration was read, the oration delivered, another hymn or ode was sung, and prayer closed the ritual."[13]
- The public fasts held during the War of 1812 "showed that the religion and politics of Americans were too closely related to be studied separately."[14]
- In 1861 the words "In God We Trust" were added to the nation's coinage, a practice inspired by the Reverend M. R. Watkinson of Ridleyville, Pennsylvania.

Additionally, the U.S. has fashioned a rather spirit-filled national anthem, insisted that their presidents take the oath of office on the Bible, established Capitol prayer rooms, proclaimed national days of prayer, brandished federal banners in churches, and talked, talked, talked . . . of God's special love for America, of America's unique responsibility to God, of a New Israel and a Chosen People, of constantly rededicating oneself to the principles of basic, Christian Americanism, and so on.

According to many observers, the 1950s was an especially curious time in the history of the American civil religion. These were the glory days of Billy Graham, Norman Vincent Peale, Fulton Sheen, anti-Communist crusades, McCarthyism, Korea, and the Cold War. But most important, it was a time when a full 62 percent of the American people professed church membership and when only one of ninety-five senators in the Eighty-third Congress reported no religious affiliation.[15] The 1950s saw, as a result, an unparalleled rhetorical escalation of the American civil religion.

Official Civic Piety: Its Power

Although many commentators have questioned the moral and theological worth of the rhetoric surrounding this national religion, the most devastating attack (with regard to its worth as a viable theoretical construct) has been issued by those who view the quasi-religious remarks of American politicians as mere ceremony, implying that no "real," tangible implications inhere in such pronouncements. "There is legal separation of church and state," such persons argue, "and there are no real punishments inflicted on those who ignore such forms of civic piety nor are there palpable rewards for embracing it."

Existential Influence

The power of civil religion lies in three domains: legal, political, and psychological. For example, the rhetoric of religiously inclined public officials sometimes helps form an indirect sort of legal precedent:

> Government proclamations of days of thanksgiving and occasionally prayer are another illustration of ceremonial acts of

government which are of slight intrinsic significance but are
of great importance in the use to which they are put as precedents to justify far more substantial encroachments of government on religious affairs or religion on government affairs.[16]

Secondly, the American people often use religious criteria when inspecting the
remarks of those who would lead them. As Cohn relates:

That summer [1952], too, many letters came to Springfield, Illinois, denouncing Governor Stevenson as an "atheist." His
offense against God is that he is a Unitarian. . . . As the campaign progressed, another deadly charge was hurled against
him. Letter writers convicted him—naturally without trial—
upon a different ground. It was that he did not mention God in
every speech he made: a failure that indicated he was not only
an atheist but also close to "godless Communism."[17]

A less obvious, but equally potent result of this admixture of religion and politics
has been pointed out by David Easton and Robert Hess. When studying the political worlds of children, Easton and Hess came upon the rather curious finding
that

not only do many children associate the sanctity and awe of
religion with the political community, but to ages 9 or 10 they
sometimes have considerable difficulty in disentangling God
and country. . . . The fact that as the child grows older he may
be able to sort out the religious from the political setting much
more clearly and restrict the pledge to a political meaning,
need not thereby weaken this bond. The initial and early intermingling of potent religious sentiment with political community has by that time probably created a tie difficult to dis-
solve.[18]

In non-rhetorical venues there is an equally long list of very real intertwining
of God and government: compulsory Sabbath laws, public support of military
and congressional chaplains, required schooling for even Amish and Mennonite
children. The list is endless. To dismiss the rhetoric of civic piety prematurely,
then, would be to ignore a legally, politically, and psychologically compelling
phenomenon.

Symbolic Influence

A second aspect of civil religion's power lies in the symbolic realm. Kendall and
Carey, for example, present a tolerably exhaustive taxonomy of "basic American
symbology" and find religious themes an inevitable part of the American political tradition.[19] In Kenneth Burke's terms, the theological wraps itself around
public consciousness by becoming a "collective poem" that undergirds civil insti-

tutions and civil polities.[20] Other writers regard this religious patina to be highly utilitarian. As Gordon notes: "As far as the author recalls, in fact, no political, social or psychological deterministic stance has yet been evolved which, in its application to groups of people, does not generate a metaphysic—or, to be more specific, does not deal eventually in spiritual and religious-ceremonial matters that usually become central to its own welfare, and, by extension, the welfare of the people at large."[21]

In short, religion provides a wealth of symbolic force for political leaders who associate themselves with such forces. Were there not power in such linkages, how could we account for the fact that *Time* magazine found it newsworthy to note that Richard Nixon held thirty-seven Sunday services during his first term but only four during his second?[22] How could we account for Norman Vincent Peale's lionizing of young Pastor Peter Muhlenberg, who ended his revolutionary era sermons this way: "In the language of the Holy Writ, there is a time for all things. There is a time to preach and a time to fight: and now is the time to fight."?[23] How could we explain the actions of the citizens' group described below were we not to acknowledge the symbolic power of civic piety?

> They called themselves the National Citizens' Committee for Fairness to the Presidency, and they assembled 1,400 strong in Washington last week to challenge what their improbable leader—a Taunton, Mass. rabbi named Baruch Korff—called "the lynching psychosis" in Congress and the media. They waved posters and flew flags; they pinned on chrome buttons that said SUPPORT THE PRESIDENCY; they roared and booed and shook their fists as speaker after speaker denounced the press as a pack of wolves or worse. And when the man they had come to rescue appeared briefly before them vowing that he would not leave until his appointed time in 1977, the room fairly rang with their chanting: "God bless Nixon! God bless Nixon! God bless Nixon!"[24]

One of the clearest statements about the symbolic importance of civic piety is provided by Michael Novak. In *Choosing Our King*, Novak says that the question is not whether the American people will have a civil religion, but rather what kind of religion it will be. He goes on to state:

> There are those who despise the notion of a civil religion out of fear that symbols of transcendence will be perverted to the uses of the state. Whether we like or dislike the notion, however, every national state generates a civil religion. For a state is not solely a pragmatic, administrative agency. The chief officers of the state perform priestly and prophetic roles, conduct huge public liturgies, constantly reinterpret the nation's fundamental documents and traditions, furnish the central terms of public discourse.[25]

Although we have separated for analysis here the existential and symbolic significance of civic piety, the twain inevitably meets. Consider, for example, the case of Ms. Carol Feraci, who was, in 1972, a thirty-year-old registered alien from Toronto, Canada, and a member of Ray Conniff's singing troupe. When the Conniff group appeared at the White House in January 1972, Ms. Feraci improvised a sermon of her own directed at that stalwart civil religionist and then president, Richard Nixon. Pulling a "Stop the killing (in Vietnam)" sign from the bosom of her gown, she stepped calmly to the microphone and said to the president and his guests: "You go to church on Sunday and pray to Jesus Christ. If Jesus Christ was in this room tonight, you would not dare drop another bomb."[26]

As might be expected, the reaction of the president's guests was swift: Bob Hope decried the homily as "shameful"; Billy Graham was reported to have a "purple" cast to his face; Martha Mitchell suggested that the aspiring preacher be torn limb from limb. The dazed Conniff, having a sense for the protocol demanded under such conditions, restored the existential and symbolic balance by ending the program with "God Bless America." That which God joins, it would seem, cannot be put asunder by woman either.

Thus far, we have used rather general terms when discussing the American civil religion. We have also focused on secondary, often popularized, accounts. We have taken that approach intentionally to show that popular norms and popular beliefs are the inexorable forces that propel such belief systems. Rhetorical failures in the civil-religious realm inevitably make news. They do so precisely because the agencies that regulate it are fundamentally rooted in American folkways. As we will see in Chapter 5, the popular constraints placed upon civic piety make it generically distinctive—communication of a certain sort. Were this not the case, Bill Bright, Billy Graham, Richard Nixon, Harry Truman, and Norman Vincent Peale would not know how to talk about America's religious heritage, and their communicative decisions would be made in a void. Too, were the ground rules that guide civic piety poorly understood, the miscues by Adlai Stevenson and Carol Feraci would have gone unnoticed. Fossil rhetoric though it may be, civic piety is important both sociologically and rhetorically and, therefore, a vital object for scholarly inquiry.

American Civic Piety: Its Panorama

In 1970, Pat Boone, George Otis, and Harold Bredesen authored a pyrotechnic pamphlet entitled *The Solution to Crisis—America*. The book is interesting on a number of fronts. It is a rare contemporary warning of Communist subversion in the United States; it is consciously reactionary in its theology; and its zealous, prophetic cast is overshadowed only by its evangelistic concern for uniting spirituality and an improved political instinct in the American people. A short excerpt from the pamphlet reveals its tones more dramatically:

> This is God's blazing message to America in this hour—and it
> is *without question its very last chance.*

This is the time to energize these spiritual weapons for the salvation of our land. It must be done *immediately, fervently, with faith, and with tears!*

If this is done by the Christian people with all of their heart immediately, and with perseverance, this land shall not only be saved, but there shall also explode from this united prayer-power the most astounding revival in all history.

MORE POWERFUL THAN
TEN THOUSAND HYDROGEN BOMBS

We have declared spiritual war on God's enemies and our enemies. NOW LET'S WAGE IT![27]

Subsequent to writing the pamphlet, author Boone (a pop culture icon of the day) passed on a copy to the president of the United States—Richard Nixon. The contrast in emotional fervor between Boone's pamphlet and Nixon's letter of appreciation[28] is a thing of beauty, as we see in Figure 2.1:

THE WHITE HOUSE
Washington

Dear Pat:

I want you to know how much I appreciate your thoughtfulness in letting me have a copy of your recording, "The Solution to Crisis—America," which you gave to Secretary Romney for me at the Religious Heritage Dinner on June 18. It was especially kind of you to remember me with this meaningful and timely message, and you may be sure I am pleased to have this evidence of faith and patriotism brought to my attention.

With my best wishes,

Sincerely,
Richard Nixon

Mr. Pat Boone
Beverly Hills, California 94710

The differences in the rhetorical styles of these two passages are significant. Where Boone & Co. excoriate, Nixon is blasé; the presidential circumspection contrasts sharply with the evangelism of the doomsayers; the traditional White House caution and optimism is nowhere to be seen in the pamphlet's gauntlet-dropping; most important, perhaps, is the obvious refusal by Nixon to match (or indirectly to give assent to) the confessional armor worn by the pamphlet's authors. The solution to America's crisis apparently did not reside in the presidential manor.

Official and Unofficial Civic Piety Contrasted

When one looks carefully at the tremendous array of God-and-country discourse in the United States one is impressed by its great variation in *Weltanschauung*, emotional drive, and political partisanship. Boone and his co-authors provide evidence of what Robert Bellah would call a "heretical byway" of the civil religion, while Nixon's rhetoric travels timidly along the American mainstream. That public rhetoric is consistently chosen to body forth such nuances is significant. If we are to believe Martin Marty, it is by inspecting such public expressions that we can differentiate among religious in-groups and out-groups:

> Americans tend to classify denominations in relation to their typical or mainstream status by a set of subtle contextual norms. Most of them revolve around the dialogue of American churches with their environment. The more exposed a group has been or becomes, the more its claims are eroded by its place in a pluralist society, the more it has been seen in harmony with main themes of national history, that much more does it belong. The more isolated, intransigent, withdrawn, the less exposed and eroded a group has been, no matter what its size and influence, the less it has come to be regarded as a normative religious expression for America. The largest remaining body of unexposed believers belongs to what is known as sects and cults, and they can best be accounted for and located by this approach.[29]

Taking Marty at his word, then, it should be possible to distinguish among those who align closely with Bellah's "official" American civil religion (instances of which we have already seen and upon which we shall concentrate in Chapter 5) and those political animals who stalk the American people from lairs far removed from 1600 Pennsylvania Avenue. Table 2.1 indicates the breadth of church-state persuasion in America.

It should be evident from inspecting the chart that church-state rhetoric "factors" in varied and complex ways. Not only do Americans speak extensively of things divine but they do so within a bevy of what Bitzer has termed "rhetorical situations."[30] Characterizations of such rhetors might proceed as follows:

1. Ecclesiastics: duly appointed or elected spokesmen for an organized body of religious believers.
2. Statesmen: duly appointed or elected governmental spokesmen.
3. Official civil religionists: ecclesiastics and statesmen who endorse the religious character of American society.

Table 2.1. Rhetorical Activities in the Church-State Sector

Spokesmen	Rhetorical Foci		
	Church Issues	State Issues	Church-State Issues
Ecclesiastics	**1** Null case (e.g., conventional preaching on scriptural themes)	**2** e.g., Quaker commentary on war-mongering	**3** e.g., Catholic lobbying on state aid to private schools
Statesmen	**4** e.g., Governmental sanctions on inter-church disputes	**5** Null case (e.g., congressional debating, political campaigning, etc.)	**6** e.g., governmental regulation of Sabbath laws
Official civil religionists	**7** e.g., Thanksgiving proclamations by nation's Chief Executive	**8** e.g., Priestly invocation at a political convention	**9** e.g., Inaugural addresses
Unofficial civil religionists	**10** e.g., American Legion campaigning for regular church attendance	**11** e.g., National Council of Christian and Jews remarking on political ethics	**12** e.g., Billy James Hargis speaking on Communist intervention
Irreligionists	**13** Null case (e.g., atheistic baiting of organized religion)	**14** Pure null case (irreligionists, as a group, are apolitical)	**15** e.g., Atheist Madlyn Murray O'Hair discussing prayer in the public schools
Anti-secularists	**16** Null case (e.g., doctrinal preaching on issues specific to the group of believers)	**17** Pure null case (anti-secularists, as a group, are apolitical)	**18** e.g., Jehovah Witnesses' refusal to engage in patriotic rituals

As indicated in the chart, a variety of dramatis personae play a role in the American civil religion. The "null cases," those activities that do not connect to mainstream civil-religious issues, are mentioned because they comprise much of the discourse visited upon the American people daily. Too, the "fringe" activities exemplified in areas 2, 3, 4, 6, 15, and 18 of the chart affect the tenor and scope of the American civil religion even though they do not relate directly to either "official" or "unofficial" civic piety. The complete story of such complexities must be told another day by other writers, however.[31]

The Rhetoric of Unofficial Civil Religion

In Chapters 3 through 5, we will concentrate primarily on what has been termed "official" civic piety, the sort of talk engaged in by mainstream or establishment persons and groups. However, the nation's political complexion is also affected by a potpourri of splinter groups or, as Martin Marty would have it, religio-political sects. The American Legion, the Catholic War Veterans, the Christian Economic Crusade, the Daughters of the American Revolution, the John Birch Society, the Church League of America, the American Coalition of Patriotic Societies, and other grassroots groups add color, intensity, drive, and ambition to the American civil religion. The fact that Bellah ignored such groups in his conceptualizing of the American civil religion mark him as somewhat patrician. His rationale for dismissing them is, ostensibly, that their rhetoric does not embody the themes and attitudes that captivate most Americans. While this may be so, the rhetoric of the sects constantly places pressure on its "official" cousins and hence vivifies what is often left subtle in the civil-religious mainstream.

The ontogeny of such sects is interesting. Apparently, the rather loose *gestalten* surrounding the official American civil religion does not provide for some Americans the forthrightness and emotional impact they crave. Some of these civil-religious sects are spawned from "high church" religion; Martin Marty describes their appeal as follows: "The thesis here is that negatively-oriented sects gain their current attractiveness from their attempt and relative success at isolating people from competing value systems; and that positively-oriented cults, usually gathered around charismatic persons or clans, succeed to the extent that they provide surrogates for interpersonal relations or attachment to significant persons in an apparently depersonalizing society."[32]

While the "sects" do not always compete with their "official" counterparts, they can draw off enthusiasm from the parent bodies. At other times they can be embarrassingly vocal, embarrassing, that is, as Pat Boone was for Richard Nixon. Such groups often consist of persons who instinctively embrace sectarianism (both political and religious), activism, and overt ideology and who, as a result, differ profoundly from their "official" counterparts. As a result, they are highly colorful when performing and almost always draw media attention. Let us examine why.

Sectarianism

As mentioned previously, official civil religion tries to affect a balance between that which is rendered to God and Caesar. Not so for the civil-religious sects. For example, the Christian Government Movement (née the Christian Amendment Movement) is a longstanding pressure group that wants to make American political life more Christian in character. The group lobbies vigorously, publishes frequently, and postures politically. The group's constitution details just such goals:

In the light of Scripture, the infallible Word of God, we hold these principles to be true:

> (1) That all of life is to be lived in service to God; and that therefore a concern for national righteousness and justice is necessary for God's people.
>
> (2) That men because of their willful rebellion against God do not know the way to political and national blessing.
>
> (3) That the lord Jesus Christ, having satisfied the demands of the law and completed His work of redemption, is seated at the right hand of God the father, and has been given all power and authority over the created universe, including governments.
>
> (4) That Jesus Christ, through His Word and Spirit, reveals the principles of true justice for all of society and its institutions and directs Christians in their efforts to bring society into conformity with God's Word.
>
> (5) That the church and the state are both institutions that have been called into being by God, and, although they are interrelated, neither should interfere with the proper functions of the other.
>
> (6) That governments should make a public acknowledgment of the Kingship of Christ and respond obediently to His Word in their policies, programs, and decisions. Failure to do either of these is an affront to God and leads to judgment.
>
> (7) That Christians are bound to make known to their leaders these principles, to make public confession for lack of obedience to these principles, and to seek true public justice and a proper acknowledgment of Christ's exalted position.[33]

When we compare such Christo-centered utterances to the bland fare usually served up at national political events (e.g., "He who, in His mercy, watches over these United States"), we begin to get a feeling for the tone of unofficial civil religion. Other groups, such as the National Association for Christian Political Action, are even less expansive in outlook. As we will see in Chapter 5, the fundamentalist perspective evidenced in the following passage (extracted from an N.A.C.P.A. newsletter) could not be more different from "high-church" civil religion:

> We are an evangelical, Bible-believing association of people who believe that Christ is Lord—Lord of all of life, wanting His servants everywhere working in obedience to Him. No work done for the Lord is in vain (I Cor. 15:58). All of life is therefore spiritual and sacred, or should be, for the Christian. There can

never be two realms for the Christian, one spiritual, one secular, for no matter what he does, it must be done for the glory of God. That's why NACPA exists, to be the Body of Christ's arm at work in politics, trying to bring justice and peace through its various educational efforts (magazine, literature, research team of Christian political scientists, film, meeting with legislators, etc.).[34]

The sectarianism of unofficial civil religion also takes a more avowedly political turn on occasion (e.g., the John Birch Society which holds a "God and Country Rally" in Belmont, Massachusetts each year). As Bellah insists, however, "For all the overt religiosity of the radical right today, their relation to the civil religious consensus is tenuous, as when the John Birch Society attacks the central American symbol of Democracy itself."[32] The John Birchers' motto replies sharply to Bellah: "less government, more responsibility, and with God's help, a better world."

Activism

Mention of the John Birch Society stimulates a second thought relative to unofficial civil religion: its viewpoint is distinctively partisan. Such groups are more than willing to act out their political and religious convictions. While not all the sects are as strident as the Reverend Dallas F. Billington, its themes are often quite hortatory:

> I want you . . . who are present to pray this prayer beside your
> bed every night: that God will kill [Madlyn Murray O'Hair]. .
> . . Now we have no right to go out and take a gun and kill her,
> but we can sure pray for God to kill her. I don't want you to
> stop there, I want you to pray to God to remove any judge or
> judges that keep us from having our Bible in our schools. . . .
> It is not wrong for you to pray God to destroy your enemy. . . .
> Is it wrong for us to pray to remove a judge that is to remove
> our Bibles? If we say for God to do it, have we committed any
> sin? No![36]

Perhaps the best known of the sects is the Christian Anti-Communist Crusade, headed by the indomitable political cleric, Billy James Hargis. Hargis, more than most "one hundred percent Americans," has seized upon the unique, activating force unleashed when God and country join together and confront the infidel:

> "I am asking one million Americans to collect a small stone
> from their rock garden (about the size of a silver dollar) wrap
> a Scripture provided on the back page of the *Weekly* around it,
> and mail it off to their impeachment-minded senators and
> congressmen," Hargis wrote.

The Bible verse Hargis selected is appropriate to the occasion: "He that is without sin among you, let him first cast a stone. That bunch of Pharisees in Jesus' time got the message, and so will these modern-day Pharisees who are willing to sacrifice the country so they can achieve their political dream."[37]

Richard Nixon did not face impeachment, it would appear, from any reluctance to act on the parts of unofficial civil religionists.

Overt Ideology

Not all such "unofficial" groups are quite so sectarian and activist. Many groups have a purely political agenda but latch onto the "God stuff" to divert attention from their quite secular ambitions, using it as a kind of "rhetorical cover." Perhaps the most obvious example of such diversionary tactics is provided by the Church League of America, a domestic fact-gathering agency headquartered in Wheaton, Illinois. Among other things, the Church League's national office catalogues the names of "thousands of individuals" who, for example, write "an article or book attacking and ridiculing a major doctrine of the Christian Faith or the American way of life...."[38] That such activities have an uncertain relationship with matters theological appears to be of little concern to the Church League. Indeed, the entire matter of religion holds little interest for them. In a three-thousand-word pamphlet outlining their aims and programs, the word church is used eleven times (in each case, it refers to the name of the organization) and the word God is used but once (in the phrase "God is not dead").[39] Otherwise, the pamphlet busies itself with the political subversives on the Left who threaten to undermine America's traditional commitments.

Other instances of such diversionary tactics abound among the political sects. Literature issued by the National States Rights Party, for example, argues that racism is the only bulwark with which to protect a "White Christian Civilization." Also, the Christian Anti-Communist Crusade, ostensibly aware that communism has become only vaguely identifiable for many post–cold war Americans, has, of late, stepped up its religious appeals. For example, from May through August of 1974, Christian Crusade leader Billy James Hargis, along with thirty young students (called the "All American Kids") from his American Christian College, trouped the country with a yankee-doodled, all-Christian, musical revue that encouraged audiences to take "a stand for Christ and conservatism."[40] The weaving and cross-weaving of God and country themes in Hargis's rhetoric creates what Berger and Pinard have called "a comprehensive universe of discourse"[41] within which the indistinct goals of the deity become enveloped by, and then equated with, the more obvious ideals of the political group espousing them. It is because of such curious marriages that Sidney Mead has warned: "God, like Alice's Cheshire Cat, has sometimes threatened gradually to disappear altogether or, at most, to remain only as disembodied and sentimental smile."[42]

To some extent, the religio-political sword cuts both ways. That nationalism can become a rhetorical cover for certain kinds of religious persuasion was well demonstrated in one of the more curious documents to be published during the bicentennial celebrations of 1976. The World Home Bible League, an organization whose political posture is often hard to distinguish, issued a paraphrased New Testament during the bicentennial, a book replete with a mawkishly patriotic cover and the title *Let Freedom Ring!* With the exception of the cover, a two-page "Americanish" introduction, and a dozen or so nondescript photos, the four-hundred-page volume contained nothing but the Holy Scriptures. Rhetorical expediency, it appears, has both political and religious attractions.

Conclusion

While we will focus in this book on mainstream civil religion, we dare not ignore the continual interfaces between official and unofficial civil religion. Imagine, for example, the turmoil caused for the American Right when in December of 1973 the traditional Nativity scene was, via the agency of the American Civil Liberties Union, banned from its accustomed place on the Ellipse near the White House. That two of the nation's most powerful images could be divorced in this manner bestirred a good many citizens. "Are we to believe that the Constitution of the United States requires us to turn away the Baby Jesus from the White House?" angrily queried some. The A.C.L.U. countered by arguing, in effect, that the presence of the crèche constituted a "sectarian, activist, and overtly religious" incursion in matters purely political. Although the day was won by the Civil Liberties Union (which essentially spoke in behalf of official civil religion), the commitment of those advocating "God, country, and conservatism" was only rekindled anew:

> And so the ancient story is repeated at the door of our national mansion. Once again, there is no room. Caesar may tax and count, posture and rule, without the annoying presence of Mary and Joseph, and the Babe lying in the manger. But let Caesar know that the Star in the East shines nevertheless. Let him know that, for all he might do, the true meaning of Christmas still swells great in the hearts of the American people. And let him be assured that he will yet have to deal with Christian soldiers.[43]

In this chapter we have noted the intensity and force of civic piety. We have noted, too, that civil-religious tenets have turned into something of a rhetorical institution in the United States. In the following chapter, we will ask how such institutionalization came about, focusing particularly on Robert Bellah's notion of an American civil religion. We will also ask how well his construct explains the phenomena we have been discussing, phenomena which, according to Gerald L. K. Smith, invariably serve to "het up" the American people.[44]

Chapter 3

Traditional Explanations of Civic Piety

"If the universe were material bound by inexorable law, still it needed a spiritual hypothesis. Even the Great Machine required a Divine Mechanic."[1] Thus did Sherwood Eddy account for the Founding Fathers' tendencies to spice their political statements with theological seasonings. Picking up on this theme, Robert Bellah has suggested that this "spiritual hypothesis" eventuated in a sort of national shadow religion, a religion used by the American people to make sense out of their collective strivings. As we have seen in Chapter 2, the lubricant used by the nation's "mechanics" was discourse of an unquestionably public variety.

But what are the roots of civic piety? Why does it exist at all? The answer to both questions seems to be that civic piety in the United States is a kind of rhetorical cognate to religious disestablishment. As such, its existence can be explained, in part, by noting the forces that also lead to the separation of church and state in that nation.

In this chapter we will examine philosophical, political, and other accounts for the church-state interactions popular in the U.S. since the Founding. Then, we will examine with some scrutiny the symbolic interpretation offered by Robert Bellah and others, an interpretation that has been well received by scholars and laypersons alike. As we move through these rival explanations we will be reminded once again that disestablishment in the U.S. has been a phenomenon of manifest importance, a facet of its national character that has been termed "a greater revolutionary event than the mere political separation from Great Britain."[2]

The Roots of Disestablishment and Civic Piety

Although most informed scholars agree that the guarantee of religious freedom in the United States is one of its most fundamental and distinctive features as a nation, there are a wealth of competing explanations for why—given the sociopolitical environment of the eighteenth century—the American people managed to escape the internecine struggles between church and state so often found in Europe. That the American people escaped such turmoil and yet were regarded as citizens of a "religious" nation could be seen merely as an interesting historical accident if its socio-political implications were not so profound. Explanations for this symbiosis of religion and politics in the United States are rife. Let us examine some of them.

Political Hypothesis

One of the most attractive explanations for church-state relations in the U.S. regards disestablishment as a cultural integrator, an agent that keeps the rival theological factions that founded the nation from lunging at each others' jugular veins. Leo Pfeffer, a preeminent student of religious freedom, suggests that the nation's earliest settlers were convinced "that the best way to keep from these shores the religious bloodshed, persecution, and intolerance that had plagued the old world was to maintain . . . a wall between church and state in the new world."[3] Other writers, however, are quick to point out that the mortice joints in such walls do not always hold. As Dennis Brogan comments, "Religion has been a notorious dividing force where it was not identified with the state. Hence the Inquisition, the Penal laws in Ireland, the waves of persecution and counter-persecution in France."[4] According to the "political" hypothesis, then, the colonists fashioned a rigorously secular government and provided it with a religious patina for largely sentimental reasons.

Many authorities do not credit the earliest Americans with such prescience, however. Some suggest that the settlers would have been just as likely to fall into the brambles had it not been for the facts of national survival themselves. For example, of the original thirteen colonies, only two, Virginia and Rhode Island, guaranteed full religious freedom to its people. Delaware and Maryland demanded Christianity. Pennsylvania, Delaware, North and South Carolina required assent to the divine inspiration of the Bible. Most of the remaining colonies demanded adherence to some sort of religious establishment.[5] As Bates notes, the resulting religious toleration in the U.S. "was never isolated, as the myth would have it, from an economic or political background."[6] According to the political hypothesis, then, the colonists used civic piety as a surrogate for an actual church-state. Whatever else they were, the Founding Fathers were pragmatists according to this account.

Philosophical Hypothesis

Other commentators explain church-state relations in the United States via different routes. For example, Higginbotham summarizes the position of many intellectual historians (like Perry Miller) when he argues that the American experiment in church-state polity was only an extension (a radical one, to be sure) of certain philosophical currents sweeping across Europe in the late seventeenth and eighteenth centuries. Says Higginbotham: "The Revolution needed religious foundations to match the political underpinnings provided by Locke and Jefferson. If the Enlightenment led educated men to rationalism or deism, traditional

Christianity still loomed large in the lives of the great majority of Americans, most of whom were Protestants of the left wing or Calvinist variety."[7]

Thus, not only was disestablishment necessary for economic and political reasons but it also provided a kind of philosophical frame for burgeoning governmental structures—a socially acceptable, ultimately political rationale for seeking independence. The effects of such a grand scheme on colonization were pronounced: "Each citizen bore responsibility, moral no less than political," argues Edwin Gaustad.[8] That the revolutionary era managed to weld the potentially competing philosophical systems of government and religion was no small feat. That it could fashion out of them a viable, pragmatic spirit of independence—of the colonies from their mother country and of church from state—was as unexpected as it was important.

Serendipity Hypothesis

When accounting for such a broad and complex movement as the American experiment in church-state relations, the simplest hypothesis may well be the most attractive. A growing number of scholars are beginning to demythologize the U.S.'s founding by suggesting that a host of confusing and often competing forces rather accidentally conspired to establish American civic piety as a viable institution. That is, while some would have us believe that the fervor with which disestablishment was sought was surpassed solely by Jonathan Edwards's holy trek into the American wilderness, others remind us that the American colonists were as a whole "not very much interested in religion, a fact which, if it did not favor the health of churches, nevertheless did indicate a spirit which could accept Jefferson's interpretation of the meaning of the First Amendment."[9]

Still, while some of the colonists may have been blasé about religion, their millenarian brethren viewed the young nation as a New Israel, a land with a religious destiny. In light of such contrasting views of the importance of religion, then, the American civil religion may well have been erected on the pedestal of happenstance, no clear-cut theological mandate for a super-religious government being apparent.

Perhaps most skillfully articulated by Bernard Bailyn, the serendipity hypothesis encourages us to view the disestablishment of religion (and, subsequently, the institutionalizing of civic piety) as emanating from a veritable labyrinth of forces—social, philosophical, religious, economic, historical, political, and accidental:

> The disestablishment of religion was neither an original goal nor completely a product of the Revolution. Its roots lay deep in the colonial past, in circumstances that Jonathan Parsons described as a "random way of settling ministers and churches, together with a vile contempt of creeds and confessions . . . all seem to jumble together, and make mere *hodgepodge*." These unplanned, unexpected conditions, lacking in

completeness and justification, were touched by the magic of
Revolutionary thought, and were transformed.[10]

This is a climate-of-the-times hypothesis, a position which holds that the
U.S. was founded by church-goers who, perhaps inadvertently, enwrapped their
burgeoning social and political systems with the mantle of religious language.
Equally, they were political tinkerers despite themselves, persons willing to experiment with unprecedented social compacts. The complex of forces acting
upon them was apparently sufficient, in any event, to replace European models of
church-state relations with a national attitude of all things in their proper places,
God included.

For a number of reasons, then, disestablishment came to the United States.
When it came, however, a void was created, a void which eventually came to be
filled by American civic piety. But for civic piety to function effectively it too
had to have special qualities. It had to do something for the American people that
could not be done by legal or constitutional means. But what?

Symbolic Hypothesis

Not surprisingly, the man who popularized the phrase, "American civil religion,"
has his own explanation for its existence. In explaining its roots, Robert Bellah
burrows for his rationale deep within the human condition when arguing that a
society must make its ideals sacred through appropriate symbolism and develop
its own metaphysic if it is to function with maximum emotional efficiency. The
U.S.'s national ethos, according to Bellah, must explain itself to itself in grand
and idealistic fashion.

Bellah's explanation thus constitutes the symbolic hypothesis for understanding American civic piety. According to such a perspective, the U.S. has had
a special (not necessarily unique) need to articulate its collective goals, its most
fundamental and demanding values, its heritage and destiny. Ostensibly, the red,
white, and blue bunting, the presidential seals, the deistic imprimaturs on the nation's coins, the Christmas messages, the Fourth of July oratory, the Lincolns, the
Eisenhowers, the Nixons, and God in His heaven, collectively offer the American
people a clear national self-understanding. According to such a viewpoint, the
emotional uncertainties created by disestablishment opened up the people to an
American civil religion.

In his research, Bellah focused almost exclusively on what we have termed
(in Chapter 2) "official" civil religion. Indeed, Bellah concentrated most of his
analysis on the high priest of the national faith, the president of the United States.
From such an exalted perspective, Bellah's explanation for the widespread existence of civic piety makes sense. Like any group of religious believers, that is,
Americans needed their prophets (e.g., Benjamin Franklin), their patriarchs
(Washington), their martyrs and redeemers (Lincoln). Americans expect their
chief executives to perform the role of shaman (because presidents devote only
part of their time to quasi-religious tasks)[11] while full-time civil religionists (like

Billy Graham) become the workaday diviners who read the will of the gods in omens:

> America's soul: patriotism, morality, respect for law, faith, so-cial justice, brotherhood among people of diverse backgrounds. This is the very soul of America but we are in danger of losing our soul, and the boys in the military may soon ask if it is worth dying for. Unless our soul is restored, the best men in America will begin to ask if it is worth going into politics for. *Unless our soul is renewed and restored.* Jesus asked the question long ago: What shall it profit a man or a nation if they gain the whole world and lose the soul.[12]

In addition to its distinct personalities, the American civil religion has its holy places (the White House), its amulets (Nixon's lapel flags), its saints (Norman Vincent Peale) and its sinners (the anti-war Berrigan brothers), its baptisms (the first grader's pledge of allegiance) and its confirmations (often administered by military chaplains). Although it is highly non-denominational, the national faith is nevertheless creedal (i.e., nationalistic). The nation's grade schools "provide the place of instruction . . . in the sacred history of the civil religion."[13] This "sacred canopy" of symbols, according to Peter Berger, performs basic and important functions: "The 'gains' of theodicy for a society are to be understood in a way analogous to those for the individual. Entire collectivities are thus permitted to integrate anomic events, acute or chronic, into the *nomos* established in their society."[14]

The popularity of Bellah's symbolic hypothesis is remarkable. As Thomas and Flippen indicate,[15] almost all the major texts in the sociology of religion have accepted Bellah's thesis, star-spangled tabernacle and all. Bellah himself has remarked somewhat immodestly, "the phrase 'civil religion in America' . . . took on a life of its own . . . has been picked up by the *New York Times* and by the popular newsweeklies, . . . has inspired books, essays, and symposia."[16] Nevertheless, some criticism of Bellah's notion of an American civil religion can be offered, the most fundamental of which centers around its conceptual worthiness for explaining civic piety in the United States.

The American Civil Religion as Theoretical Construct

Perhaps the most devastating critique to be made of Bellah's hypothesis has been offered by John Wilson, who asserts that civic piety has been incorrectly labeled a civil religion by Bellah. Employing a purist's understanding of religion, Wilson argues that the refrains Bellah found imbedded in presidential discourse do not "manifest the kind of interrelatedness, institutionalization, and coherence of expression which would warrant identifying them as positive evidence for a developed and differentiated religion" in the strictest sense of that word.[17] Wilson is even more specific in his charges when he defines "real religion" as providing for:

> (1) cultic aspects to the phenomena, i.e., provision for periodic (frequent) ceremony or ritual which provides definitive interpretation of it; (2) recognized leadership offices invested with effective authority; (3) explicitly defined means of participation in the religion (thus establishing the grounds of membership); (4) at least implicit delineation of beliefs—if not "correct belief"; (5) influence upon behavior at one or more levels and in a manifest way; (6) finally, and perhaps most important, a coherence of the above in order for the conception of religion to be applicable. Beliefs and behavior must have some manifest relationship to each other.[18]

According to such criteria, Bellah's American civil religion clearly does not pass muster.

An American Civil Religion?

The implicit response Bellah makes, of course, is that he was arguing analogically (as we have done when offering the metaphorical extensions of Bellah's conception included above). That the bulk of his argument stands on the stilt-like legs of metaphor seems not to bother Bellah:

> In a sense, and not in a trivial sense, civil religion in America existed from the moment the winter 1967 issue of *Daedalus* was printed. . . . By saying [this] I do not mean that the notion was arbitrary, fanciful, or a myth, in the pejorative sense of that word. But I do mean that it was what Alfred Schutz would have called a social construction of reality . . . [as Schutz says] "We live in the description of a place and not in the place itself."[19]

Thus, Bellah is arguing that his metaphorical interpretation has heuristic value, that the concept of "religion" provides him with explanatory power not made available via alternative conceptualizations of the same phenomena. Lest the reader become impatient with what may seem to be semantic nit-picking, it should be noted that were we not to allow Bellah the argumentative expansiveness of his religious metaphor, many of his interpretations of civil-religious discourse would fall asunder, as we shall see later in this essay.

Some resolution to the debate appears to derive from assuming a Durkheimian-functionalist approach to the question. That is, by looking at the distinctive jobs traditional religion is said to perform for the individual believer, and by judging Bellah's religion by such criteria, we can get a clearer understanding of the controversy. Listed below, then, is what Thomas O'Dea sees as the most common tasks accomplished by traditional religious organizations:

1. Supportiveness—some supra-human being provides consolation to the oppressed, the frustrated, and the deprived.

2. Priestly ministration—explicit religious doctrine and guidance are provided for the religious community.
3. Normative base—standards of judgment for determining the rightness or wrongness of conduct are provided.
4. Prophetic statements—an ethical ideal is held up by which the believer may guide his future actions.
5. Identity—the believer is defined as part of a larger community of believers who have an ultimate meaning for life.
6. Growth—the individual is helped to grow intellectually and psychologically within the framework of the religion.
7. Expressivity—important, psychologically satisfying means of expression are provided for in religious worship.
8. Renewal—through ritual, deep-seated values are refreshed and given new meaning for the believer.
9. Hope—religions oftentimes hold out the possibility that there will be a magical intervention in human affairs.
10. Predictability—patterned explanations of life are given, often by scriptural pronouncements.
11. Authority—some over-arching standard is offered which encourages or castigates alternative courses of actions.[20]

When applying such standards to Bellah's civil religion, we must keep in mind the corpus from which he derived much of his conceptualization—the inaugural addresses of the presidents of the United States, a seemingly small body of data from which to posit the existence of anything as grand as a national faith. Still, in a severely limited sense, the American civil religion occasionally performs some of the functions of traditional religion. In Lincoln's second inaugural, for example, we find elements of supportiveness, of a normative base, and of prophetic impetus for a war-ravaged people. Too, Kennedy's maiden presidential speech attempts in oblique fashion to provide identity, predictability, and renewal for the new frontiersmen he was addressing. Most of the other presidential inaugurals contain possibilities for expressivity and, on occasion, authoritative bases upon which the American people may found courses of action they are contemplating.

However, to look for aspects of doctrine, of psychological growth, or of "magical intervention" by an immanent God would be to break the back of the fragile metaphorical edifice Bellah erected in 1967. Indeed, if we apply O'Dea's criteria of interrelatedness and coherence of expression to presidential inaugurals, then even Lincoln and Kennedy would have to be viewed as playing at the religious game. As Alley correctly asserts, if there is a civil religion, "the strength of presidential personalities [tends] to construct a new civil religion in every generation."[21] To find a civil *religion* in the United States, that is, would be to distort the concept of religion unnecessarily. At the very least, Bellah has found a religion that, say, a staunch Roman Catholic, or an orthodox Jew, or an Episcopalian would hardly see as rivaling their respective faiths. At best, the American civil religion is a political version of Unitarianism.

That Bellah has found true religion in the inaugural wilderness becomes even less certain when we look at the chronology of civil religion in America. As O'Dea states, all genuine religions experience certain dilemmas when, as is their natural course, they undergo institutionalization (i.e., when their doctrines and modes of worship become modified and regularized within a definable organizational framework). That is, as a religion matures, there develop mixed motivational states within its members, routinization of ritual, internal bureaucratic rivalries, "legalization" of ethical beliefs, and sharp differences of opinion between the religion and the prevailing political order which permits its existence.[22] Most modern religions, it seems clear, have faced each of these problems in one form or another as they have moved toward institutionalization.

The American civil religion, on the other hand, appears to have undergone no such sociological adolescence. As we have seen, the motives of its citizen-believers were thoroughly mottled as far back as the 1700s. Furthermore, although ritual has always characterized civic piety, it is hardly routinized in the way that most "real" religious rituals come to be. Because the organizational structure of the American civil religion has always been amorphously defined (e.g., any mainstream minister, priest, or rabbi will "do" for the necessary invocation), the bureaucracy, whatever little bit of it there is, has always functioned rather smoothly. Also, according to any standard definition of doctrine, no such phenomenon has ever been a significant part of a national faith articulated by both a Kennedy and a Nixon in the same decade. Most important, of course, is that there has always been a highly cordial relationship between the American civil religion and the United States government itself, a fact stemming in large part from the almost total identification both entities share as civic pietists. Thus, by reverse reasoning, it appears that because it never has experienced the problems most formal religions have undergone, the American civil religion is not made of the same philosophical and sociological stuff of which religions have been traditionally constituted.[23]

In disallowing Bellah his use of the term *religion*, we are in no way suggesting that his research has been for nought. Indeed, Bellah has brought to his subject penetrating insight. Equally, our point here is not to quibble with terminology. Rather, we are suggesting that by employing the construct of religion, Bellah committed himself to all of its attendant dimensions and implications. Had he used Wilson's happier conceptualization of "civic piety," Bellah might have avoided a number of theoretical problems.

This is also not to say that Bellah is wrong and Wilson right. After all, Wilson can be charged with theoretic provincialism (possibly even anachronism) when he insists on reserving the term "religious" for those activities taking place in churches. Moreover, there is some element of scholasticism in Wilson's arguments, especially when he insists on debating the existence of a "thing" called civil religion. Ultimately, the Wilson-Bellah debate will be settled on the most pragmatic of grounds: the extent to which their respective models can explain the phenomena they observe. While the data are not yet in on Wilson, the forthrightness with which Bellah has presented his conceptualization permits us a brief examination of its theoretical worthiness.

The American Civil Religion as a Reified Construct

As mentioned previously, most of the commentary made of Bellah's essay has focused on the positive and negative valences of civil religion. However, few writers have questioned Bellah's theoretical starting point—that the religious refrains found in presidential speeches can best be understood as manifestations of a civil religion. But if Bellah's initial assumption is faulty (or insufficiently developed), then any subsequent extrapolations made from it will be logically premature. As Wilson states, Bellah has not "made a compelling case that the relevant phenomena [he identified] . . . become intelligible only in these terms."[24]

To obtain a clearer perspective of the issue, let us review Bellah's own seminal statement on the matter of civil religion: "This article argues not only that there is such a thing [as a civil religion], but also that this religion—or perhaps better, this religious dimension—has its own seriousness and integrity and requires the same care in understanding that any other religion does."[25] In talking about "this religious dimension," Bellah's errors are more than syntactical. What he meant to add, of course, is "this religious dimension *of rhetoric*." That is, Bellah discovered not "religion," but interesting rhetorical assertions. His civil religion was his own hypostatization, and Bellah, in expanding upon his "religious" hypothesis rather than upon his rhetorical discovery, opened himself up to all of the very real dangers that reification creates for all analysts of the human condition. At the risk of sounding presumptuous, it appears that Bellah was somewhat taken in by the civic piety he set out to explain. In creating his religion out of the humble stuff of which rhetoric is made, Bellah, not unlike Doctor Frankenstein himself, became the victim of his own creation.

To explain Bellah's construction of a national religion, one need look no further than his primary corpus—presidential inaugurals—which contain the most rhetorically astute, emotionally compelling, and historically sanctioned civil-religious discourse American politicians have fashioned in two centuries. At the hands of rhetorical giants like Jefferson, Lincoln, Roosevelt, and Kennedy, even an eminent twentieth-century sociologist could hardly avoid casting his analyses in sacral tones and heralding the existence of an American civil religion.

That Bellah perhaps overreacted to the discourse he inspected is understandable when one recognizes that passages like the following are likely to cause even the most hard-headed sociologist to swoon: "This is the hope that beckons us onward in this century of trial. This is the work that awaits us all, to be done with bravery, with charity, and with prayer to Almighty God."[26]

Bellah's fatal flaw of responding to his own reifications may be accounted for by his tendency to adopt a patrician perspective of the American civil religion. From the exalted position of presidential ceremonies, all appears to be right, good, true, and sacred. The expendiency of the Church League of America seems far removed from such rarified pinnacles. Viewing the American civil religion through the eyes of new presidents, however, is not unlike building sociological theory of U.S. teenagers by exclusively interviewing the acneless kids on Pepsi commercials.

At crucial points, it would seem, Bellah has sacrificed his analytical skills to speak solemnly and idealistically of the religion he found and, later, loved too well. Indeed, Bellah's own rhetoric contains many of the same reverent, hopeful tones with which presidents attempt to invigorate their maiden speeches. For example, when commenting on Native Americans, Bellah had this to say about civil religion:

> They point out to us that though we are the bearers of a tradition that has its own integrity, it is not a self-sufficient tradition. The survival of all of us on earth today, a survival that, as Norman O. Brown has pointed out, is itself only a utopian hope, depends upon our pooling of all man's cultural resources. If America can have any meaning and value in the future it is only a relative value, only as part of a greater encompassing whole.[27]

Of such stuff, any inaugural speaker would be proud.

Recently, Charles Henderson (himself a fine scholar of civil religion) has hinted at the reason for what we are here describing as Bellah's theoretical miscues.[28] Reviewing Bellah's book, *The Broken Covenant*, Henderson wrote:

> But Robert Bellah is not only writing about religion in America, he is also a spokesman for religion. He is personally involved in and committed to a particular faith which he has worked out over the last quarter century. . . . In *The Broken Covenant* Bellah writes with precisely that double vision. He speaks as a sociologist who steps back to take the long view, the analytical view; and he speaks as an advocate of the most vital elements of the religion he describes. His book records not only those thoughts and perceptions which come to him as a result of logical analysis; he speaks also from the heart.[29]

The point being made here is that Bellah's "double vision" does some amount of sociological and theoretical damage, no matter what theological benefits may inhere in his often prescient analyses.

Conclusion

Several conclusions seem warranted by this brief analysis of Bellah's civil religion. The first is that we have been talking here about *Bellah's* civil religion, a social construction of reality invented by Robert Bellah for the purpose of explaining human events. As Martin Marty notes, the American civil religion exists much as the Middle Ages exist for a scholar—both are convenient labeling devices by which human activities can be described or explained efficiently.[30] In labeling phenomena thusly, Bellah served an important function—he helpfully pointed out certain events and ideas that had hitherto been ignored completely, treated as trivial, or explained insufficiently. But because Bellah manufactured a construct, and subsequently treated the construct as if it existed in fact, he failed to investigate alternative explanations for his data. There are other methods for interpreting the religious refrains found in presidential discourse, methods which appear to be aligned closely with the observed realities themselves.

In the following pages, we will offer just such an alternative, taking our lead from historian John Wilson. In a provocative essay entitled "A Historian's Approach to Civil Religion," Wilson politely rejected the notion of an American civil religion, concluding his essay with the observation: "In a historical perspective I think it is difficult to arrive at the judgment that there is in American society an institutionalized, well-developed, and differentiated civil religion, a tradition parallel to and interrelated with other religious traditions in our culture."[31] Alternatively, Wilson muses, other models may prove to be more flight worthy than the religious paradigm constructed by Bellah.[32] As to what such models may be, however, Wilson is uncomfortably vague. In Chapter 4 we will offer a relatively explicit alternative to Bellah's model. Thereafter, we will apply this understanding to the very phenomena Bellah himself studied, asking if a rhetorical explanation of civic piety sheds new light on a topic which has become clouded. Before turning to such matters, however, we must remember that no new approach could have been envisioned had not Robert Bellah imaginatively isolated such phenomena for analysis in the first place. As Alley has commented, "Allowing his assumption, [Bellah] produces an impressive case."[33]

Chapter 4

An Alternative Understanding of Civic Piety

THIS CONTRACT, made *Each* day of *Each Month* between *the United States Government,* herein called the "first party", and *Organized Religion*, herein called the "second party";

WITNESSETH: That for and in recognition and performance of the covenants contained herein on the part of both parties in the manner hereinafter specified, let both parties recognize that: A) Religion is capable of providing an ultimate meaning system for its adherents; B) Government is able to exert coercive power on the affairs of its citizens; and C) Both government and religion wield considerable rhetorical power both within their respective sectors and across sectors.

This contract is made by the aforementioned parties and is accepted upon the following conditions, and it is agreed that each of the terms hereinafter specified shall be a condition. The breach, default, failure or violation of any one or more thereof shall entitle the innocent party to terminate this contract. In addition, should any first party official fail to abide by the stated conditions or in any other manner fail to pay tacit homage to religion, he or she shall be branded un-American and declared non-electable; and, should any member of any second party body fail to abide by the stated conditions or in any other manner to deny God's approbation of governmental policy, both foreign and domestic, he or she shall be labeled radical and denied an opportunity to offer the benedictions at political gatherings.

Let it furthermore be agreed to that:

1. The guise of complete separation between the first party and the second party will be maintained by both parties.
2. The guise of existential equality between the first party and the second party will be maintained by both parties, but the second party's realms shall be solely that of the rhetorical.

3. First party rhetoric will refrain from being overly religious and second party rhetoric will refrain from being overly political.

4. Neither of the aforementioned parties shall, in any fashion whatsoever, make known to the general populace the exact terms of the contract contained herein.

This agreement shall insure to the benefit of both parties, and their successors in interest.

WITNESS our hands, the day and year first above written.

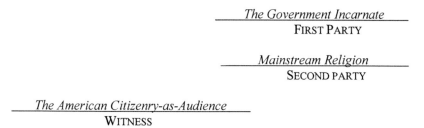

The Government Incarnate
FIRST PARTY

Mainstream Religion
SECOND PARTY

The American Citizenry-as-Audience
WITNESS

It does not take a legal scribe to determine that the above document has more metaphorical than adjudicative value. Yet as we will see in this chapter, the document is nonetheless quite "real." That is, we will argue here that (1) the contracting parties were knowing, if not conscious, signatories; (2) the apparently flaccid terms of the contract are really quite binding on those who subscribe to its contents; and (3) the contract has been renegotiated with unflagging regularity throughout American history. It is hoped that this *rhetorical* interpretation of church-state relations in the U.S. provides an attractive, alternative explanation for the genesis and perpetuation of civic piety. In Chapter 5, we will see that the functions, themes, and characteristics of civil-religious discourse can best be explained via this contractual image.

An Overview of the Contract

Should the wary reader contrast our critique of Bellah (in Chapter 3) and the contract presented above, the reader might be tempted to cry "foul!" After all, we too will be using metaphor when explaining church-state relations in the United States. Our critique of Bellah is not intended to disparage metaphorical argument per se but simply to warn against its over-extension. Here, we will use the contractual metaphor consciously, fully aware of the conceptual pitfalls such an approach entails. Moreover, we will not consider the contractual image to be probative argument, but simply one device scholars may use to illuminate complex phenomena. Finally, we will use a metaphor well suited to the fact-territory being dealt with here (public rhetoric) while still trying to avoid intentional fallacies.

The choice of the legal-contractual metaphor was not capricious. For as one looks at the amount and intensity of civic piety in the U.S., one is impressed with the frequent collusions among religious and governmental spokesmen. The timing, phrasing, and elegance of American civic piety come from people who know full well their expected roles. Civic piety in the U.S. emerges not so much from blind, momentary passion but from a knowing, pragmatic understanding of what is required when God and country interact.

The Contractual Metaphor

Haltingly, to be sure, Peter Berger has suggested that "our political life continues to be infused with religious symbols, religious rhetoric, and religious functionaries" all of which appear to constitute "a *de facto* political establishment of religion."[1] Gustav Weigel makes the point more directly: "Secular society today is trying to make a deal with the churches. It is saying: Give us your unswerving support in the pursuit of the objectives we have before us; in return we will cover you with honor."[2] Surely, such talk of *de facto* deals being made between God and country extracts much of the poetry from civic piety. That is precisely our point—that the government of the United States and its religious bodies have entered into a practical compact rooted in an understanding of what public discourse does for citizens and of its stabilizing effects on their lives.

In opting for this contractual metaphor, we are clearly taking a good number of historical liberties. The church-state story in the United States is hardly a simple one, as we have seen in the early portion of Chapter 3. Mountains of conflicting motivations, thousands of diverse personalities, and scores of historical, political, theological, and sociological currents have conspired to fashion the relationships now shared by government and religion. Thereby denied truly probative value, we use the contractual metaphor for heuristic purposes.

Yet our metaphor can teach us well. Consider, for example, the day upon which the terms of this contract were first manifested. It was a day during which the constant wrangling of the delegates to the Constitutional Convention threatened to destroy the delicate cordiality that had been built among the delegates. Local interests and personal ambitions promised to bring down the new nation just fashioned after the war with Great Britain. In-fighting, political intrigue, and home-grown American contrariness loomed ominously in 1787. In the midst of this rancor, an elderly gentleman rose from his chair at a crucial moment. It was "Benjamin Franklin, the elder statesman"[3] who made the following address:

> Mr. President: The small progress we have made after four or five weeks of close attendance and continual reasonings with each other—our different sentiments on almost every question, several of the last producing as many noes as ayes, is methinks a melancholy proof of the imperfection of the human understanding . . .
>
> I have lived, Sir, a long time, and the longer I live, the more convincing proofs I see of this truth—that God governs in the affairs of men. And if a sparrow cannot fall to the ground without His Notice, is it probable that an empire can rise without His aid? . . .

> I, therefore, beg leave to move that, henceforth, prayers
> imploring the assistance of Heaven, and its blessings on our
> deliberations, be held in this assembly every morning we pro-
> ceed to business, and that one or more of the clergy in this city
> be requested to officiate in that service.[4]

Benjamin Weiss, apologist for the American civil religion, remarks that subsequent to Franklin's address "the members of the Convention soon demonstrated a
different attitude of willingness to give and take and the Constitution began to
take form."[5] Apocryphal though the specifics of the tale may be, and specious
though Weiss's casual argument may appear, Franklin's speech is surely a
benchmark in the history of civil-religious discourse in the U.S.

Franklin's address evidences many of the traits we associate with contemporary religio-political rhetoric: (1) it achieves its fullest expression during moments of crisis; (2) it taps a dimension—religion—that is compelling for many
Americans; (3) it reduces inordinately complex issues to their most basic, patently religious, understructures; (4) it reaffirms the coordinated, but separate,
roles people and the Deity play in the affairs of the nation; and (5) its grand abstractness creates a totemic structure around which all Americans may happily
rally. No matter what cynical historians may say about Franklin's speech being a
clever diversionary tactic (a harbinger of labor-management's cooling-off period?), God has been asked to settle many a crisis in U.S. history.

While some may still cling to the view that Franklin's speech was (in the
language of the American civil religion) a "genuine outpouring of deep religious
commitment," it would be unwise to dismiss the strategic dimensions of his act
or Peter Berger's interpretation of such sacred canopies:

> If one imagines oneself as a fully aware founder of a society, a
> kind of combination of Moses and Machiavelli, one could ask
> oneself the following question: How can the future continua-
> tion of the institutional order, now established *ex nihilo*, be
> best ensured? [The answer seems to be to] let the people for-
> get that this order was established by men and continues to be
> dependent upon the consent of men. Let them believe that, in
> acting out the institutional programs that have been imposed
> upon them, they are but realizing the deepest aspirations of
> their own being and putting themselves in harmony with the
> fundamental order of the universe. In sum: Set up religious le-
> gitimations. There are, of course, wide historical variations in
> the manner in which this has been done. In one way or an-
> other, the basic recipe was followed throughout most of hu-
> man history. And, actually, the example of Moses-Machiavelli
> figuring the whole thing out with cool deliberation may not be
> as fanciful as all that. There have been very cool minds indeed
> in the history of religion.[6]

The coolest of such minds in colonial history may well have been that of the gentleman from Philadelphia.

Rhetorical Nature of the Contract

In the latter part of this chapter we will address the specific terms agreed to by the spokesmen for God and government. Before doing so, however, let us to examine two of the more general features of the agreement: its rhetorical nature and its flexibility.

If our contractual metaphor has any value, it is that of pointing out how often the American people have relied on public rhetoric to extricate themselves from uncomfortable political binds. Perhaps because rhetoric is such a useful entity, Americans have long agreed to the maxim: that which we cannot accomplish de jure we will effect per rhetorica. Thus, if the U.S. could not survive amicably as a totally secular state, it had to be provided with a religious mantle through the agency of public discourse. If organized religion demands a say-so in the political and ethical life of the nation, it must be given just that—a say-so. And if the rhetorics of government and religion clash, resolution or sublimation must be effected through more rhetoric.

That public discourse has been chosen to maintain the delicate relationship between church and state is no happenstance. The very nature of rhetoric itself earmarks it as a perfect candidate for such a task: (1) while rhetoric's effects are sometimes painfully tangible, rhetoric itself is thoroughly ethereal; (2) rhetorical engagements are transitory events, genuinely evanescent; (3) rhetorical power can be placed in the hands of many persons (especially in large, heterogeneous society) without existential conflict necessarily ensuing; (4) given the correct emotional and attitudinal circumstances, rhetoric is an incredibly potent force which can advance and retard a culture's ideologies. Because it has such qualities, rhetoric is a useful tool for propelling a society's facts as well as its fictions.

While irreligionists like Madlyn Murray O'Hair have long decried the inroads religion has made in American political life,[7] history shows that rhetorical contracts, not legal ones, have been the nation's most dependable allies. Thus, although Reinhold Niebuhr may have been justifiably upset by the goings-on in the White House, he was ill-advised to base his critique on legal grounds:

> We do not know the architectural proportions of Bethel. But we know that it is, metaphorically, the description of the East Room of the White House, which President Nixon has turned into a kind of sanctuary. By a curious combination of innocence and guile, he has circumvented the Bill of Rights' first article. Thus, he has established a conforming religion by semi-officially inviting representatives of all the disestablished religions, of whose moral criticism we were naturally so proud.[8]

Richard Nixon, it would seem, not Madlyn Murray O'Hair or Reinhold Neibuhr, best understood America's rhetorical history. Richard Nixon knew, as Benjamin Franklin knew, that rhetorical engagements lie well beyond the arm of the law. The Bill of Rights placed very few sanctions on the rhetorical behaviors of worshiping presidents. Indeed, no matter what the separationists may claim, Richard Nixon's Sunday services abided by both the letter and the spirit of the First Amendment. As Robert Bellah has stated, "the separation of church and state has not denied the political realm a religious dimension."[9]

While some scholars may be unwilling to distinguish so readily between the legal and the rhetorical, most Americans seem able to do so. Americans have allowed their Continental Congress, for example, to ingest "God or one of the numerous synonyms of the Deity into most all of its documents and promulgations," but they have demanded that "the Constitution emerging from the Convention [contain] no such invocation or reference."[10] As Leo Pfeffer once observed, "The omission was not inadvertent; nor did it remain unnoticed."[11] "Let religion and religious politicians have their rhetoric," reason most Americans, "but don't force us to sign loyalty oaths, require us to join an established church, or demand that we recite prayers in public schools." As long as organized religion is armed exclusively with rhetorical weaponry, most Americans appear willing to reaffirm the covenant described by Sidney Mead:

> (since the public welfare was to set the limits even of religious freedom, and the public welfare is a matter for the state to define) the way was left open for the state, if and when it judged that the religious sects were inadequate or derelict in the matter, to defend itself by setting up the institutions or machinery necessary to guarantee the dissemination and inculcation of the necessary beliefs. . . . The free churches accepted, or had forced upon them on these terms, the duty and responsibility to define, articulate, disseminate, and inculcate the basic religious beliefs essential for the existence and well-being of the society—and of doing this without any coercive power over the citizens at all, that is, armed only with persuasive power.[12]

The nature of the church-state compact in the U.S. is seen in sharpest relief when we look at the nexus between the legislative and the rhetorical. In 1956, for instance, Senator Styles Bridges of New Hampshire introduced a bill that asked Americans to "perpetuate renewed observance throughout the world, by nations and individuals, of the Ten Commandments."[13] As Paul Blanshard notes, since such a resolution would only be emotionally binding on Congress, it was assumed that, were the resolution to pass, no one would test its constitutionality.[14] Essentially, the bill called for nothing more than renewed rhetoric on behalf of the American civil religion, and hence, little concern was voiced over its potential to compromise church-state separation. Thus, although Bridges' motion adhered closely to the tenets of the civil religious compact, the affair was not without its procedural difficulties:

When Bridges introduced his resolution in 1956, there was a moment of embarrassed silence while Senate officials pondered the question of which committee had jurisdiction over the Word of God and the Ten Commandments. Congress, of course, has no standing committee on the relations of church and state or the general extension of moral principles to world society. Finally, the Senate sent the resolution to the Committee on Foreign Relations.[15]

Fluctuating Nature of the Contract

Although the "contract" was first written in Revolutionary times it has been constantly renegotiated over time. Indeed, one of the most distinctive elements of the civil-religious covenant is the flexibility with which it meets changing exigencies. That is, while the quantity of "official" civil religious discourse may not change from age to age, the intensity with which it is preached—and hence the extent to which the terms of the contract are enforced—are quite variable indeed.

As we have seen in the early portion of Chapter 3, very real and very practical reasons drew God and country together in the early days of the nation. With British sabers rattling and with internal strife in the colonies being significant, the rhetorical power of organized religion was first unleashed on behalf of the young nation's independence. The Reverend James Otis and his "black regimen" of colonial ministers "preached up" the Revolution "in innumerable 'fast day' and recruiting sermons."[16] Generally, though, they did so politely, not idolatrously; nor were they especially chauvinistic about their soon-to-be nation.[17] In any event, religion paid its rhetorical dues in colonial America, and later on, as Gribbin notes,[18] both Northerners and Southerners were treated to renewed sermons on nationalism by America's clergymen turned patriots during the Civil War. Too, as Ray Abrams details in *Preachers Present Arms*, the American clergy used rhetorical machine guns when rearticulating the contract during World War I. The following excerpt from a speech by the Reverend Charles A. Eaton may well be representative of war-time preaching in the early 1900s: "When [the spy] comes sneaking around with a bomb, don't say 'Let us pray,' but take him out there on the marsh and tie him down and place the bomb on his chest. Light it and stand off and watch him blow to his Kaiser—to Hell! Be regular he-men."[19]

The contract has not always been honored with such intensity. Indeed, except for World War I's rhetoric and that displayed during the highly emotional 1950s, most Americans have been rather blasé about their civic pieties. Sidney Mead suggests that this change in emotional tempo resulted from the burgeoning nationalism of post–Civil War America. Says Mead: "American nationalism finally was rendered pervasive and secure by the Civil War. Just as the older Federalism disappeared in a new and unprecedented assertion of central power, the former dedication to the Union gave way to a novel but irresistible sense of organic unity. This nationalism no longer had the same need for the older mythic unity supported by religious sanctions."[20] Coupled with rising industrialization and the scientific era, America's nationalism could thus take on a more casual tone, the existential need for such rhetorical support having now been diminished.

In other words, there have been undulations in the emotional intensity of civic piety over the years. This is not to say that the rhetoric has become less plentiful. Today's presidents still go through their paces as do the members of the clergy joining them at state functions. Yet as Paul Blanshard notes, the prayers of Congressional chaplains now go almost totally unheeded, sometimes being delivered to a congregation of no more than six persons.[21] In other words (as we will see in Chapter 5), the pragmatic need for civil-religious discourse has been replaced by ritualistic exigence. So, while the terms of the contract are still adhered to faithfully, habit rather than burning conviction seems to drive it. Says Frederick Fox:

> Despite all his elaborate staging, President Johnson's Prayer Proclamation got scant attention. It was lost in a whirlwind of activity—a stroll with his dogs around the White House grounds, luncheon at the National Press Club, supper for the Congress, signing other bills and proclamations (for example, "White Cane Day," October 15) and greeting callers like Sharon Moline of Salt Lake City, also known as "Miss Wool of America." The day ended, with a series of last minute conferences before driving out to the Naval Hospital in Bethesda for a gall bladder operation.[22]

Terms of the Contract

When reviewing the contract presented earlier, the reader's attention is directed to the three principles upon which it is based: (1) that religion provides an ultimate meaning system for its adherents, (2) that government can exert coercive influence on the affairs of its citizens, and (3) that both government and religion wield considerable rhetorical power. By accepting such assumptions, the specific terms of the contract become easier to see.

The first principle is perhaps the most subtle. Essentially, we are arguing here that organized religion sets a certain "tone" in the U.S., a respect for faithfulness and a commitment to higher values. Government is an unimaginative, spiritless oaf in contrast. Government builds roads, outfits people for battle, regulates the country's shipping, subsidizes its farms, computerizes its tax forms. Religion, in contrast, posits transcendent verities, takes a stand on other-worldly issues, discourses about the intangible, points citizens toward over-arching ethical standards, and retrieves them from the miasma of ordinary existence. In short, religion gives people faith in faith. And when religion shares the motivational cosmos with government, it becomes only a short emotional step from faith to patriotism and from God to country—presuming, of course, that the nation's political leaders have their rhetorical wits about them.

Because traditional western religions answer ultimate questions with some degree of authority and provide (through their respective eschatologies) a sense of destiny for their believers, it is small wonder that government courts them so ardently. Too, religious bodies have usually been insightful enough to reckon with the awesome power possessed by the State Incarnate—power to fill its coffers, to send its sons off to war, and to punish crushingly those who refuse to do so. Government, for all of its attractiveness, is a brawny, stubble-faced suitor. Finally, it must be remembered that the philosophical power of religion and the coercive influence of the state are buttressed equally by their ability to use rhetoric often and well. Indeed, the two combined may well constitute the most important rhetorical institution in the contemporary United States (much to the dismay of such spurned rhetorical rivals as Black Power, feminism, consumerism, and so forth).

But if organized religion and the United States government have joined together in holy wedlock, the relationship promises to be a curious one: marital roles are carefully proscribed and prescribed; a sharp imbalance in power exists between the newlyweds; and, cruelest cut of all, the marriage cannot be announced in the local papers. Though she may have made an honest man out of Sir Government, Madam Religion lost more than her virginity on that fated day in 1787 when Preacher Franklin tied the knot for all eternity.

The Guise of Complete Separation

Thomas Jefferson notwithstanding, the American people have never witnessed total separation between their government and their religious bodies. Franklin Littell makes the case more precisely:

> That men of different religious covenants may live together as good fellow citizens is a fact—and also a profoundly important theological event. It means that the religious covenants and the political covenants are separated. And that is the first phase of the guise of the American experiment—not "separation of church and state" (a misnomer, for we have never had it) but separation of the religious and political compacts. Our theoretical understanding has not, as yet, caught up with our experience.[23]

Government and religion have had their own spheres of influence in the United States, a set of conditions that many commentators would describe as "the genius of the American experiment in the disestablishment of religion." Still, although both parties have willingly agreed to maintain the fiction of separation, they have constantly colluded with one another, as atheist Madlyn Murray O'Hair has exhaustively detailed (here presented in modified fashion):

1. The United States government is especially liberal with regard to copyright requirements for religious publications.
2. The U.S. Office of Education publishes a booklet entitled *The Declaration of Independence and Its Story* which acknowledges the hand of God in the fashioning of the American republic.

3. Religious services and prayer breakfasts are frequently held in the White House and in other governmental buildings.
4. Congress has proclaimed April 30 the National Day for Humiliation, Fasting, and Prayer.
5. Congress has incorporated such organizations as the Boy Scouts and the Veterans of Foreign War even though such groups require belief in God for full membership.
6. Military chaplains, who perform a wide variety of religious functions, are salaried by the United States government.
7. The phrases "In God We Trust," "Under God," and "So Help Me God" have been legislated into official governmental language.
8. Catholic hospitals receive federal funds and yet refuse to perform legal abortions for taxpayers.
9. The United States Department of the Interior and the United States Department of Agriculture permit church groups to hold religious services in national parks and recreation areas.
10. Texas school boards often inquire whether or not applicants for teaching positions believe in a Supreme Being.[24]

This is only a partial listing of the numerous interactions between the U.S. government and organized religion. At the same time, however, students of religious freedom can respond with an equally long list of principles and practices that separate church and state in the U.S.:

1. There is no national religion which requires the membership of the American people.
2. Job discrimination on the basis of one's faith has severe punishments attendant to it.
3. No frankly religious precedent may be employed in the adjudication of a case in a court of law.
4. Prayer in the public schools has been banned.
5. Federal and state assistance to religious educational institutions—as religious institutions—is prohibited.

And so on and so forth.

As Littell, Bellah, and O'Hair would argue, however, the separationists' case is primarily a legal one, not a sociological one or, as we would have it, not a rhetorical one either. That is, the rhetoric of governmental officials is often openly religious in tone (as we have seen in Chapter 1). At the same time, however, these same political leaders will claim, paradoxically, that theirs is an areligious country where persons of all (or no) faiths are treated equally under the law.

Both sides are right in part—Americans are an areligious people even as they ardently admire civic piety. Notice, for example, that of the eleven "violations" O'Hair identifies, only two (numbers 8 and 11) are bereft of a rhetorical dimension. Numbers 2, 3, 4, 7, and 10 refer to rhetorical concessions government makes in behalf of religion—proclamations are issued, public space is made available, religious language is added to public rituals, and God is mentioned occasionally in federal documents. Notice, too, that few funds are expended to support such activities, no concomitant legal sanctions are imposed, and nobody is really compelled to do anything in particular. Finally, it should be remembered that sentimental forces (e.g., number 1), traditional forces (5), psychological forces (6), and political forces (9)—not binding legal ones—have motivated most of the other violations O'Hair identifies.

All of this is not to say that rhetorical violations do not run counter to the spirit of the First Amendment or that there are no tangible violations of its letter in the United States today. Nevertheless, the American people have largely fashioned a legal disestablishment and replaced it with the rhetorical trappings of civic piety, thereby safeguarding the alternative that all human interactants have at all times—that of not listening to one another.

The Guise of Existential Equality

"It is distinctive of our country that we have developed a relationship in which church and state can cooperate without the one dominating the life of the other: government not dictating to the church; and the church, on the other hand, not dictating to government."[25] Thus opined the Reverend Oswald C. J. Hoffman when, in the early 1960s, he addressed the Pentagon Protestant Pulpit, a weekday series of noon-hour services conducted by members of the clergy in the Concourse of the Pentagon. In this section, we will see that the Reverend Hoffman was half right: the church does not dictate to government.

Of all the charges that can be leveled at the American civil religion, the most strident is that it saps the dignity and prophetic spirit of more traditional religious bodies. That is, the nation's congregations have agreed to a contract that even a first-year law student would find degrading and manipulative. American religion is being used, such persons argue, for the greater honor and glory of the United States government. As we shall see later in this essay, these commentators are often correct.

Before getting into such polemics, however, it seems useful to survey the facts in the case. Are religion and government existential equals? Had both reached the age of consent when signing their John Hancocks (and Jonathan Edwardses) to the contract they devised? The answer to both questions is clearly no. While the church in contemporary society has significant emotional influence over the lives of its adherents, it does not possess the coercive, adjudicative, tax-making power of its contractual partner. The church's realm is clearly the rhetorical—it can make words about social conditions and governmental priorities but it cannot enforce its will directly and immediately as can government. This is not to disparage the power of discourse, for, as the United States government knows full well, the rhetorical influence of the churches makes them a prized ally. Yet, when government can require even conscientious objectors to fight in its wars, when government can make laws relative to tax-deductible religious contributions, and when government can compel the churches to insure that their buildings conform to health and fire codes, it is clear who wields the existential club, as has been rather sardonically pointed out by sociologist Bernard Bell:

> Certainly no competent sociologist or political scientist, no scholarly observer of our country who is not himself a professionally ecclesiastical person, says or thinks that the Church has much to do with the complexion of the contemporary American picture. Instead, their usual conclusion is that most Americans regard the Church as promoter of a respectable minor art, charming if it happens to appeal to you, its only moral function to bless whatever the multitude at the moment regards as the American way of life.[26]

Things were not always so, of course. In the early days of the U.S. the church had considerable tangible influence. But as historian Alan Heimert notes, things began to change in the nineteenth century:

> To be sure, the campaign of 1800 clearly marked the beginning of a more secular era in American politics. With it began an era in which the lay orator, rather than the preacher, increasingly took over the task of expounding public issues for and to the popular mind. . . But in the aftermath of the war, the clergy seemed to retreat into a self-imposed ecclesiastical exile, thus completing a transition that had begun, even before the war, with the rise of lay spokesmen to eminence in American political life.[27]

At this point apparently, the existential-rhetorical balance began to shift. The roles of the contracting parties became more sharply defined; new job descriptions were written; and the coordination of religious rhetoric and governmental action was effected. To the dismay of some, organized religion thus became a rhetorical lackey—indoctrinating the tribe's warriors as they went out to battle;[28] providing a "spiritual embellishment" and a "useful sustaining force" to governmental policy;[29] and generally becoming something of a factotum in American life. As Will Herberg sadly notes:

> In this reversal the Christian and Jewish faiths tend to be prized because they help promote ideals and standards that all Americans are expected to share on a deeper level than merely "official" religion. Insofar as any reference is made to the God in whom all Americans "believe" and of whom the "official" religions speak, it is primarily as sanction and underpinning for the supreme values of the faith embodied in the American Way of Life. Secularization of religion could hardly go further.[30]

While theologians may cringe at such a set of conditions, the church probably effected the best deal it could. Unbalanced though the contract was, it was a
contract nonetheless, with significant dividends accruing to both the greater and
lesser of the two equals. Because, as Loren Beth indicates, the church did "not
contain all of the citizens of the state, and therefore [did] not have jurisdictional
rights coextensive with those of the state,"[31] it grabbed what it could—rhetorical
jurisdiction. The church reserved the right to advise, to admonish, and often to
advance governmental policies and behaviors, and the state agreed to provide a
very public forum for the espousal of mainstream civil-religious viewpoints.

Thus, the genius of the compromise should not be understated. Because of it,
church leaders were accorded rhetorical access to heads of state, allowed to set the
agenda for discussions of moral issues, and generally treated with respect, if not
obeisance. Rather than incorporate church in state, with all of its attendant abuses,
and rather than relegate the church to third-class status, the American people permitted religion to occupy an honored place in the national sun. By carefully modulating the existential/rhetorical balance between church and state, Americans
thereby avoided the Scylla of irreligiosity and the Charybdis of pure theocracy.

As a conclusion to this section, it might be helpful to consider the alternatives
the American people had to institutionalizing civic piety, to not agreeing to the
contract being explicated in this chapter. Loren Beth provides a handy summary
(here modified for brevity's sake) of the various church-state options confronting
the American colonists:

1. Pure theocracy—a situation in which actual political authority
   is held and exercised by the heads of the ecclesiastical establishment.

2. Total separation—complete and unalterable divorce of church
   and state functions.

3. Mixed theocracy—the state is regarded as subordinate, even
   in temporal affairs. It is allowed such autonomy as the church
   is willing to grant it.

4. Total identification—a situation in which every citizen is subject to the state, politically, as well as to the national church.

5. Total conflict—often witnessed in quasi-totalitarian countries,
   this is a system in which church and state aggressively attempt
   to vanquish each other.

6. Erastianism—a condition in which the state is accorded control of religion in order to secure religious peace, thereby establishing a national religion.

7. Totalitarianism—situation in which organized religion is totally vanquished by the state and where the opportunity for religious observance is denied.

8. Partial separation—most commentators see this as the American system, in which the dignity and jurisdiction of both
   church and state are respected by both parties.[32]

When placed in perspective, then, the contract being described here makes considerable sense. History had shown the colonists that total separation was impractical for a nominally religious people, mixed theocracy not feasible for a diverse citizenry, total identification and pure theocracy philosophically repugnant for a people attempting to escape such systems, and total conflict and totalitarianism unacceptable on any reasonable grounds. That left partial separation . . . and erastianism.

In short, the American people happened upon a church-state system even more curious than that of partial separation—they created a kind of symbolic erastianism in which the state was granted existential jurisdiction over its citizens (and their various religious institutions) and the church allowed to share in rhetorical jurisdiction over the American people. Concomitant with this arrangement was an agreement to maintain the fiction of total separation through the agency of civic piety.

Naturally, there are those who might argue that this is too reductionistic a view of church-state relations in the U.S., too dismissive of religious authority. There are those who might argue that religious groups have sometimes dragged government kicking and screaming into certain arenas of social reform. Nevertheless, it seems clear that government, not religion, has affected most social reforms in the U.S. While its ear has often been bent by religious groupings during such moments, it is equally clear who has done the urging and who has done the acting across the broad sweep of U.S. social history.

Maintaining Rhetorical Balance

With the twin proposition the "First party (government) rhetoric will refrain from being overly religious and second party (religion) rhetoric will refrain from being overly political," we come upon the most important feature of the contract being described here. Political and religious leaders have had to constantly juggle things because of the contract they signed. During the tribulations (and later, trials) of Watergate, for instance, mainstream churches largely circumnavigated the matter. Although some civil-religious pagans (like the Reverend Peter Christianson) passed out petitions among their congregations calling for the impeachment of Richard Nixon, "moral outrage from the pulpit was not as widespread as it might be."[33] John Cardinal Krol, Roman Catholic prelate to Philadelphia, "skirted any specific mention of Watergate, lumping it with other evils as part of 'a serious departure from ethical and moral principles.'"[34] Also, when American Episcopalians gathered for their triennial general convention in Louisville in October of 1973, they failed to go on record regarding Watergate. Even groups as disparate as the Christian Church (Disciples of Christ) and the Union of American Hebrew Congregations failed to issue a strong statement on Watergate. The American civil religion, it seems, is largely a fair-weather religion.

By and large, it has always been so. As scholar Harry Kerr indicates, even the fast and thanksgiving sermons preached in colonial times were uncharacteristic of the usual fare served up to the colonists: "Published sermons indicate that ministers seldom forsook Christ for long, and even if the political enthusiasm of an occasional minister caused him to neglect his religious role, at least he retained an audience. Considered in this light, fast and thanksgiving sermons present the rare picture" of the colonial preacher.[35] Alan Heimert agrees with Kerr when remarking that "with the exception of John Davenport (and, for a few years in the 1680s, Increase Mather and his fellow critics of moderate government), few New England preachers had publicly stood as spokesmen against the standing order."[36]

This being the case, pacifist preachers are especially interesting. Like their fellow ministers, pacifists are obliged by the terms of the contract to refrain from being excessively political. If they do mention politics, they are asked to reaffirm the standing political order. Those pacifist preachers during World War I who refused to abide by the contract met with a number of unfortunate circumstances: some were despised for disobeying "the tribal gods"; most were barred from their churches; some were never able to find another pulpit; and others gave up the ministry entirely.[37]

It is this matter of being overly political that most clearly distinguishes the rhetorics of "official" and "unofficial" civic piety. When preachers talk about political matters, they often relinquished their claim to the dividends of those who follow the straight and narrow. Anti-establishment ministers are especially feared by church officials who implicitly realize they are doing violence to the contract. On the other hand, excessive establishmentarianism by religious leaders is also feared by politicians and viewed with a jaundiced eye by the electorate. Because these constraints are so tight, the following tale amuses: "Father Taylor during an exciting election campaign once prayed, 'O Lord, give us good men to rule over us, pure men who fear Thee, righteous men, temperate men, who—pshaw, Lord, what's the use of veering and hauling and boxing around the compass? Give us George N. Biggs for governor.'"[38]

The rhetorical sword cuts both ways—politicians should be religious but not too religious. They must pay homage to America's God but avoid being gushy about it. In 1972, for example, George McGovern took great pains to "hide the fact (and ban the photo) of himself as pastor of a Methodist church,"[39] even though he did, of course, make occasional theological allusions in his speeches. Similarly, both Presidents Johnson and Nixon were careful not to identify "Vietnam policy with the designs of God in whom Americans professedly trust."[40] As Richard Neuhaus declares, such a gaffe "would have occasioned a severe conflict between the churches and American civil religion and inflamed a public debate about 'the purposes and meaning of our beloved nation'" which would have been both "intense and corrosive."[41]

Kennedy belonged to a church that was often quite public in its professions. The ornateness of Catholic architecture, the ostentatious nature of traditional Catholic services and ceremonials, and the clannishness and ethnicity of its worshippers all conspired to depict them as capital-R religious. In contrast, the

American civil religion has been largely Protestant in design and execution since its inception.

Thus, while sociologists and political scientists may argue that it was the essence of Kennedy's Roman Catholicism that frightened the American voter in 1960, it seems just as reasonable to suggest it was the rhetorical tone of Catholicism that made people suspicious. Catholicism, with its traditional claims to theological supremacy, its non-egalitarian private schools, and its mysterious religious formulas, typically only gave grudging respect to the American civil religion. Apparently aware of such prejudices, Kennedy himself displayed a somewhat cavalier attitude toward religion in an attempt to affirm the civil-religious contract:

> Some have termed John Kennedy a "spiritually rootless modern man." Others have spoken of him as a secular man. These references point to his unwillingness to adapt himself to institutional religion. JFK accepted religion as a part of his life, but his closest associate, Ted Sorenson, could say: "But not once in eleven years—despite all our discussions of church-state affairs—did he ever disclose his personal views on man's relation to God." Sorenson also informs us that Kennedy cared "not a whit for theology." He apparently saw the Bible as a good source for quotations, but with no more reverence than he might have had for other great literature, and possibly less than he had for Jefferson. As one historian phrased it, he "wore his religion lightly."[42]

Whatever he may have felt personally, John Kennedy did his utmost to respect the terms of the contract his forebears had signed.

The Future of the Contract

That we have been discussing God and patriotism with a legal metaphor may offend some readers. The hushed, reverential tones with which Robert Bellah speaks of his civil religion surely has greater poetic value. We hope to have shown, however, that figuratively at least, the U.S. government and organized religion have made a deal, a transaction based on the division of existential and rhetorical roles. In arriving at this contractual metaphor we perhaps have not drawn on the better tendencies of humankind. But we have drawn on very human instincts, instincts rooted in a practical understanding of how a large, pluralistic democracy must be simultaneously religious and areligious for it to function properly. In demystifying the discourse some Americans prize most, we have tried not to debunk it even though we have grounded our understanding in the rough-and-ready, thoroughly practical nature of the American people. That Americans have chosen to maintain a collective fiction of church-state separation while simultaneously building bridges between them is hardly condemnatory even if it is profoundly paradoxical.

As we approach the latter part of the twentieth century, however, there is growing evidence that the contract will be honored with less zeal in the future. Already, we are beginning to see growing concern over the imbalance between the contracting partners. For example, when "Cardinal Spellman of New York described our armed forces in Vietnam as 'soldiers of Christ' and declared himself in favor of 'my country right or wrong,' he was severely censured by most of the religious press."[43] Similarly, although the Clergy and Laymen Concerned About Vietnam were composed of, at best, 10 percent of the American clergy,[44] the very existence of the group indicated that some were chafing under the contract's restrictions. Also, with ministers, priests, and nuns now being elected to state and national offices, there seems to be growing sentiment to turn the country in a new direction. Moreover, we are now hearing some theologians decry civic piety and asking for a more demanding civil-religious rhetoric and, even, for less talk and more action. As these voices grow louder and more insistent and as more and more members of the clergy ask to renegotiate the contract, it is conceivable that people will begin to heed the warning Franklin Littell issued in 1962:

> If "the American religion" continues to emerge, bringing with it the hearty and uncritical affirmation of everything American, the time may yet come when believing Jews, Catholics, and Protestants will have to face up to tribal religion in its more demonic form. In that day they will learn, as has been learned by the religious remnants who have remained faithful in the face of other totalitarianism, that they have much in common besides a goodly land.[45]

Chapter 5

Rhetorical Features of Civic Piety

The rhetoric associated with American civic piety is a complex thing. As we have seen, such discourse derives its rationale from a potpourri of human motivations. Too, its manifestations are as variable as its authors are numerous. Yet when treated as a body of rhetoric, civic piety is composed of a distinctive and consistent pastiche of elements even though it is fueled by personal predilections, to be sure.

To a large extent, the rhetoric of the American civil religion has become—in our times, at least—what Kathleen Hall Jamieson calls generically calcified.[1] That is, it responds more surely to its own "antecedent rhetorical forms"[2] than to the peculiarities of the exigences to which it responds daily. Frederick Fox has pointed out, for example, that proclamations issued by American presidents on national days of prayer are distinguished more by their similarities than by the unique rhetorical personalities of their creators. It does not take a cynic, implies Fox, to note the isomorphic qualities of Kennedy's and Eisenhower's proclamations:

> *Eisenhower:* "This Nation, under God, arrived at its present position by the toil and sacrifice of many citizens who subordinated personal interests to the common welfare . . . in the unconquerable spirit of a free people . . . to work toward goals of human betterment which may be attained only beyond our span of years."

> *Kennedy:* "This Nation under God has achieved its great service to mankind through the toil and sacrifices and subordination of personal desires to common welfare, . . . in the unconquerable spirit of a free people . . . to work for goals of human betterment that lie beyond our span of years."[3]

That a Catholic Democrat should borrow so faithfully from a Protestant Republican in preparing his remarks reveals both the universal nature of the American civil religion as well as the inventional constraints willingly observed by its spokesmen.

The story of civil religiosity in the U.S. is a story that has been told many times previously in the pages of rhetorical history, a story of the substitution of commonplaces for *topoi* as aids to rhetorical invention, of speakers' dependence upon stock phrases rather than ideas developed for the unique communicative situation at hand.

In this chapter, we will look carefully at the distinguishing aspects of civil-religious discourse, attempting to see whether Gabriel Fackre's phrase, "the musak of civil religion,"[4] is an accurate (or needlessly precious) description of American civic piety. More specifically, we will examine four features of civil-religious discourse which give it a distinctive, even formulary, flavor. We will argue here that civil religious discourse in the U.S. is characterized by its expedient complexity, its non-existential content, its ritualistic presence, and its prosaic animus. Although such traits appear to accord themselves with Fackre's rather cynical description, we will see that no facile designation alone captures the rhetoric of civic piety.

Expedient Complexity

Expediency

Although many commentators have accused politicians and clerics alike of being venal when it comes to civic piety, rhetorical facts marshaled in support of such charges have been few and far between. For at least one American politician, Richard Nixon, allegations of religious opportunism seem to be partially justified.

Having collected a sample of 201 public speeches delivered by Richard Nixon between 1948 and 1974, we proceeded to search each address for civil-religious themes. Keying exclusively on references made to America's "God(s)," we found that 28 speeches (18 ceremonial, 10 non-ceremonial) of the 201 contained god-references, while 173 did not. Of the 56 god-references, 12 were found in introductory portions of the speeches, 9 in middle segments, and 35 in concluding remarks.

It does not take a rigorous statistician to see to the core of Nixon's inclinations regarding matters theological. Less than 14 percent of Nixon's speeches contained divine allusions. Of the fifty-six identifiable references made to (or about) God by Nixon, thirty-five (or 62.5 percent) resided in his perorations. Of the remaining references, the majority were used by Nixon to pry open his addresses. Equally interesting, there was no easily discernible chronological pattern to Nixon's deployment of the heavenly hosts. Rather, Nixon mentioned God selectively throughout his career, his choices apparently being dictated by the demands of the rhetorical situations he faced.

Almost 65 percent of the speeches containing theological refrains emanated from ceremonial situations. Three of the speeches were eulogies, three were convention acceptance addresses, three were remarks made at religious gatherings, two were State of the Union Addresses, two were holiday proclamations, and, of course, two were his presidential inaugurals. The remainder was commencement addresses, remarks made at memorial dinners, and election day speeches.

Of the ten non-ceremonial addresses, four were "crisis" speeches (on Vietnam, on Watergate, and on the economy), four discussed the "communist problem," one was a campaign speech (delivered in 1974), and the last was an instance of the "One America" speeches Nixon gave from time to time during his career. It is particularly noteworthy that almost none of Nixon's theologically embellished speeches dealt avowedly with partisan politics, welfare, higher education, international diplomacy, the natural environment, or the other workaday vicissitudes of American life. For Richard Nixon, at least, God was a comrade to be relied upon infrequently but dramatically.

Although others may argue to the contrary, there is little reason to suspect that Nixon's strategies were singular. He, like most American presidents, was a nominally religious person. Reared a Quaker, Nixon revealed a modest and decorous respect for his nation's politico-religious heritage throughout his public life. As we shall see shortly, Nixon's rhetoric was rather typical of his political predecessors and will probably be typical of his successors as well.

Complexity

Naturally, no mere quantitative description of civil-religious rhetoric will alone explain its suasory characteristics. Rather, it is the content of the civil pietists' remarks that provides us with the best understanding of the phenomena being described here. More specifically, it is by attuning ourselves to the pantheon of Gods guiding the American civil religion that we can discern most clearly its theological essence as well as its rhetorical methodology.

It will be remembered that when Robert Bellah first remarked about the American civil religion, his database was generated largely from the maiden speeches of America's presidents. While Bellah has stimulated a wealth of research on the topic, no scholar, curiously enough, has returned to examine the initial sources of many of Bellah's insights. Therefore, a systematic examination was made of each of the forty-seven presidential inaugurals with an eye peeled to the kinds of gods mentioned by the chief executives. The results are as fascinating as they will be, for some, disturbing.

America's Gods: Numerous observers have remarked about the "God who guides this great and good nation." Such comments sometimes contain a full measure of outrage: "The 'God' referred to [in patriotic messages] is only an abstraction, a digit in political computations, a football in political maneuvers."[5] More cerebral commentators have been equally concerned with two questions: Does America have one God or many Gods? Upon what theological axis does America's God(s?) turn?

In response to the first question, Robert Alley relates a story about arch civil religionist Billy Graham. During an interview, Graham was once asked: "What God, by your definition, would be equally acceptable to Jew and Christian alike?" Alley reports that "Graham was somewhat flustered when he responded with a question, 'Do you mean the God up there or the God in Christ?' He [Graham] became quite aggravated as he dismissed the questioner with obvious displeasure, passing to safer ground with another reporter."[6] Alley sees such a vignette as having significance for the American civil religion: "Of course, Graham is not a dualist in his views, he does not believe in two Gods, and he was using a figure that snared him. Nevertheless, he was asserting what amounted to a dualism, which he regularly affirms on occasions when he moves from his 'Hour of Decision' to a White House Prayer Breakfast. Billy Graham is only one of many evidences of a burgeoning national cult in the United States."[7] As we will see, Graham—as a civil pietist—is neither a monotheist nor a dualist. Rhetorically, he and his fellow apologists for civil religion in America are polytheists of the first order.

As for the characteristics of America's God(s), a number of designations have been offered, the most cogent being that of Bellah himself: "The God of the civil religion is . . . on the austere side, much more related to order, law, and right than to salvation and love. Even though he is somewhat deist in cast, he is by no means simply a watchmaker God. He is actively interested and involved in history, with a special concern for America."[8] Bellah's notion of a godhead with multiple dimensions is borne out when we carefully examine the rhetoric expended on His (or Their) behalf.

The American Pantheon: Bellah, of course, was right when he asserted that each American president has used God as a footnote in his inaugural address (save one—a brief one—Washington's second). What Bellah did not report, but what a systematic inspection of the inaugural addresses reveals, is that in the forty-seven inaugurals (Ford's address at his swearing-in ceremony being considered an "inaugural" for our purposes), numerous and varied descriptions of America's God are presented. Of the 183 descriptions of the deity offered by U.S. presidents, five general themes emerge. These include:

1. *God the Inscrutable Potentate*—This is a powerful and protective God, one who oftentimes, but mysteriously, directly intervenes in the affairs of the American people. According to Washington, He is powerful—the "Invisible Hand which conducts the affairs of men."[9] According to Jackson, He is also protective of the nation-state; He is the "Power whose providence mercifully protected our national infancy." According to Grant, He is rather arbitrary as well, one who "in His own good time" would make war-torn America one again. And according to Lincoln, one who had much experience with this mysterious, oftentimes fickle God who seems to delight in caprice, His succor would be garnered for America when "God wills" it in "His appointed time." Thus, God the Inscrutable Potentate is a God to be reckoned with, but he is equally a God with whom it is difficult to know how to reckon. He is, according to McKinley, a cosmic wheeler-dealer: "[God] will not forsake us so long as we obey his commandments and walk humbly in His footsteps."

2. *God the Witnessing Author*—Here in our pantheon we find the Creator God who authors things both human and divine

and watches His creations from afar. This is a silent, onlooker God, a non-participant in human affairs. He was, for George Washington, the "Great Author of every public and private good," and for Polk, He who fashioned our democratic form of government. He is an "ever-watchful" God who looks "down upon us all," one who is an especially obliging witness to our national ceremonials. According to some of the nation's presidents, God the Witnessing Author is the *deux ex machina* for the nation's social apparatuses.

3. *God the Wise and the Just*—This is an increasingly popular God in the national pantheon, one whose counsel and ministrations provide a reservoir of knowledge and justice for humanity. He is a Receptacle God from whom presidents and preachers alike draw their human portions of wisdom. This is the God who provided Franklin Roosevelt with "Divine guidance," the God who watched over Taft in the "Discharge of [his] responsible duties," and the "Almighty Providence" who helped Herbert Hoover handle the "ever-increasing burdens" of the White House. In addition to dispensing wisdom, this is a God who became John Adams's "Fountain of justice" and Lyndon Johnson's rather stern, Old Testament-like overseer: "God is harshest on those who are most favored." However, from the standpoint of the inaugurals, God the Wise and the Just was a rather reluctant wellspring of justice, rarely threatening His minions in LBJ's style. More often, He contented Himself with enlightening the minds of His servants and leaving the business of justice to more human agencies.

4. *God the Genial Philanthropist*—This is a rabidly partisan deity. God the Genial Philanthropist dispenses both material and emotional gifts to the deserving. As a result, His blessings have often been recounted by America's chief executives consistently over the years. Unlike God the Wise and the Just, this is an active God who dispenses prosperity (five times in the inaugurals), wisdom (five), strength (four), peace (three), mercy (two), and freedom (two references). This divine assortment of benefits has accrued uniquely to Polk's "Heaven-favored land." According to Ulysses S. Grant, His munificence has even included the most tangible of bounties: "providence [has] bestowed upon us a strong box in the precious metals locked up in the sterile mountains of the far West."

5. *God the Object of Affection*—Only occasionally can God the Object of Affection be seen in the inaugural rhetoric of

U.S. presidents. This is a God who deserves, but who does not demand, expressions of love and obedience from His faithful. Only in the occasional remarks of the more contemporary presidents do we find anything resembling a full-bodied declaration of gratitude to this rarest of America's Gods. Harding, Truman, FDR, Eisenhower, and Nixon (repeating FDR verbatim) have briefly expressed the nation's gratitude and affection. Most presidents have concentrated instead on initiating or renewing their divine bargains rather than thanking God for services previously rendered (or promising Him future obeisance, for that matter).

These, then, are the nation's gods. That they are mentioned but briefly by U.S. presidents is probably less important than they are mentioned at all. And their relative popularity should not go unnoticed. Table 5.1 reports the collective weight they have been accorded in presidential inaugurals.[10]

TABLE 5.1

REFERENCES TO GOD IN PRESIDENTIAL INAUGURALS

Deity	Percentage of Times Mentioned		
	All Inaugurals	**Early Inaugurals**[a]	**Later Inaugurals**[b]
God the Inscrutable Potentate	33.5	45.4	21.0
God the Witnessing Author	17.1	14.1	19.9
God the Wise and the Just	16.1	8.6	24.3
God the Genial Philanthropist	28.6	29.7	28.2
God the Object of Affection	4.7	2.2	6.6

[a] From Washington's first through Cleveland's first
(roughly the first half of the inaugurals).

[b] From Cleveland's second through Ford's swearing-in speech.

As might be expected, God the Inscrutable Potentate and God the Genial Philanthropist led the field during the earliest inaugural addresses. Most presidents, however, have sampled equitably within America's pantheon (with the exception of God the Object of Affection). Of all the presidents, Washington, Lincoln, and Eisenhower made the greatest number of references to the deity, while ten of the presidents made but one allusion. No president chose to mention all five of the Gods being described here and most appeared to have had a "favorite" heavenly consort (e.g., in his second inaugural, Lincoln focused special attention on God's inscrutability).[11]

Some interesting temporal differences are revealed in our quantitative analysis, however. The apocalyptic God (which understandably captured Lincoln's attention) appears to hold less interest for more contemporary presidents. Balancing that is a growing rhetorical concern for the wisdom and justice of God, perhaps reflecting a decreased fascination with the God of the Old Testament, perhaps reflecting nothing more than personal choice.

Most likely, however, such a shift in heavenly emphasis reflects a growing confidence in America's ability to solve her own problems, a confidence that precludes the necessity of a transcendent God. A receptive God, an inactive God, a "font of wisdom" God may well be on its way to becoming America's most popular God. And unless the trend reverses itself dramatically in the future, it appears that God the Object of Affection—the God who receives—will continue to be shunted aside for gods less obviously self-centered.

Several conclusions seem warranted by our brief examination of presidential rhetoric:

1. America's God is multi-faceted, containing numerous (sometimes competing) traits.
2. America's God is not vengeful nor does He typically punish those who transgress His laws.
3. America's God is, by and large, a passive God whose name is invoked *after* the nation has set its sights in a particular direction.
4. America's God is more an immanent than a transcendent God, one who reinforces America's political destiny and becomes its stalwart companion during its national trek.
5. America's God is people-centered; man—"in his individual and corporate being—is the beginning and end of the spiritual system of much of present-day American religiosity."[12]

Above all, God is not an object of divination for U.S. chief executives. They do not attempt to discover the "will and intention of the gods, and thereby to foretell the future, or explain past events."[13] Rather, "God is conceived as man's 'omnipotent servant'"[14] by most of them. At least as presented rhetorically, America's God is an expedient God, one who watches over His people as they set about their various tasks. Moreover, He is a complex God who provides a multitude of inventional resources upon which *civil* religionists (and, sometimes, civil *religionists*) can draw. Finally, He is an expediently complex God whose pieces and parts are so intricate, so plentiful, and so delightfully contradictory that they can provide rhetorical support for any number of sainted or diabolical schemes.

One final note of caution. In opting for this polytheistic explanation, we have been operating exclusively on rhetorical grounds. That is, our inspection of presidential rhetoric has revealed that five different Gods (or, at least, five quite different features of the same God) have been employed as rhetorical helpmates by America's chief executives. This is not to say that the American people "really believe" that their national destiny is guided by a heavenly quintet. It is to say, however, that these are the Gods who have been introduced to them quadrennially.

While such expedient complexity may be fascinating to the textual scholar, there are many who decry its philosophical and theological implications. U.S. Senator Mark Hatfield, for one, has lashed out bitterly at such rhetoric. Speaking at the National Prayer Breakfast in February of 1973, Hatfield told the members of his audience (one of whom was Richard Nixon) that, the rhetorical efficacy of America's Gods notwithstanding, serious moral implications inhere in the usual brand of civic piety: "If we as leaders appeal to the god of an American civil religion, our faith is in a small and exclusive deity, a loyal spiritual Advisor to American power and prestige, a Defender of the American nation, the object of a national folk religion devoid of moral content. But if we pray to the Biblical God of justice and righteousness, we fall under God's judgment for calling upon His name, but failing to obey His commands."[15]

Non-existential Content

In suggesting that the content of "official" civil-religious rhetoric is non-existential, we are suggesting that an active concern for the tangible exigencies of the moment is generally not characteristic of such discourse. Rather, it busies itself with the past and the future more than the present. Additionally, it is richly symbolic, reveling in a world of images rather than practical policy. That such characteristics distinguish official civil-religious discourse from its (comparatively tawdry) unofficial brethren seems undeniable. That such features dovetail with the contract as outlined in Chapter 4 also seems true.

The non-existential features of civil-religious discourse are manifested in the quiescent, nostalgic, and millennial emphases to be found within it. Typically, it is these specific features that usually come under attack by detractors of the "American civil religion." From our vantage point, however, it is these same features that allow it to function effectively in American society.

Quiescent Nature

When the 1976 bicentennial celebration of the American republic was being planned, many of its architects in Washington feared two things: that the nation's churches would not participate in force (thereby insuring the failure of the national celebrations), or that the churches would participate in untoward—that is, in activist—ways. In our lexicon, it was feared that American prelates would not uphold their halves of the contract and that the activism that had swept through even establishmentarian churches in the 1960s would continue apace, thus insuring no (or, worse yet, an untraditional) civil-religious commemoration. In short, it was feared that American preachers would become exhortative rather than accommodating.

In fact, there was little need to worry. In detailing his bicentennial suggestions for the Church of the Covenant, however, Joe Williamson admitted that such non-contractual thoughts had run through his and his colleagues' minds:

> Early in our conversations about the possibilities of this event we became convinced of the importance of disassociating ourselves from the "official" Bicentennial programs which are devised in Washington. Those programs are being set up to reinforce the tendencies of "civil religion" in America. That form of religion weds the religious rhetoric of faith to the policies of the political establishment and seeks to sanctify those policies in the name of God. We felt it of paramount importance to do just the opposite. We affirmed the need for a new "declaration of independence," specifically a declaration of independence by the churches from the state.[16]

However, after waxing on in this same article about the church's historical position on such matters, Williamson concluded with a rendition of the bicentennial plans finally adopted by the Church of the Covenant:

> We have begun to develop an alliance with other religious people who share our sense of things. We have developed a funding proposal which will provide money to help us carry out our plans. We would like to help other churches recover their sense of history as well. These histories will be written into pamphlet forms which can be distributed to visitors who come to Boston during 1975–76. We also intend to create a series of dramatic and artistic presentations which tell the story of our past and call us to respond faithfully to that past in the present. Street theater, multimedia, music, mime, and dance are all being explored as ways to do this dramatic representation. We would also like to construct a major convocation in the city of Boston which will call for the intersection of religious vitality and political commitment.[17]

Thus, despite the temptations of radical thought, Williamson's church, at least, opted for the historically sanctioned course in such matters—completely symbolic, non-activist events. The contract continues.

Most American churches followed suit. The Baptists, for instance, sponsored a series of sermons on the topic "Let Christ's Freedom Ring," assemblies and programs on the bicentennial themes, pageants, dramas, and choral work celebrating America's history, the publication of local church histories, bicentennial "heritage" rallies, and a sedentary-sounding Christian Citizenship Workshop whereby "church members [can] become more actively involved in the processes of government."[18]

The Baptists, of course, were not alone in sponsoring such quiescent events. (Nor are they to be censured unless one advocates substituting action for rhetoric and the complete overturning of the contractual applecart.) Even the American Jewish community—hardly a group reluctant to put forth its religio-political beliefs—contented itself during the bicentennial by preparing a portfolio of drawings by Mark Padwal depicting highlights of the American Jewish contribution during the last two hundred years, a series of lectures on Jews in American society, as well as other symbolic activities.[19]

The preparations made for the nation's celebration by religious groups serve as models in high relief of the usual rhetorical fare served up by civil religionists. The religio-political establishment in the U.S. was founded, as we saw in Chapter 4, upon a bedrock rhetorical assumption—that blatant political activism by the churches and the refusal by government to participate with the church in dialogue are eventualities to be eschewed. If the American civil religion is a religion (and, as we have seen, there is little reason to suspect that it is), it is a largely symbolic religion. As a "religion," it does not take verifiable action. It does not give alms to the poor. It does not even hold bingo games. Rather, it is a religion which exists within and because of discourse. Since it *does* nothing it is doomed to tag-along status existentially. On the other hand, it owes its very preservation to the fact that it does nothing. For when ritualistic rhetoric becomes something other than ritual, it too must open itself up to the scrutiny, actions, and potential rebuffs of all who inhabit the marketplace of controversy. For the theological establishment in the U.S. to become more active would be to lose the very tangible benefits that accrue to faithful handmaidens of government.

That civil-religious rhetoric is designed to operate largely symbolically is notably revealed in the U.S.'s founding documents. Kendall and Carey, among many others, have noted that legal proclamations in particular will have no part of a church-state, no matter what that state will permit on more patently rhetorical fronts:

> The Declaration of Independence, with its references to the Creator, to the laws of nature and of nature's God, to Divine Providence, appears to be the declaration of a religious people, or, more specifically, a *Christian* people. The Constitution and the Bill of Rights, by contrast, have in them not one word that could not have been written, and subscribed to, by a people made up of atheists and agnostics. The Declaration seems to be the declaration of a people who wish to make clear above all else their commitment to work the will of God; the Constitution and Bill of Rights seem to be the expressions of a people whose exclusive concern is with the things of this world.[20]

Not all persons are as willing to distinguish so sharply between the existential and the rhetorical. Alarmists such as the Veterans of Foreign Wars have worried constantly about the tangible import of the Supreme Court's decisions relative to church and state: "If we were to drop God from our vocabulary we would have quite a job. How would we do it? Would we take a razor blade and cut 'God' from our

Bibles? Must we eliminate the mention of God in our Declaration of Independence, Pledge of Allegiance to the flag and in our national anthem? Must we destroy all money on which appears the words 'In God We Trust?'"[21] While the VFW may well worry about such evisceration, they miss the genius of the civil-religious contract when reasoning to their conclusion: "If we go to these ridiculous extremes we might as well finish the job by closing all the churches, imprison their spiritual leaders and follow the communists' adoration of Lenin."[22] Despite such concerns, cooler heads in the nation have been able to distinguish existential from rhetorical reality throughout its history.

It equally distorts the contract, however, to argue from rhetorical premises to existential conclusions. The Reverend Joseph Costanzo, a Jesuit apologist for greater state aid to religious institutions, often based his arguments on rhetorical grounds:

> Wholly in accord with this original corporate and unofficial profession of the religious foundations of American democracy are the individual official pronouncements of the highest government officers from the very beginning of the Republic. To discount the long tradition of presidential utterances, especially the presidential Thanksgiving Day proclamations, as expedient and pious exhortation is to testify to the strength of the American consensus that the nation's religious foundations must be officially acknowledged and promoted.[23]

The typical reply made to such charges is akin to that of disestablishmentarian Leo Pfeffer: "Government expenditures of tax-raised funds for religious institutions cannot easily be justified on the basis of . . . meaningless acts of ceremonial obeisance."[24] Although Pfeffer's argument does indeed have both practical and historical appeal, he has surely underestimated the considerable power of public rhetoric when describing its manifestations as "meaningless."

All of this is not to say that to act rhetorically is not to act at all. In J. L. Austin's terms, civil-religious rhetoric is performative.[25] That is, the very fact that the Church is accorded rhetorical status equal to that of government is a tangible affirmation of the importance of church-state harmony in America. For clerics and statesmen to share the speaker's platform during the nation's bicentennial celebrations was to continue to work out a very old and very necessary rhetorical compromise. Were the church to include existential punch in its rhetoric by calling, say, for Congress to redistribute national wealth, it would have dallied unadvisedly with a completely workable rhetorical compact. Little is really lost, the civil-religious lobby would argue, when those at the U.S. military academies are compelled to attend chapel. For, as United States Solicitor General Erwin Griswold has remarked, "no cadet or midshipman is required to believe what he hears."[26]

Containment: The natural, rhetorical result of the bifurcation between the suasory and the existential was touched on briefly in Chapter 4. American civil-religion largely produces an accomodationist rhetoric, one that tacitly supports the political status quo. Typically, it legitimizes the current political order, a task not unlike that performed by many revolutionary era preachers who used their pulpits to preach all manner of sedition against the British oligarchs.

In post-revolutionary times, however, the established church in the U.S. has demonstrated real genius for discovering by whom, and on what side, the national bread was being buttered. Conrad Cherry explains such accommodations in the most pragmatic of terms: "It is now a sociological and historical truism that any religion which becomes a vital part of its culture is inclined to maintain the status quo of that culture. When the motifs of the national faith are invoked, therefore, it is frequently for the sake of uncritical endorsement of American values and tasks."[27] According to Wallace Fisher, such syncretistic behavior runs directly contrary to the sectarian ideologies built up by many religions over centuries of activism: "civil piety and religion-in-general blur the particularistic genius of the Reformation and Catholic traditions."[28]

Perhaps Fisher is right, but he has failed to reckon with the political fallout of failing to legitimize the current national ethos—that of being relegated to insignificant rhetorical status. For all of his fulminating, Billy James Hargis (a most unofficial civil religionist) obtained scant access to the corridors of power in Washington. By paying their rhetorical dues, however, and by delicately bringing to bear the considerable collective influence they have, establishment prelates consistently hold open the possibility of modulating the socio-political environment. Whatever the philosophical costs of tacit legitimization—and its tacitness should not be forgotten—it is the only politically astute game in town, as has been pointed out, grudgingly to be sure, by Fox:

> Even though he [the President] invites preachers of different faiths to speak in the White House—distinguished Catholics, Jews, and Protestants—they all tend to bring him the same message. Few would dare to criticize him under his own roof as Nathan the prophet once criticized David the King for sending a soldier to death in combat so he could have his wife, Bathsheba. Nixon's clergy never criticize him for sending bombers over North Vietnam. They mainly come to encourage and inspire.[29]

It is for these and other similar reasons that we find no truly prophetic God in America's civil-religious pantheon. No God of Abraham opined during the bicentennial celebrations. Rather, God becomes what Andrew Greeley calls a "senior partner" to American interests,[30] a God whose rhetorically necessary immanence precluded Him from having a transcendent voice. In civil-religious terms, America's God is largely a God who watches the American people as they march their leaders in and out of office. The realities of power being what they are, He could not be otherwise, lest He be made to reside in generously taxed churches. Apparently, such a set of conditions has never been attractive to the American people. Hence, the contract abides.

Those who denounce this accomodationistic God too often forget that, in societal terms, there are many other rabidly prophetic Gods inhabiting the rhetorical marketplace. While the nation's God may tacitly sanction "the massacre of Indians . . .

the lynching of Blacks . . . the atom-bombing of Japanese . . . [and] the napalming of Vietnamese children,"[31] it cannot be forgotten that there were many other Gods speaking out all the while, Gods who were true to their denominational heritages. It also cannot be forgotten that we are talking here about a national God, one who is conjured up by a chorus of priestly voices. Finally, it should not be forgotten that the contract has never been as one-sided as many of its detractors would have us believe. Government needs its religion-tinged rhetoric just as surely as the church needs the tangible benefits of governmental affiliation. As Peter Berger has observed, "Religion legitimates so effectively because it relates the precarious reality constructions of empirical societies with ultimate reality."[32] Thus, while its content may have few activist implications, civil-religious rhetoric is an imperfect but reliable guardian of the very tangible relationship shared by church and state in the United States.

The Curious Case of Doctor King: When commenting upon an earlier draft of this manuscript, a colleague objected to what seemed to be a rightist bias implicit in our analysis. He argued, for example, that a person like Martin Luther King, Jr. stood in sharp contrast to the accomodationists being described in this essay. King, with his mass marches, his sundry civil disobediences, and his fitful exhortations seems—at first glance—to fly in the face of the careful choreography being described here. That is, King's notion of a judgmental God who smiles benevolently on social activism seems to give the lie to our analysis.

The most obvious response to such an argument is also the least satisfactory: Martin Luther King, Jr. was an anomaly in the pages of civil-religious history. A more telling retort might be that King, for all of his reverence for God the Wise and the Just, never completely severed the bonds between himself and the political establishment in Washington. Most important of all, King was a member in good standing of the rhetorical establishment. It is not an accident of history that King is best known for his "I Have a Dream" *speech* and his *letter* from the Birmingham jail. Nor can we forget that King used public discourse as the focal point for almost all of the civil rights demonstrations he engineered. And it is important to remember that the Black Power movement was launched by those who sought to fill in the behavioral-existential void created by King's willingness to effect change through *rhetorical* agencies. King was a preacher. He did not throw bombs.

Naturally, had he lived, Doctor King would have objected to the quiescent bicentennial celebrations held in the U.S. in 1976. Nevertheless, it is hard to imagine that he would have failed to participate in them. It is equally certain that he would have found some way of breathing fire into the nation's festivities. Thus, while King may have rejected much of the civil-religious contract, it seems clear that he respected its underlying rhetorical essence.

Nostalgic Nature

Perhaps because it has now become institutionalized, American civil-religious discourse tends to turn in upon itself, often using its own ancestral rhetorical forms to provide it with both a rationale and psychological momentum. As a result, civic piety is largely antiquarian. In 1954, William Lee Miller observed that Americans' faith "is not in God but in faith; we worship not God but our own worshiping."[33] In a similar vein, we are suggesting here that civil-religious discourse is often meta-rhetorical because it constantly dredges up kindred remarks made previously. If there is a civil religion in America, it is not a faith in faith (as Will Herberg would have it) but a faith in statements about faith. Most religio-political rhetoric—of both the official and unofficial varieties—exhibits such meta-rhetorical features. For example, the Christophers, an association of Catholic laymen, once published a widely distributed tract entitled *Every President Invoked God's Help*.[34] The eight-page pamphlet is little more than a random collection of religious remarks made by America's presidents. What is most interesting is that, except for a two paragraph introduction, no original material appears in the pamphlet. It is as if the Christophers' civil-religious invention had been sapped long ago, as if there were no longer a pressing, ongoing need to deal with new circumstances.

Such meta-rhetoric has its obvious benefits: (1) it facilitates rhetorical invention for spokespersons by eliminating the need to search potential *topoi*, allowing speakers to depend on ageless themes instead; (2) it provides its authors with a sense of security because it grounds itself in purely rhetorical precedents; (3) it helps to raise the emotional impact of the discourse by reveling in the past, thereby reinforcing civil-religious myth; and (4) most important, such an approach displaces purely denominational or partisan underpinnings. All of these benefits, no doubt, add to the heart-warming glow of the heart-warming glow described by Clarence Manion:

> There is a heart-warming glow around the conjunction of "God and Country." The expression stirs the stimulating sensation of patriotism down to and through its deepest roots. At Gettysburg, Lincoln prayed that "this nation, under God" might have a new birth of freedom, and in saluting the American flag today, we all repeat the declaration that this nation shall stand, "under God, with liberty and justice for all." This conjunction of God and Country runs like a bright golden thread in and throughout the entire fabric of our political and constitutional history.[35]

The meta-rhetorical nature of much civil-religious discourse also betrays its cosmological overtones. Unlike much contemporary talk, religio-political rhetoric continually examines its beginnings when explaining (or to explaining away) contemporary challenges. It draws its strength from its revolutionary roots, even though it often distorts those roots in a salad of querulous historical allusions. Like any cosmological rhetoric, it "defines the power of the supernatural, guides human behavior, provides a system of norms with ethical implications, and upholds and sanctifies the values of society"[36] by featuring the past. As a result, the pages of *The Military Chaplain* have a certain breathy quality to them:

> If our Bicentennial is to be a true celebration of 200 years of our history, and a springboard to a "New America," a "New Spirit of '76," all the national, statewide, city and village organizations

and plans underway to mark that anniversary and to make America live anew, vibrant with hope and opportunity, had better "look back" and remember that God has been a part of our history since our founding and, undoubtedly, the source of the manifold blessings this land has enjoyed.[37]

According to Philip Hammond, such rhetoric raises "to hagiologic stature the persons thought to have conceived and instituted the [democratic] procedure: the Washingtons, Jeffersons, and Lincolns."[38] An understanding of the cosmological nature of civil-religious rhetoric allows us to understand why, of the three main bicentennial themes in the U.S.—Heritage '76, Festival '76 and Horizons '76—it was the first that received the overwhelming attention of America's religious leaders. Perhaps because the oblique lessons, personae, and myths of the past cannot rise up to contradict statements made today, the past is a comfortable (for many, an emotionally compelling) receptacle of public thoughts. Rhetorically speaking, then, Ezra Taft Benson chose well when exulting:

> Let us not permit these admonitions of our living prophets to fall on deaf ears. Let us, as they direct, learn the meaning and importance of our God-ordained Constitution. Let us rededicate ourselves to the lofty principles and practices of those wise men whom God raised up to give us our priceless freedom. Our liberties, our salvation, our well-being as a Church and as a nation depend upon it. This nation has a spiritual foundation—a prophetic history. Every true Latter Day Saint should love the United States of America—the most generous nation under heaven—the Lord's base of operations in these last days. May we do all in our power to strengthen and safeguard this base and increase our freedom.[39]

Millennial

Besides rushing pell-mell into the past, civil-religious spokespersons often skirt the practicalities of the moment by speaking in millennial terms. Many observers trace these millennial themes to ideas first set afloat during the Great Awakening. While some scholars argue that Johnathan Edwards was not himself responsible for spreading a messianist understanding of the American mission,[40] notions of America as a Redeemer Nation were made popular during his time. As Sydney Ahlstrom notes, the millennial concern "was on men's minds on the first Fourth of July, and in somewhat more secularized form it would become an enduring feature of American patriotic oratory."[41]

Whether because of its Judaeo-Christian roots or its prideful people, civil-religious rhetoric often points to a Golden Age when the U.S. would lead the world's children out of darkness. In an excellent essay, J. F. Maclear has traced millennial themes throughout that nation's history, ultimately finding them to be one of its most emotionally abiding features.[42] In revolutionary times, sermons of the ilk of

"The American States Acting over the part of the Children of Israel in the Wilderness and Thereby Impeding their Entrance into Canaan's Rest" (preached by Nicholas Street in 1777),[43] set the millennial tone. Later, according to Maclear, the most successful years of postmillennialism were those between 1815 and the Civil War, but even during Reconstruction such themes continued to compel the American people.[44] Too, Ray Abrams credits much of the success of the pro-war rhetoric prior to World War I to its millennial undertones and overtones.[45]

In more contemporary times, the children of a New Israel were on the march once again. Note, for example, the strong messianic strain in the remarks of Harry Truman:

> Religion should establish moral standards for the conduct of our whole nation, at home and abroad. . . . For the danger that threatens us in the world today is utterly and totally opposed to all these things [spiritual values]. The international Communist movement is based on a fierce and terrible fanaticism. It denies the existence of God and wherever it can it stamps out the worship of God. . . . Our religious faith gives us the answer to the false beliefs of Communism. . . . I have the feeling that God has created us and brought us to our present position of power and strength for some great purpose.[46]

Although millennial attitudes may compel contemporary Americans as individuals, themes of a virtuous nation leading its lesser brethren in the world to some pre-envisioned eschaton is typically too rich for today's cosmopolitans. As a result, such trumpery is being replaced by a kind of demythologized pragmatism, a belief that the nation's destiny has already been assured by dint of social technologies. Thus, while futuristic themes still distinguish civil-religious discourse, the Great Awakening's motifs have been replaced by more urbane fare.

Whatever it has become, however, civic piety continues to circumnavigate the present. As we have seen, preachers assiduously avoid activist or policy-oriented themes, focusing instead on the safer terrains of the past and the future. So, for example, when he resigned the vice-presidency in 1973, Spiro Agnew's humiliation did not preclude him from showing that he was a diligent student of civil-religious rhetoric:

> But I can't help thinking tonight of James Garfield's words to an audience in New York just following the announcement that Lincoln had died. Garfield, who was later President himself, was only a young Army officer at the time of that great tragedy in 1865, but he saw clearly where his country's strength lay, and he expressed it all in these few words to a frightened crowd. He said: "Fellow citizens. God reigns, and the Government in Washington still lives." I take leave of you tonight, my friends, in that same somber but trusting spirit. God does reign. I thank Him for the opportunity of serving you in high office, and I

know that He will continue to care for this country in the future
as He has done so well in the past.[47]

Ritualistic Presence

Much of what has been said thus far has revealed the ritualistic understructure of
civic piety. As we have seen, there is a certain sameness to the divinities invoked, a
tendency to resort to standard themes on standard occasions, and a marked avoidance of contemporary problems. In all these ways, civic piety finds its fullest expression in ritual. As a result, it is a rhetoric forged by political necessity, tempered
by religious pluralism, and polished by ritual of a most public sort. It is, according to
Duane Litfin, "a kind of periodic tipping of the hat to God to appease Him; a sort of
national knocking on wood."[48]

Ritualistic Forms

In their simplest forms, rhetorical rituals do two things: they resolve ongoing exigencies (e.g., the need for commemoration) in stylized ways and provide a familiar,
collective vehicle for expressing certain powerful human emotions. These twin
functions of ritual show why civic piety has reveled in ritual since its beginnings in
the Thanksgiving and Election Day sermons of the colonial U.S. The religious experience, says Thomas O'Dea, is "spontaneous and creative"; institutionalizing that
experience through rhetorical ritual reduces "these unpredictable elements to established and routine forms."[49] Such routinization makes for predictability, for the sure
knowledge that God is in His sky and watching over the American people. That
these thoughts have to be rekindled from time to time through ritual does not gainsay the depth of such sentiments. In fact, it is the functional repetitiveness of civil-
religious discourse—the God Day Rallies, the Washington Prayer Breakfasts, and
the Fourth of July services—that keeps the religio-political machinery in the U.S.
well oiled and operational.

Ritualistic Events: Civic piety deploys ritual in two primary ways. Sometimes,
the entire rhetorical interaction is structured on ritualistic premises. The tabernacle,
the congregation, the deacon, and the sacred scriptures of nationhood combine to
obliterate all outside exigences. On such occasions and in such places, God's America receives the exclusive billing.

These productions are often large-scale affairs. Take, for instance, the God Day
Rally sponsored in 1973 by the Catholic War Veterans of Brooklyn. The Veterans
announced their event in an upbeat manner: "Plan God Day Rally at St. John's University in September, Ten Thousand Expected to Attend." "With the blessing and
prayerful endorsement of Bishop Francis J. Mugavero of the Brooklyn Diocese," the
event was heralded as one "paying homage to God and allegiance to Country
through a Prayer Rally and special patriotic observances."[50] The dignitaries at the
God Day Rally included leaders of the church and of civic and governmental
groups, as well as a member of Congress (Lawrence J. Jogan, R. Md.—the sponsor
of the "Human Life Amendment" in Congress).

The color and pageantry expected on such events was amply provided by the United States Army Band, the Young Americans Drum and Bugle Corps, the St. Agatha Glee Club, St. Ephrem's Choir, and the Patron Nations' Festival Dancers. The highlight of the celebration was a "God Day Mass" concelebrated by various dignitaries of the Church. Thereafter, an assortment of civil-religious activities was administered by fifty religious leaders (of countless religious persuasions) and "forty lay-leaders of civic, patriotic, veteran and pro-life groups."[51] A parade through the University's grounds and a prayer rally provided the capstones for the three and a half hour affair.

Such brobdignaggian productions are not atypical. Especially during the bicentennial celebrations of 1976, such extended rituals were the rule rather than the exception. That thousands upon thousands would willingly expose themselves to such religio-political oratory probably says as much about their regard for the inherent attractions of collective celebration as it does about their fervor for linking the temporal and the divine. "Those who would dismiss the sacred ceremonies as mere antiquated conventions, and the rhetoric of ceremonies as an insincere attempt to marshal the support of pious people," claims Cherry, "would miss the cultural significance of these occasions of worship."[52] They would miss, too, the colorful continuity provided the nation's civil religion by drama and ritual.

Ritualistic Themes: The less histrionic (and more common) manifestation of civil-religious tenets is the passing references found in political and religious oratory. Inaugural addresses, religious invocations, benedictions at political rallies, and the like are the workhorses of civic piety in America. As we saw in Chapter 2, these themes are now so thick in American political discourse as to be almost invisible. While such themes do not prick the collective consciousness as vividly as the grand rituals just described, they do to remind audiences of their obligations to God and Caesar.

As we saw with Richard Nixon, though, certain ground rules must be observed when deploying such themes: (1) they must be brief, (2) they must commence or terminate an address (but usually not both), and (3) they must normally (i.e., during peacetime) be appended to ceremonial, as opposed to policymaking or policy-endorsing, speeches. According to some observers, these stringencies can denude genuine religious sentiments: "God, says the unwritten glossary of American politics, is a word in the last paragraph of a political speech."[53]

While God may be something of a cosmic afterthought in American political discourse, He is inevitably present. When groups like the American Legion deploy such themes they serve at once as an affirmation of popular sentiments and a reflection of an insatiable need for pageantry: "[Local Legion posts] are urged to close Communion Breakfasts, Post Installations, etc. with the following but simple ceremony to give greater glory to God and a greater respect for our country. Use simple birthday candles and at the close of the gathering have everyone light them and hold them above their head. The person in charge of the gathering shall lead or choose someone to lead the people in the song, 'God Bless America.'"[54]

Ritual, however, carries certain liabilities. With sameness can come somnolence. The following vignette of the National Day of Prayer, Eisenhower-style, illustrates the point well:

> When October 2 arrived, it turned out to be a dud, at least as far as public praying was concerned. The President saw this first hand. He attended a special morning service in his local Presbyterian Church and was very disappointed by the turnout. As he said afterwards, he found himself praying among "only a handful of people."
>
> When he returned to the White House, he began an immediate investigation; that is, his secretary phoned me to find out what had gone wrong. Why had the Day been so poorly observed?
>
> I [his consultant for religious affairs] immediately got State on the phone and asked them to tell me why. They assured me they had mailed the President's August 8 proclamation "to fifty major religious press services and periodicals." Many of these had reprinted the text in full but, as I said earlier, the popular press gave it scant notice. Even the Presbyterian churches neglected to use it in their Sunday bulletins. It simply had zero grass roots appeal.
>
> As I reported this to the President, he gritted his teeth. He did not like to be beaten on any front. If the Congress required him to proclaim an annual Day of Prayer, he was determined to have it heard the length and breadth of the land.[55]

On the other hand, the alternative to *not* regularizing civil-religious events and themes is highly unattractive: "The only other possibility [for scheduling the National Day of Prayer] would have been to save it for the best crisis of the year. . . . But then, the proclamation might become more unnerving than inspiring; the people might await its annual issuance with some dread."[56]

Such problems notwithstanding, ritual often functions well. But contrary to what Costanzo feels, ritualized discourse has not "set an incontrovertible historical record of the religious presuppositions of our national existence and endurance."[57] Rather, such rituals serve to reinforce, to revivify, and to resanction the covenant made by church and state decades ago. Naturally, when the American people find the contract to be attractive no longer, they will urge their religious and political leaders to abrogate the agreement. What is more likely, however (given the rather dire consequences of such a decision as outlined in Chapters 3 and 4), is that the American people will choose to continue their religio-political rituals.

And the suasory power of ritual should not go unnoticed. "It does not matter that we are a practical and sophisticated people, no longer (we think) influenced by symbols, myths, or rituals," argues Michael Novak.[58] We do respond to such entreaties and we do reject would-be presidents should they not measure up to our ritualistic standards:

Eugene McCarthy is quick to see through and to deflate the American civil religion, its rituals and its deficiencies. . . . Even astute commentators have been unable to understand McCarthy's refusal to believe. *They* believe. His agnosticism affronts them. They called him lazy, moody, irreverent, unpredictable, irresponsible, not serious, a poet, a dreamer. Whereas, in fact, he is merely hard-headed, a skeptic, who refuses to accept the rituals, to confess the mysteries, to pretend to the powers. [McCarthy once said] . . . "Take the magic out of it. I'll take the issues before the people. That's all it takes." He was wrong, of course.[59]

Ritualistic Features

Shortly after he became America's thirty-third president, Richard Nixon initiated a series of weekly worship services in the White House. Because the services were held in the White House, the American civil religion was given a ritualistic shot in the arm on a biweekly basis. The program detailing the service of June 29, 1969, is particularly instructive, as we see in Figure 5.1:[60]

	June 29, 1969
Prelude	
Opening Remarks	The President
Doxology	
Prayer	Dr. Louis Finkelstein
	Chancellor, The Jewish Theological
	Seminary of America
	New York City
Hymn	"We Gather Together"
Anthem	Members of the Christ Lutheran Church Choir
	"Now God Be Praised in Heav'n Above"
	by Melchoir Vulpius
	Director: Mr. Geoffrey Simon
Hymn	"O God, Our Help in Ages Past"
Benediction	
Postlude	

We see here the same sort of ritualistic structure described earlier. We see, too, a certain theological anomaly. In commenting on the White House services, columnist Edward Fiske remarked: "The nondescript nature of the liturgy that is followed was evident when no one saw any contradiction in asking Rabbi Louis Finkelstein, a chancellor of Jewish Theological Seminary and preacher on June 29, to stand by while the congregation said the Doxology in praise of the Christian Trinity."[61]

In the remainder of this section, we will investigate why a Jewish rabbi was able to participate so gracefully in a nominally Protestant service. In part, the answer is that the level of abstraction imbedded in civil-religious discourse is normally so high that even obvious contradictions can reside peacefully under its sacred canopy (to borrow Peter Berger's happy phrase).

Having observed that civil-religious discourse is both ritualistic and quiescent, we can easily understand its abstractness. Its abstractness does not make it feckless but it does depend on its devotees to ferret out precise understandings and moral implications. And yet some scholars would disagree with that statement. Robert Bellah, for one, seems to find great specificity in the American civil religion. He implies, for example, that a sentence fragment from Kennedy's inaugural ("the revolutionary beliefs for which our forebears fought") contains an explicit suggestion that the United States should be about the business of solving its "greatest domestic problem, the treatment of the Negro American."[62] Bellah also suggests that Kennedy's exhortation that God's work be our own work is an explicit, "very activist and non-contemplative conception of the fundamental religious obligation, which has been historically associated with the Protestant position."[63]

While there is little doubt that John Kennedy's sympathies lay with African Americans, and while it is reasonable to assume that many Protestants could find favor with Kennedy's inaugural address, the specificity Bellah finds in Kennedy's remarks could also have come from an unconscious attempt by a Berkeley sociologist to validate his own understanding of the nation's self-understanding. Surely the phrase, "God's work must truly be our own," could, if uttered by a Richard Nixon, be seen as yet another Republican plea for decentralizing the federal government and asking volunteers to take on duties now assumed by the State.

Our take is that most civil-religious discourse is quite abstract and necessarily so.[64] Moreover, we will argue that such abstractness serves three very practical functions, all of which dovetail with the contractual metaphor used to explain the existence of civic piety in Chapter 4.

Symbolic Unification: One of the inescapable facts of U.S. history is that it has been a theologically pluralistic society from the beginning. Even in the relatively homogeneous (by contemporary standards) American colonies, civil-religious discourse functioned to integrate diverse sentiments and to fashion from them a political consensus. According to Winthrop Hudson, for example, the earliest version of civic piety in the U.S. paid its inventional debt to the Old Testament: "This faith of the new republic was neither sectarian nor parochial. Its roots were Hebraic. Its explication was cast in Hebraic metaphors—chosen people, convenanted nation, Egyptian bondage, promised land. Its eager millennial expectation was expressed in the vivid imagery of the Hebrew prophets."[65]

Contemporary Americans have learned these lessons of history well. The need for a symbolically compact and integrative discourse, a rhetoric around which all denominationalists and partisans can rally, continues to press upon them. According to Bernard Bailyn, religious-sounding discourse provides a "higher justification, a breadth, generality, and intensity,"[66] unavailable in more specific, and more political, rhetoric. Because pluralism reduces "matters of ultimate commitment to matters of personal preference,"[67] the rhetoric of civil religion must be quietly evocative:

> "Service to God and Country" is basic Americanism. It is not a fostering of religious worship in order to appease any element of our citizenry or to draw attention from any less desirable social activities. Since it is essentially basic Americanism, it is strictly non-denominational, non-sectarian. It is not intended to act independently of religious groups but to cooperate with them to the end that the American people might never forget that God is the source of all their rights and privileges.[68]

On this same score, Murray Edelman has suggested that when one person uses a phrase like "governmental control" and another refers to "private enterprise," we learn "nothing from their speech about political economy but we do learn something important about the group values with which each identifies."[69] Similarly, to lace one's speech with the metaphors of civic piety is to acknowledge a national consensus without identifying the existenial import of that consensus. Thus, there was little need for Rabbi Finkelstein to feel offended by the Protestant doxologists in the White House since they all spoke the same meta-language, a language shared by American Catholics as well:

> In his inaugural address Kennedy avoided the articulation of any specifically Roman Catholic doctrine or references to Jesus Christ and the Church. Participation in the ceremony was invited through appeal to such beliefs as "the rights of man" that come from the "hand of God." A similar, but less absolute, differentiation occurred in the funeral for Robert Kennedy. There specifically Christian doctrines were articulated, but the eulogies of both Senator Edward Kennedy and Archbishop Cooke dwelt mostly on civil religious themes. The upshot of the ceremonial differentiation between the civil religion and other American religions is that an American may be a Methodist, a Conservative Jew or a Roman Catholic and at the same time participate in the celebration of the civil religion—but without insisting that the civil religion be expressed specifically in Methodist, Jewish or Catholic terms.[70]

Ambiguous Delineation: Having observed (1) civil religion's passive themes, (2) the abstractness of its language, and (3) that "only 24 percent of American Protestants feel that it is right for clergymen to discuss political candidates or issues from the pulpit,"[71] we are left with an interesting dilemma: Having ruled out so much, how can civic pietists talk at all?

With calculated ambiguity. Rarely, these days, do we find the forthright language of Bishop Theodore S. Henderson of Detroit who, when addressing a Methodist conference at Atlantic City in March 1918, urged his fellows to "get in touch with our War Council, should you find anybody of pro-German tendencies in your community. Let us locate, eliminate, and exterminate every pro-German in this country."[72] Such confessional zeal for the national religion is surely out of step with the more delicate fare served up by today's preachers. For example, in "specifying" what it means to "keep this a nation under God," the Christophers suggest that the shibboleth reminds us that:

- Men derive their rights directly from God.
- The authority of all government comes from the Lord by way of the people.
- The function of government, consequently, is to act as the agent of the people in securing their God-given rights and in promoting the general welfare.[73]

If this quotation typifies the optimum level of specificity to be found in official civil-religious discourse (and we believe it does), it is small wonder that such messages are normally quite brief.

The ambiguity in civil-religious discourse is such that (according to Cherry) there probably never has been "a consistent meaning of [our] national symbols."[74] Even in Revolutionary times, claims Harry Kerr, "it was fortunate . . . that the preachers avoided specific applications to current problems. Whatever such applications might have added to the interest and impact of the [Election Day] sermons would likely have been offset by the irritation of auditors who felt that they were being told how to conduct their business."[75] As Kerr is quick to point out, this reluctance to be specific was not characteristic of the ministers when they spoke on other occasions.

On the contemporary scene, most mainstream preachers are typically unspecific when discoursing about civil-religious matters. No matter what concrete referents words such as church, state, establishment, free exercise, and separation may have for some, when civil religionists use them they are used ambiguously. "Even the word God," says Sidney Mead, "had become so ambiguous long before theologians announced his death that the Federal Communications Commission was led to declare in July 1946 that 'so diverse are these conceptions that it may be fairly said, even to professed believers, that the God of one man does not exist for another.'"[76]

Mystification: Although the language of civic piety is typically ambiguous, it is more than that—it is richly ambiguous. That is, within its ambiguity lie conceptions of the national ethos grander than those which ordinary Americans could articulate for themselves. National myths allow average Americans to transcend the banalities of day-to-day life, making them part of a larger and more satisfying social enterprise.

It comes as no surprise, then, that the American civil religion's rhetorical energy derives from its capacity to ennoble ideas. The myths of a New Israel, of a God-fearing people, of strict separation of church and state, of the Holy War, and the like function as do all myths: "The myth, then, is a comprehensive view of reality; it explains it, interprets it, provides the ritual by which man may maintain his contact with it. . . ."[77] Thus, when terms like freedom, democracy, and providence lost their specificity for the American people, says Cherry, they actually increased their utility as conjurers of grand images.[78]

According to Irving Kristol, the mystification of life through rhetoric holds special appeal for the American people. As Kristol wryly points out:

Just imagine what our TV commentators and "news analysts" would do with a man who sought elected office with the promise that, during his tenure, he hoped to effect some small improvements in our condition. They would ridicule him into oblivion. In contrast, they are very fond of someone like John Lindsay, who will settle for only the finest and most glowing goals. Public figures in our society get credit for their utopian rhetoric—for their "charisma," as we now say—and only demerits if they emphasize their (necessarily modest) achievements.[79]

Whether Kristol is right in his ethnocentric view of mythification is, of course, a matter for some debate.[80]

No sub-theme in the catalog of civil-religious discourse has been turned into myth more richly than that of a bellicose America. Although he is too simplistic when arguing that World War I's "back-the-war" rhetoric only had "to be couched in holy phraseology to bring forth the desired responses from the church people," the mythical themes reported by Ray Abrams are familiar and powerful ones indeed:

> The Old Testament, with its war-god, Jahweh; the Holy Wars of the Israelites, the Imprecatory Psalms, and the Day of the Lord of Amos; the heathen in his blindness versus the Christian, the false versus the true gospel; the Christian crusades, the war hymns of the church; the example of Jesus driving out the money changers from the Temple and rebuking the Scribes and Pharisees; the sufferings of little innocent Serbia and Belgium and the cross of Christ, the symbol of sacrifice for others and world redemption through the shedding of blood—these and a hundred other symbols were utilized to take advantage of the religiously motivated individuals, while the awful struggle was painted as the Battle of Armageddon or the Holiest War of all the Ages. Thus were the Christian hosts mobilized for battle.[81]

Even in contemporary times we find a kindred sort of martial mystification. When surveying educational materials distributed by military chaplains, Berger and Pinard happened upon a compelling myth of the American fighting man:

> Peace is a profession of conviction. The military man has a definite reason for what he does and for the uniform he wears. As an American he has learned so much about how to live he has tended to forget why he does so. He does not want to live for himself alone. He is granted life by a God who wants peace and understanding among men. His reason for living is, in essence, to advance that peace. Into whatever situation his military status takes him he goes in the spirit expressed by Air Force Captain Edwin G. Shank shortly before he was killed in Vietnam: "To do the best job possible for our country"—we would add, for our God.[82]

Those who suggest ritual trivializes religion and patriotism and renders them impotent have missed the sociological mark. For a great many people, God-and-country rallies are both rhetorically attractive and psychologically rewarding. On the other hand, Americans are not so foolish as to fail to notice the neutering of the discourse they hear at such gatherings, the opportunism displayed at times by civic pietists, the gushing emotionalism of the ceremonial events, or the querulous myths they are asked to accept. In all of these things, however, Americans seem to take a delightfully pragmatic stance, acknowledging such discourse for what it is—an amalgamation of poetic images and cultural yearnings. The willing suspension of disbelief, we observe, is not reserved exclusively for Broadway openings.

Prosaic Animus

Our inspection of civil religion indicates that, on the civil side at least, the esoteric continually loses out to the prosaic. Civic piety is largely homocentric—it is constructed for and about mortal human beings. Indeed, Moberg would have us believe that these non-theistic themes are characteristic of all American religious discourse: "Worship for many people is partly or wholly homocentric. We worship God to serve human needs; we implore the Deity to shape our own ends; we seek guidance in human affairs; we beseech God to give us peace and security amid the uncertainties of life; we seek immortality when life seems broken by death. In theory worship is theocentric; in practice it involves many homocentric goals and motivations."[83]

Quite obviously, a national faith rooted in theocentric assumptions could not, as can the American civil religion, place its Godhead on the dollar bill or on a rainbow of bumper stickers. By featuring its homocentricity, however, we can understand why proposed federal legislation has urged the canceling of "In God We Trust" stamps with "Pray for Peace" designata.[84] And these prosaic impulses have been with the American people for some time. For example, Clark found starkly non-contemplative references to God in the nineteenth-century oratory of Bishop Matthew Simpson:

> He saw the hand of God in the invention of new ploughs, drilling machines, reapers, all designed to husband labor; he saw God in the building of the railroads so that the West was able in the hour of crisis to send its produce to the Eastern cities; he saw God in the simple matter of the sewing machine, in the discovery of the electric telegraph, in the starving of the poor in England at the time when they sympathized with the rebellion; he saw God in the sending of food by the North in "beautiful fulfillment of the Scriptures."[85]

It is understandable that such refrains would be found in a society long noted for its pragmatism. There has never been a clear-cut bifurcation between the sacred and the secular in American theology: "American religion is . . . non-theological and non-liturgical; it is . . . occupied with the things of the world to a degree that has become a byword among European churchmen," says Will Herberg.[86] If that is true of

American religion in general, it stands to reason that it would be even truer of civic piety in particular. Rather than finding metaphysical flights from the "Alone to the Alone" in such rhetoric,[87] we find it to be imbued with the most practical of stuff:

> A contrivance called "God's Float" was rushed to completion [for a parade], but there was considerable embarrassment because of the shortage of appropriate materials. The float could not look Catholic, Protestant or Jewish—at least not *too* Catholic, Protestant or Jewish. It would have to be given some dignified place of honor in the parade. But where? Finally, it was put first, and at the heart of the display was placed a rather innocuous and not-quite-denominational building surrounded with mottoes reading "In God We Trust" and "Freedom of Worship."[88]

Sociologists might explain the practical (some would call it profane) flavor of civic piety by featuring the capitalistic and ruggedly individualistic nature of the people who sustain it. Theologians might account for such features by noting the non-contemplative roots supportive of American theology in the main. Historians would offer still other explanations. We suggest a rhetorical interpretation. By accepting the notion that civic piety is largely a public affair and that it is surrounded by simple, but strong, motivational vectors, we can better understand its hyper-functionality.

Publicness

At least one way of explaining the prosaic nature of civic piety is to realize that the bargain struck by church and state in the U.S. was a contract regulating mass emotion. The compact was conceived by, and for, *national* religious and political leaders. It is more an historical curiosity than anything else that its themes have also been appropriated by local congregations of the national religion. Failing to appreciate the public nature of civil-religious discourse in the U.S. is to miss its very raison d'etre.

Support for such a claim is provided by the distinguished historian, Winthrop Hudson, who declared: "'Civic religion,' the 'religion of the republic,' was *public* religion, a religion available to all through natural reason. 'Spiritual religion' was *private* religion, an 'experienced' religion that was intensely personal. The one was preoccupied with the nation and its mission; the other was preoccupied with individuals and their redemption."[89] The implications of Hudson's distinction are apparent—it is inappropriate to apply private criteria when assessing a public institution like American civic piety. That is, it is entirely legitimate for devout Roman Catholics to castigate the Jansenistic remarks made in church by a local pastor. However, were they to react with equal outrage at the pastor's participation in an Arbor Day ceremony, they would be confusing what should be quite distinct (private and public) priorities.

In actuality, of course, most Americans make just such distinctions each day. Most Americans do not expect to find a confessional stance in the remarks of their elected officials. Most Americans assent to Gerald Ford's rhetorical priorities: "My faith is a very personal thing. It is not something one shouts from the housetop or wears on his sleeve. For me, my religious feeling is a deep personal faith I rely on for guidance from my God."[90] Most Americans, it seems clear, were unconcerned that Dwight Eisenhower's personal religious sentiments were out of sync with his presidential piety, as was once reported by Billy Graham:

> When he becomes President, [Eisenhower] brought a strong sense of dedication to his office. He introduced a prayer he wrote himself into his inaugural address and began the practice of devoting a minute of silent prayer at the beginning of cabinet meetings. Many of the cabinet meetings he had opened in prayer.
>
> He joined and regularly attended the National Presbyterian Church in Washington. Before he became President, he was not a member of any church. He called Dr. Ed Elson, the pastor of the church, and Dr. Elson gave him several hours of private Biblical instruction and teaching. The President of the United States was baptized and made a public profession of his faith in Jesus Christ. He became one of the most dedicated churchmen in the nation.
>
> I talked to him many times about this experience, and I am convinced that he made his personal commitment to Christ as a boy; but he made it publicly after he had become President of the United States.[91]

Dwight Eisenhower knew, as most Americans know, that a public rhetoric like civic piety must acknowledge the sundry philosophical predilections of its hearers and seek the most common denominators if it is to be effective. Civic piety must sacrifice the delicate individuality of a particular theological and/or political system for one which will motivate members of a bewilderingly diverse audience. Because it cannot rely on sectarian and partisan arguments, civic piety often takes on the ritualistic, non-existential, and expedient features described in this chapter.

Politicians, then, must be vigilant about their private and public personae. In this connection, Richard Nixon's White House tapes did the unthinkable—they permitted his private morality to be displayed in public. His civil-religious heresy was not so much that he crossed the indistinct line of ethical principle but that he was not publicly circumspect. As adherents of a national civil religion, Americans can forgive many things in their national leaders but public gaucheness is not one of them. As adherents to private ethical systems, of course, they rendered other (usually, more denunciatory) judgments of Mr. Nixon's Watergate behavior as well.

Emotional Hardiness

The prosaic cast of civic piety also derives from its use as a helpmate to the American people during times of crisis. Civil-religious themes act as prime agents of disaster relief and have always acted thusly:

> In the presence of a storm or a cannonade at sea or in the exigencies of combat in the field, and notably in the great exigencies of national destiny such as a presidential assassination, the extraordinary range of American denominational religiosity is pretty much contracted into the essentials for men in peril, wherever and whatever their religion.[92]

That is not to say that civic piety provides tangible palliatives. Rather, it encourages an audience to view the crisis at hand as but a momentary tribulation for a nation whose grandeur has long been assured:

> America became great, not because of any material wealth, but because of the spiritual fiber of our forebears regardless of creed. In every crisis and emergency in our Nation's history, Americans, from the leaders on down, have called on God to aid, comfort and guide them, and their pleas have always been answered. SO MAY IT EVER BE![93]

As Herbert Schneider reports, Woodrow Wilson and Franklin Roosevelt often resorted to civil-religious themes during wartime. According to Schneider, these rhetorical choices served to give "a general religious solemnity to the struggles and to suggest officially that 'in God we trust.'"[94] In addition to mythifying the particular conflagration at hand, such rhetoric illustrates the "primordial impulse to invoke the symbols of social unity" during times of conflict.[95] Thus exalted and befriended, the American people can then make greater sense out of their uncomfortable empirical realities—or so goes the hypothesis of civic piety. Understanding the "crisis function" of such rhetoric helps explain why so many unofficial civil religionists (like Billy James Hargis and Fred Schwarz) tried to co-opt themes of civic piety when combating the Communist menace.

Optimism: A truly distinctive feature of civic piety is its zealous and enthusiastic spirit. The American civil religion has never been popular among Sartrian crepehangers. Instead, Americans are attracted to a rhetoric asserting that they can attain almost anything. Will Herberg credits such simple optimism to the idealism found within the Judaeo-Christian traditions from which it sprang and by which it is nourished.[96] The rhetorical explanation for such themes is less complicated: any discourse attempting to unify a diverse population could hardly be otherwise. "The true and operative religion of America is not that of the churches at all, with their pessimistic general confessions," argued Willard Sperry in 1946, "but that of the state with its declarations of independence."[97]

Sperry's thesis is attractive in contemporary times as well. After all, the market on optimism has not been cornered by election-year politicians alone. A generous share belongs to church leaders like Ezra Taft Benson. Note in the following passage (from a speech Benson gave on December 4, 1973, to students of Brigham Young University) that no manner of hardship can prevent a Holy Nation from triumphing:

> Yes, we have a rich heritage, but may I remind you that nations often times sow the seeds of their own destruction even while

enjoying unprecedented prosperity, even before reaching the ze-
nith or the peak of their power. I think history clearly indicates
that this is often the case. When it appears that all is well, oft-
times the very seeds of destruction are sown, sometimes unwit-
tingly. Most of the great civilizations of the world have not been
conquered from without until they have destroyed themselves
from within by sowing these seeds of destruction.[98]

But,

> Every true Latter-day Saint should love the United States of
> America—the most generous nation under heaven—the Lord's
> base of operations in these last days. May we do all in our power
> to strengthen and safeguard this base and increase our freedom.
> This nation will, I feel sure, endure. It is God-ordained for a glo-
> rious purpose.[99]

Civic piety, it would appear, always ends on the upbeat.

Emotional Simplicity: "The Pilgrim Fathers," intoned Norman Vincent Peale,
set forth in "little ships across a stormy sea, driven not by the winds that raged the
Atlantic and caught the sails of their little boats, but by the mighty conviction that as
sons of God nobody could make slaves of them."[100] Cynics, of course, could argue
that such emotional simplicity is typical of Peale's unique faith in hope. This does
not appear to be the case, however. While civic piety is often more sophisticated
than Peale's, it is rarely intentionally complicated. It relies on straightforward commonplaces, hitting hard at the listener's basic motivations and depending for its effect on the audience's adherence to certain simple, archetypal themes—God meets
nation, God loves nation, God sustains nation—and seeks only to create telling (if
necessary, local) variations on such themes. "The religion of Washington politicians
stops with this simple identification of goodness and faith," writes Paul Blanshard,
"controversial theology is completely taboo"[101] in civic piety.

To understand why such dictates are followed carefully we need only to be reminded of the exigences which call forth civic piety. The stock themes of "justice
and magnanimity, humanity and valor, the virtues of the heart before the head, a
simple trust in God"[102] and so forth are found in civil-religious rhetoric for the same
reasons that they are found in other forms of popular communication. Such themes
are compelling to us collectively, no matter how vapid they may appear to us as individuals in private. While scholars and theologians may denounce these themes as
just so much emotional sop for an ignorant audience, the richer, albeit divisive,
themes of sectarian religion and partisan politics wait in the wings . . . beckoning
unbecomingly.

Unless the American people suddenly prove willing to tear down the political
edifice described in this essay, civic piety will have to do. By accepting its emotional simplicity as well as its other features described here, Americans are accepting what is for many of them a valued public heritage. By keeping the civil-religious
contract in its proper perspective, taking it just as seriously as good sense and social

realities warrant, they are doing what Americans have always proved willing to do—go with what works.

Conclusion

When concluding his seminal essay on civil religion, Robert Bellah urged that the ethnocentricity of American civic piety be replaced by a more cosmopolitan, indeed international, self-knowledge. Said Bellah:

> So far the flickering flame of the United Nations burns too low to be the focus of a cult, but the emergence of a genuine trans-national sovereignty would certainly change this. It would ne-cessitate the incorporation of vital international symbolism into our civil religion, or, perhaps a better way of putting it, it would result in American civil religion becoming simply one part of a new civil religion of the world. It is useless to speculate on the form such a civil religion might take, though it obviously would draw on religious traditions beyond the sphere of Biblical relig-ion alone. Fortunately, since the American civil religion is not the worship of the American nation but an understanding of the American experience in the light of ultimate and universal real-ity, the reorganization entailed by such a new situation need not disrupt the American civil religion's continuity. A world civil re-ligion could be accepted as a fulfillment and not a denial of American civil religion. Indeed, such an outcome has been the eschatological hope of American civil religion from the begin-ning. To deny such an outcome would be to deny the meaning of America itself.[103]

Attractive though Bellah's goal-state may be, the realities of cross-cultural un-derstanding and, more important, of misunderstanding, seem to threaten his project at the very start. If we have described *American* civic piety accurately in this chap-ter, could its international counterpart be more efficient, less shot-through with compromise and equivocation? Would the qualities of an international deity be more specific than those possessed by the U.S.'s own twenty-eight-flavored God? Given the diversity of its myths, could the world devise a civil-religious contract that would be both functional and uplifting? Could a satisfactory formula for describing international destiny be devised that would have equal meaning for an Israeli and a Palestinian? If an American Catholic and a Protestant fundamentalist can abide one another only under the occasional canopy of public ritual, can we expect more from a destitute Moslem and a well-fed German? Obviously, these are all highly rhetori-cal questions about unquestionably rhetorical matters. As such, they will be further burdened by the vagaries of native languages and dialects. Thus, while the globe may be turning into a more compact village because of telecommunications, it seems unlikely that anything as fallible as civic piety can easily overcome the myr-iad problems attendant to truly international discourse.

Throughout this essay, however, it has never been our intention to quibble with Bellah's goals. Surely it is wise for the American people to reckon with the press of international responsibility, with the mistreatment of minority groups, and with the philosophical emptiness native to so much of the popular discourse heard daily. But to subscribe to Bellah's ideals is not to condone his several reifications of political life in the United States. While it may make for adequate shirt-sleeved philosophy to speak of a single American civil religion, it makes little sense to deny the very real cultural diversity that constantly threatens to embarrass such homogenizing rhetorics. Nevertheless, Bellah persists:

> No one has changed a great nation without appealing to its soul, without stimulating a national idealism, as even those who have called themselves materialists have discovered. Culture is the key to revolution, religion is the key to culture. If we win the political struggle, we will not even know what we want unless we have a new vision of man, a new sense of human possibility, and a new conception of the ordering of liberty, the constitution of freedom.[104]

Noble sentiments all. But implicit in Bellah's vision is a type of ideological imperialism, a demand for a set of symbols which will suffice for all Americans. Most likely, the American people will have none of this. Oh, yes, they will allow their preachers and politicians to talk of a uniform national will, a universal American ideal, but they will not easily forget, it seems to us, that all of this is talk. Because it is talk, Americans can revel in it, carp at it, demand new versions of it, glorify it, dismiss it. But should some prelate or politician fail to observe the strictures contained in the civil-religious contract described here, the American people will come a-marching.

As a people, Americans take delight in the concept of religion. It is the details, the applications, of religion that they distrust. And so let both clergyman and congressman be warned—civic piety, not civil religion, will always be the order of the day in the very tenuously united states of America. No matter how anachronistic some may find his politics to be, no matter what variety of reductionism others may detect in his theology, and no matter how vague the existenial implications of his remarks may appear to some, Billy Graham's brand of civic piety is probably as much a harbinger of the future as an echo of the American experience:

> This is all a part of the American heritage—a nation that believes in God, a nation that flies the Christian flag, a nation that believes in the providences of God in her national life.
>
> Who of us can forget the picture of George Washington in prayer at Valley Forge, and then his taking his small army and routing the British, thus bringing about our victory in the war of the Revolution? Who can forget the words of Benjamin Franklin as he called the Constitutional Convention to prayer and out of that prayer meeting came the Constitution of the United States?

Who can forget Abraham Lincoln and his cabinet on their knees many times during the Civil War, not praying for victory, but asking that God's will be done? Who can forget the great epochs in American life in which we have honored God and recognized God? I say that it is the secret of America's prosperity, America's strength, and this is the hope of America's future.[105]

Chapter 6

Postlude

In this essay, our central contention has been that to deny the rhetorical nature of American civic piety is to deny its essence. Like many things human and like most things American, civic piety does not simply exist. It exists because the American people have decided to wage their struggles of church and state on symbolic battlegrounds, realizing that the casualties of rhetorical war always live to speak another day. They have realized, too, that public rhetoric is an incredibly potent vehicle through which the "social symbiosis"[1] of religion and government can be effected, maintained, and made palatable.

In this essay, we have observed a commonplace and important feature of life in the United States. We have witnessed a panorama of civic piety, discourse that is both variegated and possessed of subtle hues. We have seen that to view such rhetoric through Robert Bellah's notion of a civil religion is to distort its value as a highly pragmatic adaptation to very real political problems. And we have noted that a contractual view of civic piety offers useful insights into how Americans live their lives. More recently in this essay, we have pointed up four specific features of civic piety: its expedient complexity, its non-existential content, its ritualistic presence, and its prosaic animus.

Given these qualities, some may be inclined to declare civic piety an eternal emptiness. One California clergyman, for example, has likened it to "spiritual aspirin," since "it doesn't cost much, doesn't do much, and isn't worth much."[2] We find this too frontal a criticism. Our cleric is right, of course, in suggesting that American civic piety doesn't cost much. Except in the eyes of the staunchest denominationalists and separationists, little is lost when the nation's chief executive requests the help of a God in whom he may have little personal confidence. Also, the participation of the nation's religious leaders in Orange Bowl rituals requires only a small measure of grace and good sense on the parts of fans as they bow their heads waiting for the kickoff. When the occasional indignities of civic piety are contrasted to the religious wars that have torn nations apart throughout human history, a political benediction or two seems a small price to pay when providing a sense of collective harmony and national destiny to people who need them.

To suggest that civic piety doesn't do much or isn't worth much is, as we have seen, both right and wrong. Because civic piety is normally devoid of existential punch—finding its rationale in the world of myth and symbol—its tangible accomplishments are sometimes hard to discern. As has been suggested throughout this essay, however, the American people have had almost no experience with anything but a surrogate church-state. Yes, there has been a wall of separation between religion and politics in the United States but it has been the rituals of civic piety that have kept that wall from becoming a nagging, national problem.

Although the American people may have turned Jefferson's wall of separation into a semi-permeable membrane, the edifice has withstood the tests of time and partisanship. And while Richard Fenn is undoubtedly right that civic piety has not (especially in recent times) performed a truly integrative function for American society[3] it has kept all rival "integrators" at bay, forcing them to vend their wares in more local, and less dangerous, marketplaces.

Recently, however, commentators have suggested that the death knell of civic piety is being sounded, that church and state will abrogate the rhetorical contract they have signed and constantly renewed. Typically, three strains of argument have been offered to support that claim: religious, political, and sociological. Some observers feel, for example, that because American Catholics have been frustrated in their attempts to receive public aid for their private schools, they soon will swear off the nation's civil-religious ceremonies. In addition, fundamentalist Protestants bemoan prayerless public schools, Jews have never been regarded as swimming in the civil-religious mainstream, and, as Conrad Cherry has indicated,[4] atheists and agnostics too have a right to expect participation in any *civil* religion that calls itself American.

American civic piety may also have to wage battles on political and sociological fronts. For example, the Vietnam War was the first major American conflagration whose holy purpose could not be easily discerned by many American clergymen. Too, unofficial civil religionists like Carl McKintire, Billy James Hargis, and Fred Schwartz are becoming more insistent that the accomodationistic rhetoric of mainstream civic piety be curtailed and that the U.S. assume a more messianic role in the world. Finally, separationists are warning that the rituals of civic piety compromise the nation's long-standing distaste for even pseudo-theocratic governmental structures.

These are all serious charges. Yet like so many of the comments that have been made about such matters, these charges credit civic piety with more importance than seems sensible. If the last two hundred years have taught us anything it is that the American people can tolerate, even relish, legion cultural anomalies. No matter how vociferous contemporary Catholics, Protestants, Jews, antiwar activists, Communist baiters, and separationists may become, they are no louder, or more diverse, than was the "movement which began with the first settlers at Jamestown," as Ernest Bates pointed out more than thirty years ago:

The American faith . . . was a complex, an amalgamation, of hundreds of warring faiths. It could not possibly be closely knit or approach a logical unity such as we find in medieval Catholicism or in modern fascism or communism. Tolerance of diversity was one of its essential characteristics. At its basis was a kind of residuum of common qualities found in nearly all of its constituent movements. Above that were elements, adopted now from one group, now from another, because they proved to possess, for one or another reason, survival value. It was bound to be shot through with logical contradictions. Such unity as it possessed, over and above a certain basic identity of spirit, was largely a union of opposites. Its method was compromise, its result assimilation. It was not "thinly dieted on dew," but lived like an organism through the neutralization of poisons.[5]

The conditions which Bates specifies hold today as well. Compared to Jamestown, bicentennial America is neither more beset nor less beset by cultural and religious incongruities. Unless the American people suddenly choose not to accommodate one another through ritual or to re-promulgate their national myths with regularity or refuse to honor the rhetorical contract they have enforced upon church and state, civic piety of a changing yet changeless variety will continue to distinguish the cultural and symbolic landscape of the United States.

Unit 3

Contemporary Reaction

Chapter 7

The Force of Religion in the Public Sphere

Ronald Lee

Twenty-five years ago, Roderick Hart in the *Political Pulpit* proposed an "alternative understanding" of the rhetorical relationship between religion and government. In doing this, he took as his point of departure sociologist Robert Bellah's work on civil religion. Hart conceptualized the difference between their views by distinguishing between the transcendent and the pragmatic. For Bellah, references to the sacred in public affairs have religious import because they justify governmental action on ultimate grounds. For Hart, these references are not religious at all, but rather practical responses to the American constitutional separation of church and state.

For Bellah, the public arena demands moral justifications that are grounded in the divine. "Though the will of people as expressed in majority vote is carefully institutionalized as the operative source of political authority," he writes, "it is deprived of an ultimate significance." He continues, "The will of the people is not itself the criterion of right and wrong. There is a higher criterion of right and wrong."[1]

For Hart, civic piety emerges "from a knowing, practiced, thoroughly pragmatic understanding of the suasory arabesques demanded when God and country kick up their heels rhetorically."[2] He argues that Bellah "discovered not 'religion,' but interesting rhetorical assertions" that through "his own hypostatization" became "civil religion."[3]

The centerpiece of Hart's analysis of the pragmatic use of religion is his employment of the metaphor of the "contract." He characterizes the sacred-secular rhetorical relationship as an unstated, but enforceable contract between government and organized religion. The rhetorical behavior of public officials and religious leaders can then be understood as the carrying out, in a quite self-interested way, the terms of this contract. Hart's contract has four parts: (1) "The guise of complete separation between the [United States Government] and [Organized

Religion] will be maintained by both parties." (2) "The guise of existential equality between the [United States Government] and [Organized Religion] will be maintained by both parties, but [Organized Religion's] realm will be solely that of the rhetorical." (3) "[United States Government] rhetoric will refrain from being overly religious and [Organized Religion's] rhetoric will refrain from being overly political." (4) "Neither [United States Government nor Organized Religion] shall, in any fashion whatsoever, make known to the general populace the exact terms of the contract contained herein."[4]

The contract, Hart argues, is enforceable because violators face serious sanctions. If representatives of the church become too political, they lose their privileges as honored members of the national community and their access to political leaders. If, on the other hand, politicians mix too much religion into public affairs, they will appear out of the mainstream and lose their influence.[5] Now precisely where the political culture draws the sacred-secular line is a matter of constant renegotiation. Crises, for instance, are occasions for more fervent religious discourse from public officials and for more political pronouncements from spiritual leaders. But in general, over time, Hart suggests that there has been a diminution in the religious tenor of American public discourse. "Coupled with the rising industrialization and the scientific era," he writes, "America's nationalism could thus tilt its religious cap at a more rakish angle, the existential need for such rhetorical support having now passed."[6]

I have read and admired Professor Hart's work for many years. As with any influential critic, the reader becomes familiar with the writer's voice. On re-reading *The Political Pulpit*, I heard a voice that I hardly recognized. This persona is rather cynical and flippant, quite different from the contemporary Hart. Whether intended or not, the author's tone turns pragmatic "civic piety" into a ruse. No one seems sincere in this book; there is no place for genuine devotion. Instead, everything is about stability, the status quo, and doing what is conventionally expected. Above all, religious faith never provides moral justification for social change. It is almost always portrayed as a dance among God, country, and established interests. For Hart, God's most important political function is to justify the way things are.

Of course, in one sense, Hart is absolutely right. Religion is a set of rhetorical conventions that reinforce the linkage between God and country, where the church does not impose sectarian political demands on the state nor does the state regulate the church. But I do not believe this is the whole story. The transcendent element of religion, the genuine appeal to the sacred, has a greater influence on contemporary politics than Hart recognizes. I believe there are two causes for our varying interpretations. First, the political-religious activity of the last quarter century has made the presence of genuinely religious appeals in public affairs more obvious. Second, and more importantly, Hart's methodology tends to minimize the influence of the sacred. He examined references to "God" in presidential speeches and other political documents.[7] He also looked for rhetorical "commonplaces" or "stock phrases" that speakers depend upon in invoking the divine. In describing these phrases, he summons Gabriel Fackre's saying, "the musak of civil religion."[8] By contrast, I am interested in the connection between religion and narrative form in political affairs.

In what follows, I examine four examples of political discourse that I believe can only be adequately explained by reference to the transcendent. Their meaning cannot be exhausted by understanding them as conventional expressions meant to pay homage to the church-state contract. The first example Hart mentions himself, Martin Luther King, Jr.'s "Letter from Birmingham Jail." The other three—Dan Quayle's discourse of family values, Bill Clinton's explanations of the Monica Lewinsky affair, and George W. Bush's inaugural address—occurred after the publication of *The Political Pulpit*. In each case, I will argue that the narrative form itself is shaped by transcendent religion.

Martin Luther King, Jr. and the Letter from Birmingham Jail

There is an odd caveat buried in the middle of *The Political Pulpit*. Although it is only three paragraphs long, it has its own section heading: *"The Curious Case of Doctor King."*[9] Here Hart discusses the comment of a colleague who had read an earlier draft of the book. The colleague "argued . . . that a person like Martin Luther King, Jr., stood in sharp contrast to the accomodationists" that had been described in the book. "[O]ne might suggest," Hart writes, "that King's conception of a highly judgmental God (who smiles kindly on social activism) clearly gives the lie to my analysis."[10]

Odder still is Hart's reply to this criticism. First, while admitting that the "most obvious response . . . is also the least satisfactory," he writes that King "was clearly an anomaly in the pages of civil-religious history." Second, he argues that a "more telling retort" is that "for all of his reverence for God the Wise and the Just," King "never completely severed the bonds between himself and the political establishment in Washington." Third, Hart contends that "King was a member in good standing of the rhetorical establishment" and that it is "not an accident of history that King is best known for his 'I Have a Dream' *speech* and his *letter* from the Birmingham Jail." Finally, he claims that it is "important to remember that the Black Power movement was launched by those who sought to fill in the behavioral-existential void created by King's willingness to effect change through *rhetorical* agencies."[11] This leads Hart to conclude that "while King may have rejected much of the civil religious contract, it seems clear that he respected its underlying rhetorical essence."[12]

I must admit I simply do not understand these replies. They seem to have little to do with the issue at hand. To say that King "never completely severed the bonds" with the political establishment and that he was "a member in good standing of the rhetorical establishment" begs the question. Moreover, it makes the very point Hart is trying to deny with the contract. King appealed to the transcendent in a serious way and yet was within the bounds of the political establishment.

The fact that King and the Black Power movement disagreed on tactics does not prove anything. Facing the fire hoses, filling up the jails, losing your children to bombings, and all the other associated costs and consequences of nonviolence hardly seem to justify the phrase "behavioral-existential void."

The "Letter from Birmingham Jail" is a powerful expression of King's justification for social action and this justification is grounded in theological conviction. In answering the argument that he should "wait," because "all Christians know that colored people will receive equal rights eventually, but it is possible that you are in too great a religious hurry," King provides an explanation of the way God works in history.[13] He does this by narrating three different time frames in the "Letter"—recent time, historical time, and spiritual time. He then explains how the different senses of conscience work in each of these time frames.[14] King believes that God moves history toward justice, but He does so through individual, heroic acts of conscience. It is in this way that King can reconcile providence and freedom. Together they bring forth what King calls the "beloved community" (or the "Dream").

The "Letter" stands as an important counter example to Hart's pragmatism. First, it was a religious refutation of the call for stability. In the context of 1960s Birmingham, King was using religious justification for social change. This is most obvious in King's contention that "I submit that an individual who breaks a law that conscience tells him is unjust . . . is in reality expressing the highest respect for law." Second, King presents a coherent vision of God's work in history. This is an ideological and theological vision, not a mere stringing together of conventional phrases. Religious commitment shaped the very form of the story he is telling. Of course, someone could go through the "Letter" and point to the fact that the term "conscience" or the "will of God" is a common phrase in political speech. What one could not deny is that the narrative structure, of which these phrases are essential parts, is formed from a deeply religious vision.

Finally, Hart might say that he began by admitting that King was an anomaly and so this objection has little force. But the martyred saint who gave the country the words by which to understand the meaning of freedom can never be a mere exception. He is arguably the most important American orator of the century. Since he is the touchstone by which all others are compared, he can never be dismissed.

Dan Quayle and Family Values

Vice President Dan Quayle delivered his maiden family-values address to the Commonwealth Club of California in the aftermath of the South Central Los Angeles riots. His purpose was to justify the Bush administration policies on poverty in urban America. Quayle[16] diagnosed black family dissolution as the leading cause of racial turmoil and urban despair. Family dysfunction, he argued, was encouraged by a welfare system, which created an ethos of dependency and hampered the ability of the underclass to "take advantage of opportunities America offers."

Less than a month later, in a speech to the Southern Baptists' Convention, Quayle[17] said that the family "is not only '*nature's* masterpiece,'—it is God's masterpiece." For him, family is society's natural moral regulator and any dysfunction in its operation has dire consequences for the community. Genesis, as Christian conservatives traditionally interpret it, is both the story of the Fall and the depiction of the first family.[18] It narrates the creation of man and woman, explains the institution of marriage as the union of one man with one woman, and traces the family genealogy through Noah. After expelling Adam and Eve from the garden, God gave humankind the institution of the family to establish moral boundaries. By submitting to these moral boundaries, humans are given the means of salvation.[19]

While admitting that the rhetorical surface of family values discourse usually does not explicitly announce religious commitments, I contend that the narrative form of the discourse is only understandable by an appreciation of its religious roots. The very phrase "family values" is nonsensical if not understood in religious terms.

There is something peculiar about the social-conservative use of the term "family."[20] For social conservatives deploy the term in ways quite different from its rhetorical connection to public policy in the immediate postwar period. In the 1950s, government funding helped families buy homes and supported transportation policies that encouraged the creation of the American suburb. Freeways were built and sewer lines were laid.[21] Through these policies, government *acts* improved the family *scene*. The social-conservative conception of family is not a scene; it is not a material condition that can be improved or endangered by simple acts. For family, although still scenic in the trivial sense that particular families can still be located, is essentially an *agency*. Yet, not a simple agency—not merely a neutral tool—but an agency that is guided by a *telos*. A healthy family will fulfill certain moral ends. This agency will, by its very constitution as a healthy family, generate correct values or, perhaps more accurately, inculcate and perpetuate a particular set of virtues.

The characterization of family as organic connects values, not to utility, but to human nature. Values are not relative to situations, but rather intrinsic to human disposition. Thus, they are not calibrated on a gauge of usefulness, but instead pronounced healthy or sick. Organic metaphors aptly depict the social-conservative view of the family. Marriage is a seedbed that brings children into the world; the subsequent family provides a nurturing environment for raising the young; and if the ground is fertile and the garden well tended, morally healthy adults will be produced. Like the plant seed, the human seed has within it a planned design and that design will be realized if the garden is protected from the weeds, insects, and bad weather that afflict the environment.

The *telos*—the connection between purpose and human nature—is understandable only by reference to religious commitment. This is why the Christian Coalition and before that the Moral Majority cared so much about issues of the family. This is why the Family Protection Act was introduced by Paul Laxalt during the Reagan administration and why Vice President Quayle focused on family in the 1992 presidential election.

To put my point succinctly, the dominant narrative form of social-conservatism is understandable only with reference to the sacred. Without the conception of the Fall and the subsequent place of the family in salvation history, the narrative is incoherent. If, as Hart did, rhetorical analysts search only for particular words or commonplaces, they will miss the way in which religion underwrites the narratives of prominent political discourses.

Bill Clinton and the Monica Lewinksy Affair

In 1998, President Bill Clinton gave three speeches in which he explained the events surrounding the Monica Lewinsky affair. The first was a brief five-hundred-word national address on the evening of August 17. In a nearly unanimous verdict, the press framed this rhetorical effort a failure. Clinton delivered the second speech on the occasion of the 35th anniversary of the March on Washington in Martha's Vineyard on August 28. In this address, he apologized for the bitter words he had spoken on August 17. Finally, at the National Prayer Breakfast on September 11, Bill Clinton gave a speech that followed the ritualistic demands of a sacramental confession. This last speech was widely hailed as a sincere and eloquent plea for forgiveness.

From August 17 to September 11, Clinton made successive inventional choices that moved away from the secular language of rights to the religious language of sin and reconciliation. Interestingly, the press evaluated all three speeches using a religious frame. The failure of August 17 and the increasingly more satisfactory discourses of August 28 and September 11 were evaluated in terms of a sacramental confession.[22]

On September 11, President Clinton was the final speaker at the nation's annual Prayer Breakfast. This occasion, inaugurated in 1953 by Dwight Eisenhower, brings the religious and political worlds together. Attended by government officials, religious leaders, and diplomats from around the world, the prayer breakfast has become "one of the center pieces of civil religion."[23]

The White House let it be known that the President wrestled with this difficult address, staying up until 4:00 a.m. reading the Bible. He had refused to consult with anyone about what he was going to say. In other words, Clinton had been engaged in an examination of conscience. At the beginning of the fifteen-paragraph speech, he says, "I may not be quite as easy with my words today as I have been in years past, and I was up rather late last night thinking and praying about what I ought to say today. And rather unusual for me, I actually tried to write it down. So if you will forgive me, I will do my best to say what it is I want to say to you—and I may have to take my glasses out to read my own writing." In the next paragraph, he says, "I don't think there is a fancy way to say that I have sinned."[24]

In the body of the address, Clinton relies on the imagery found in Psalm 51. This part of the scripture is based on King David and his petition to the Lord to forgive him after committing adultery with Bathsheba. The Psalm is centered on "broken things." Clinton states:

> But I believe that to be forgiven, more than sorrow is required
> —at least two more things. First, genuine repentance—a de-
> termination to change and to repair breaches of my own mak-
> ing. I have repented. Second, what my bible calls a "broken
> spirit"; an understanding that I must have God's help to be the
> person that I want to be; a willingness to give the very for-
> giveness I seek; a renunciation of the pride and the anger
> which cloud judgment, lead people to excuse and compare
> and to blame and complain.[25]

In the latter portion of the speech, Clinton discusses the Yom Kippur liturgy.[26] He then reads an extended passage from this text, which highlights both
the difficulty and rewards of seeking forgiveness. "Turn us around, O Lord, and
bring us back toward you. Revive our lives as at the beginning, and turn us toward each other, Lord, for in isolation there is no life."[27]

Finally, he asks for the audience's prayers: "I ask you to share my prayer
that God will search me and know my heart, try and know my anxious thoughts,
see if there is any hurtfulness in me, and let me walk by faith and not sight" and
concludes by saying "God bless you."[28]

This address is not a simple apology; it is a sacramental confession. The
secular press framed the speech in just these terms. James Bennett, writing in the
New York Times, argues that Clinton made his most "abject confession of personal failure . . . and for the first time . . . asked for forgiveness."[29] "Clerics who
attended the breakfast," he continues, "said they were moved by Mr. Clinton's
words of contrition, in language that drew on both Christian and Jewish traditions."[30] One rabbi in attendance is noted as observing that "he was impressed
that Mr. Clinton's remarks had followed the basic steps required for repentance
on Yom Kippur, the Day of Atonement: a candid admission of wrongdoing, an
apology to those wronged, and a plea for forgiveness to avoid such behavior in
the future."[31]

Also writing in the *New York Times*, Gustav Niebuhr points to Clinton's "remarkable fluency with religious language."[32] The President, he states, offered a
"frank admission" of his sins, "but the most resonant moment for clergy members may have come when Mr. Clinton said the process of forgiveness demands
'what my Bible calls a broken spirit.'"[33] Niehuhr explains that both "Jewish and
Christian tradition" considers this psalm as evidence of the "appeal David makes
to God after God has sent the prophet Nathan to rebuke the king for having
committed adultery with Bathsheba, and for sending Bathsheba's husband,
Uriah, into battle to be killed."[34] David is later told that his offering to God
should not be a literal sacrifice, but "a broken and contrite heart."[35]

Laura Goodstein, also of the *New York Times*, notes that the "Roman Catholic lectionary for yesterday took up the story of the wayward Prodigal Son who
spends his inheritance on prostitutes and yet is forgiven. Jews on Saturday night
celebrated the Selichot service, a midnight ceremony marking the beginning of
the High Holiday season of introspection, self-examination and repentance."[36]

In his three Monica Lewinsky addresses—August 17, August 28, and September 11—the President moved from characterizing his transgressions as mistakes to calling them sins; he moved from angrily blaming others for this troubles to asking forgiveness for his pride; and he moved from the liberal language of rights to the moral language of virtue. Mirroring this movement, the secular press went from stinging criticism to warm praise.

Again, as in King's *Letter* and Quayle's family-values discourse, the sacred guided the narrative form of the President's National Prayer Breakfast address. Calling on both Christian and Jewish tradition, Clinton followed the prescribed steps of religious confession. This was hardly a political commonplace, for the speaker was self-conscious about the meaning of the ritual. He quoted the scriptural sources that underwrite the sacrament. Hart may argue that the National Prayer Breakfast is an unusual occasion that calls forth atypical political discourse. This may well be true in general, but it is a more difficult argument to sustain in the case of Clinton's confession. This speech's content guaranteed it widespread attention and it also assured that it would be understood as part of the President's month-long journey to seek forgiveness. In this case, the Prayer Breakfast address was not simply another epideictic occasion, but a public address that dealt with the most significant issue of the day. I believe Clinton's progressive rhetorical choices from August 17 to September 11, and the accompanying press reaction, stand as an important and telling exception to Hart's understanding of the American church-state contract.

George W. Bush's Inaugural Address

The Bellah-Hart disagreement begins with their very different reading of presidential inaugural addresses. Bellah finds, especially in John Kennedy's speech, the justifying of American political action on the ultimate ground of the divine. Hart argues that Kennedy's religious appeal was tepid at best because he was never willing to speak in the language of Roman Catholicism.[37] This is a moment of frustration for me. Hart seems to have reshuffled the argumentative deck. Apparently, he is equating the failure to articulate a specific denominational theology with a pragmatic political appeal. I do not understand why one condition is necessary for the other. I am a Roman Catholic who has often shared, what I took to be, genuine moments of religious devotion with Protestant evangelical friends. Our appeal to a transcendent God overcame our doctrinal differences. The transcendent does not give way to the pragmatic merely because believers do not share perfect common ground. For Bellah, all they must share is the conviction that God is the ultimate source of moral justification.

I believe George W. Bush's recent inaugural address makes my objection even more salient. As I have argued in the previous three examples, the narrative form of the address can only be understood with reference to the sacred. Throughout the speech, he speaks of a "flawed and fallible people" pursuing, yet often stumbling along the way, "grand and enduring ideals."[38] The President is confident that these ideals are within "our reach because we are guided by a power larger than ourselves, who creates us equal, in His image."[39] Near the end of the address, he adds, "We are not this story's author, who fills time and eternity with his purpose."[40] The next to last line reads, "[A]n angel still rides in the whirlwind and directs the storm."[41]

All of this, Hart would probably say, is rather standard providential boilerplate for inaugural addresses. What makes this different is Bush uses this *telos* to provide a sacred justification for compassionate conservatism.[42] He does this by constructing the inaugural around the parable of the Good Samaritan. "And I can pledge," he says, "our nation to a goal: When we see that wounded traveler on the road to Jericho, we will not pass to the other side."[43] "[H]is purpose is achieved in our duty. And our duty is fulfilled in service to one another."[44] The largely unspoken but obvious theme of the address is racial reconciliation. The speech is almost completely occupied with the perfecting of domestic society. Bush's address mirrors King's "Dream" of the beloved community. It has the same postmillennialist commitments to an ever more just society that is guided on its providential journey by people of conscience. "In the quiet of American conscience," Bush says, "we know that deep, persistent poverty is unworthy of our Nation's promise. . . . Abandonment and abuse are not acts of God; they are failures of love"[45]

These references to the sacred are not just catch phrases—not merely salve for soothing the parties to the church-state contract—instead, they represent words that form a powerful American narrative about nation, God, justice, and community. In the ideological writings of the architects of compassionate conservatism, religion is the indispensable element for addressing social pathology.[46] It is the shape and meaning of the story, not just the mention of religious terms, that create a civil religion.

Conclusion

Scholars have spilled a great deal of ink on the relationship among myth, narrative, and ideology.[47] Burke argues that myth provides the indispensable first principles for ideology, usually expressed as an appeal to a "mythic ancestry."[48] For instance, both Hobbes and Locke found it necessary to build their political philosophies on an appeal to a mythic "state of nature."[49] So, too, do American political rhetors have to build their visions upon myth and these myths are frequently religious.

Put differently, these myths provide the essential rhetorical material for jumping the is-ought gap. Ideologies explain how we ought to govern ourselves, but they do so based on a characterization of what kind of "people" we are. The characterization of us as a "people" is provided by myth.[50] These ideological narratives are frequently structured by religion. Many of our most prominent American political discourses are explainable only by reference to the transcendent.

Hart, on my view, dramatically understates this relationship. Because he works so much with the surface of the texts (especially with word choice), he minimizes the importance of religion to the narrative/ideological underpinnings of American political rhetoric. To use a linguistic analogy, it is the difference between exploring semantics and examining syntax. It is in the "syntax" of political discourse that one can find the commitments that justify the label "civil religion."

Chapter 8

A New Scholarly Dispensation for Civil Religion

Carolyn Marvin

Ever since Robert Bellah introduced the term "civil religion" in the late 1960s to describe the transcendent communal impulses of patriotic rituals and speeches, American scholars have debated its existence and place in our national life.[1] Despite the pointed suggestion of the label, most scholars who use the term "civil religion" have backed away, often emphatically, from calling it a "true" religion. This includes Rod Hart, who portrays civil religion as explicitly rhetorical in his 1977 book *The Political Pulpit*.[2] In one of the periodic reconsiderations that Bellah's notion has occasioned, Hart joins in viewing civil religion as the poor and ineffectual pretender to religion it has been seen as by most of its commentators.

There are other views. Following the Gulf War, David W. Ingle and I argued for a bolder concept of civil religion.[3] We argued that nationalism, patriotism, or civil religion—all descriptors of the same thing—is religion through and through. In fact, civil religion may be the most authentic religion in the modern West. In the wake of events of 9/11, it may be time to look at these arguments again.

Whatever the status of civil religion, religion as a category of human endeavor is never gestureless rhetoric cast adrift from human actions. It is a system of lived engagement grounded in the most profoundly meaningful of acts— offering up the real lives of true believers to secure the moral and physical survival of the group. Religion is what Jesus did on the cross, what holy warriors undertake for Islam. Religion is the bodhisattva renouncing his own salvation for that of others.

I believe scholarly ambivalence about the status of civil religion turns less on the adequacy of notions of civil religion than on Americans' historically conditioned experience of religion, the model that underlies our understanding of civil religion. At this historical moment, American denominational faiths occupy a morally diminished historical status. Designed to separate national from sectarian religious authority, disestablishment as constitutional doctrine weakened U.S.

denominational faiths at their core by depriving them of authority to command the sacrifice of their followers' lives. Though it may seem disrespectful to say so, I contend that contemporary American notions of religion are hard pressed, in consequence, to project a compelling vision of sectarian faith as the source and guarantor of group life.

It is no surprise that scholarship in the Bellah mold fashions U.S. civil religion as a pale echo of already pale denominational faiths. By describing denominational religion as pale, I mean it acquiesces in its state-mandated role of offering little more than a carefully contained system of polite ethics. I will argue that a rhetorically focused conception of civil religion follows quite comfortably from denominational religion's self-conscious retreat from life and death authority over believers. As part of this aloofness, denominational faith cultivates an aversion to violence that is at odds with religion historically considered. This is central to the practice of modern denominational faiths in the United States and flows from the historical deference of denominational to civil faith as a system of blood sacrifice.

If denominational religion is pale, U.S. civil religion is bright in American life. It is expressed through an elaborate system of sacrificial and regenerative beliefs, gestures, artifacts and words that bind citizens into a community of moral obligation. Though aspects of this obligation are articulated in law, its spiritual compellingness depends on the affective submission of citizens, their willingness at any moment to be so bound.

Religion certainly has a rhetorical face. But if rhetoric were the essence of religion, it would be hard to distinguish from advertising. Genuine religious expression is always connected to real stakes of death and sacrifice. These invest religious rhetoric with truth and moral authority. Gestures of life and death are primary in religion; rhetoric is secondary.

Two conditions are especially important for generating and sustaining the religious impulse. One is that the survival of enduring groups depends on the willing and, if necessary, coerced expenditure of members' blood and treasure (though acknowledgements of coerced sacrifice always signal a crisis of faith). The second is that death, the most serious threat to group existence, is mostly beyond our control. Religion is the search for the true source of killing power. Surrendering to it, we hope, will secure its blessing or its mercy, or harness it against other, illegitimate killing powers.

In the industrialized West nations take the decision to wage peace or war. On the grand scale life seems secure or chaotic largely in concert with the fortunes of the nation to which we belong. For contemporary Western sensibilities, legitimate, demonstrable authority to kill is claimed primarily on behalf of the nation. The U.S. looks with horror on those who attack it while claiming God for authority. Though our own killing often makes an ally of God, it is ultimately justified by appeals to national authority. This is so despite the strong connection of American culture to sectarian traditions from which it has historically wrested the power to enforce ultimate truth on the bodies of believers. Relations between civil religion and its sectarian adversaries or allies do fluctuate. Civil religion may amplify, compete, or cooperate with sectarian religion. It may do all these things at once. If truth in any culture is very simply what is worth dying for, the crucial point is that civil religion is the dominant partner in any contest between national and sectarian power. At least, this is the case wherever the group as a whole grants the nation the final power to decide which citizens will be sacrificed and when. To sustain itself as the embodiment of unassailable truth, the nation calls for citizen sacrifice. The discourses that support this claim may fairly be called religious rhetoric, but their moral authenticity rests on a foundation of past blood offerings. These are enlisted to create a willingness to offer more blood in the future.

Where citizen bodies are not fully committed, rhetoric may well be in play but not religion, since the most moving rhetoric cannot hold a society together on its own. Societies are held together by believers who so agree on what is fundamental (namely, who has the right to sacrifice group members) that they will offer their own lives and their children's to defend it. To this end the nation cultivates a sacrificial class tasked to lay down its lives whenever group killing authority is in peril. This special class is the military, organized along lines familiar to any monastic community. It patrols the physical and psychic borders of the group and defends them with blood. (The home front brigade of this class consists of policemen and firemen. During the 9/11 crisis, which lacked significant sacrifices of U.S. lives abroad, firemen and policemen played the most visible and mythically compelling sacrificial roles.)

The abiding focus of civil religion, like that of religion generally, is death. So understood, civil religion is no set of optional beliefs for its citizens. In moments of crisis, disloyalty to the national god is intolerable. The need for devotion to the national purpose and its instruments is so compelling and immediate that action may righteously be taken against those who fail to demonstrate sufficient piety. More important is that the authority of the national god to dispense life and death to believers is at stake. Threat therefore provides the crisis and justification for the nation to sacrifice its own. Sacrificing citizen lives on behalf of the national god re-claims for the nation the sole prerogative to control the life and death of its own members from false gods who challenge it. By this means the national god reigns supreme.

Because their models of sectarian faith have been de-fanged and domesticated, scholars of American civil religion have underestimated its hold on believers. When denominational religion went head to head with nationalism beginning roughly in the seventeenth century in Europe, denominational religion lost much of its power to command or inspire sacrifice. Disestablishment was the settlement of that struggle in effect if not always in name. In consequence of this historical process, denominational religion in the U.S. was constrained to avoid armed challenge to the killing authority of national religion. Though it fights a rearguard action for moral superiority by arguing that violence is never justified, it is expected to rally round, and usually does, when the national god asks for sacrifice.

If less orthodox denominational offshoots occasionally venture forth from their subordinate place to try and seize killing authority for themselves, as David Koresh did in the 1993 Branch Davidian uprising, the national god stands ready to demonstrate whose killing authority is supreme. Though denominational religion retains elaborate rituals for commemorating the sacrifices that anchor its past, and though on occasion it enters the political arena to cheer on or criticize civil religious practice, its claims on believers are subjunctive and metaphorical. Few in the U.S. truly expect believers to give up their lives for the Methodists or the First Church of Christ.

Rendered weak, denominational religion allows national religion to exercise unrivaled command of group hearts, minds, and bodies. Indeed, it has little choice. Denominational religion is not so much protected by the state as carefully monitored to make sure it stays within the boundaries assigned to it. So constrained, denominational religion may offer profound meaning to its own faithful. But it is so inessential for the life of society as a whole that it is a matter of official indifference whether or not people believe in it. Belief systems of such casual consequence are not fully realized religions in the sense argued here, but simply among the available options for U.S. citizens within the bubbling stew of pluralism.

Denominational religion offers meaning, comfort and solace. These are not small gifts. Nevertheless, contemporary U.S. sectarian faiths demand little from their followers beyond piety and occasional volunteer efforts. Where religion demands more, as democratic civil religion does, spiritual doubt is a constant danger. Belief that demands the bodies of believers is serious business. It must be vigilant against skepticism concerning the ends for which death is demanded. Such skepticism is salutary and risky. It is salutary in providing a popular check on the sacrificial demands claimed by leaders for the national god. Only causes for which believers will actually sacrifice their children can be thoroughly prosecuted. This inhibits, if it never quite banishes, a level of adventurism that heedlessly spends blood and treasure. But such skepticism is also risky. Where groups are unwilling to undertake critical sacrifices, their prospects for survival diminish.

The uneasy conviction that there are few causes for which U.S. citizens are willing to shed their own blood demonstrates a classic dilemma of empire. Historically, empires have failed to inspire the intense loyalty of national faiths whose believers share a common language, land, and blood. Client or slave states typically provide the blood that secures the borders of empire. Hesitation to offer the faithful in defense of empire hints at a limit to spiritual commitment that will sooner or later be tested by those who serve other gods. Nor can advanced technologies of communication and travel provide a cohesion that will match the unifying intensity of blood ties. Indeed, technologies of distance are likely to increase rather than reduce the scale of blood sacrifice in the long run. If Clausewitzian total war has been necessary to generate a sacrificial scale adequate to tribally bind the citizens of industrial nation-states, what will global communities need to unify in their own defense? Empire builders facing the dissolution of communities made fragile by technological links operating in the absence of bodily intimacy may be tempted to call forth unity through sacrifice amplified on a terrifying scale.

Whatever the future of American empire, American civil religion has been resilient within its national borders. Like other religions, it has seen periods of more and less active belief and commitment. Since World War II unified a generation, devotion to U.S. civil religion has been manifest in short-lived bursts of solidarity engendered by presidential elections, the moon landing, the Gulf war and 9/11. It has also been marked by periods of malaise and divisiveness. The most visible class of apostates in contemporary American civil religion is found among intellectuals. This is partly because current intellectual modes of analyzing culture are not well equipped to recognize or credit genuine religion. The unfashionable master narrative, for example, constitutes the heart of religious thinking.

Still, the discomfort of contemporary scholars with the idea that civil religion exists, or ought to, suggests more than the vagaries of intellectual fashion in two important ways. The first is that intellectual authority proceeds from a textual rather than bodily base. From this perspective modernity may be seen as a struggle between textual classes that preserve the bodies of their own members from being used up for group survival by means of their skills in producing and manipulating texts, and body classes whose cultural value is the muscle-work they perform, particularly in war. Textual authority conceals, even from the textual classes, their dependence on and domination of the body classes who are required to expend their blood in the service of the group.[4]

There is a more profound reason that scholars have failed to recognize or respect the religious intensity of U.S. nationalism: namely, the official testimony of patriotism that it is not religious at all. This is the claim of the U.S. Supreme Court, the highest arbiter of the Constitution as the most sacred and foundational American holy charter. In *West Virginia State Board of Education v. Barnette*, (1943) the Court refused to make flag worship compulsory for schoolchildren by granting a constitutional right not to say the Pledge of Allegiance. The first time it faced the question of the pledge in *Minersville School District v. Board of Education* (1940), the Court ruled that schoolchildren could be compelled to say the pledge. It recanted in *Barnette*, recognizing that compulsory flag worship explicitly equated civil religion with denominational faith. In twice deciding by the narrowest possible majority (*Texas v. Johnson*, 1989; *Eichmann v. United States*, 1990) that citizens could legally burn the American flag, the Court barely refused to establish a category of desecration that would render officially holy the central artifact of U.S. civil religion.

Perhaps this refusal to confer official sanctity on U.S. civil religion is the best evidence of its secular nature and a decisive challenge to the account of civil religion I propose. Durkheim famously defined the sacred as what is kept apart from the profane. He regarded this distinction as the bedrock of all social organization. By refusing to call itself sacred, civil religion cannily distances itself from what is conventionally considered religious in U.S. life, though this conventional faith makes no compelling claim on the lives of believers. By officially repudiating its own religious status, civil religion protects the sanctity of the national god by refusing to speak its real name. Thus it separates itself from proximate religious competitors. This is the deep structure of disestablishment. The national god tolerates denominational gods if they agree not to demand believers' lives to guarantee their own claims to truth. So long as custom confers the title "religion" on sectarian faith, civil religion has reason to distance itself. To do otherwise would cede moral equivalence to competitor gods. Meanwhile, the sanctity of civil religion is gesturally manifest in ceremonial acts from naturalization to war. Language, too, offers clues to the real situation. "God may show you mercy," said Sen. John McCain, of Osama bin Laden's heretically monstrous challenge to the killing authority of the United States, "We will not" ("Terrorist Attacks"). In a moment of crisis, a sacrificial war hero asserts the respective killing authority accorded to national and sectarian religion.

The frequent appearance of sectarian language in the ritual vocabulary of national appeals for God's favor and mercy also casts doubt on a religious account of patriotism. If national religion is paramount, why does it use the vocabulary of sectarian religion at all? One answer is that U.S. civil religion inherits the rituals and symbols of Christianity historically shared by the majority of its founders. Denominational language invests civil religion with familiar religious forms. Civil religion thus deploys a recognizable religious register while shielding itself from challenge and unbelief. It is also true that conqueror religions often incorporate the indigenous faiths they dominate. As Catholic Spain absorbed the gods the shrines and ceremonies of Aztecs and Incas in South America, American nationalism incorporates and pacifies Christianity.

The religious status of patriotic ritual and belief has been challenged on the grounds that it lacks cults of divine beings, organized churches and priesthoods or their equivalent, and doctrinal explanations and consolations for death. In fact, these elements figure prominently in U.S. civil religion. I have already discussed the doctrine of sacrifice. The state and its officers constitute the church and priesthood of the nation. In the broad sweep of religions, the expression of divine principle takes different shapes. Some religions model it as a single personality with human attributes; others (Roman Catholicism and the mystery religions of Greece, for example) boast multiple divinities. Other traditions treat the divine principle as a force immanent in nature or the universe. The divine principle of American nationalism is manifest in the nation and the flag. Mystically speaking, all citizens partake of the flag, the holy corporate body, the most sacred artifact of U.S. civil religion. As a non-material numinous entity, the flag encompasses all believers, living and dead. Material flags also stand in for sacrificed citizens who are joined to it in the role of supernatural, bloodthirsty guardians. In a group crisis these transformed but watching dead call for the sacrifice of living generations. The sacrificial class is ritually called to offer its blood to avenge and nourish previously sacrificed, now divinely embodied, generations. The occasion that demands this response is the sacrificial crisis described by Rene Girard.[5] If false or competitor gods are permitted to challenge with impunity the nation that presides over life and death, the nation as divine principle may not be all-powerful or worthy of obedience. The sacrificial blood of believers removes this threat and restores its power.

Debates about the existence and value of civil religion are especially compelling to those who engage them from the perspective of professing one or another sectarian allegiance. Civil religion may then be cast as earnest but second-rate—not, after all, impressive compared to earlier religious traditions. Seen in this light, American civil religion may appear theologically shallow and ignobly chauvinistic compared to denominational faiths. The usual conclusion is that in its weak state American civil religion aids communal solidarity, but claims to a more central identity or moral focus would be unfortunate. This analysis simply fails to acknowledge the religious dominance of U.S. nationalism, which justifies and explains the death of sacrificial believers in a way that sectarian faith has not been permitted for two centuries. Americans rightly cherish their country's avoidance of the corrosive sectarian strife that convulsed Europe from the sixteenth to eighteenth centuries. The so-called wall of separation between state and religious authority in the U.S.—a phrase that both stands for and conceals the subordination of sectarian to national religion—secured internal peace through the triumph of national religion. Church and state separation is an article of faith in the democratic catechism and a source of national pride.

Rod Hart argues that the social contract between secular and religious authority is two-pronged. Sectarian religion provides a rhetoric of moral legitimacy, and the state provides enforcement. David Ingle and I argue that both the rhetoric of civil religion and its actions in the strong sense described here can be at least as usefully understood within a framework of religious nationalism. Denominational religion must bow to this authority in order to exist in the contemporary United States. Resistance by sectarian faiths within the national community is thus regarded with alarm. Witness the fate of David Koresh, who competed for killing authority with the nation. This is what denominational religion may not do. The fundamental elements of nationalism—rhetoric and action—may point less to the covenant between separate social domains that Hart argues for than to an integrated national system that makes patriotic sacrifice its religious focus.

That said, Rod Hart surely has a good part of the analysis of civil religion right. He convincingly argues that inferences from presidential rhetoric alone, from which Bellah and his colleagues made the case for civil religion, are evidentially inadequate. He calls for expanding the range of evidence within which civil religious talk and observance could be located. But he perhaps overlooks the limitless range of patriotic talk, rituals, and practices in which Americans daily ground and rehearse the claims of civil religion. To complicate Bellah's account of civil religion, Hart focuses on the indifference and hostility that are part of the social response to it and to all religion. And by limiting his observations largely to the comments of ecclesiastics competing with civil religion for the loyalty of believers, he leaves others to explore the implications of his insight that civil religion is society-encompassing, not simply a debate among presidents and clergymen. He discerns the elements of the settlement between civil and ecclesiastic authorities, the one supplying the muscle of nationalism, the other offering go-along rhetoric—though I believe the rich rhetoric of patriotism is far more central. It is found in ceremonies and talk about the Fourth of July, in presidential elections, in rituals of war and every other national ceremony. It flourishes in mediated representations of American life including news, films, politics, advertising, and every form of popular culture. In this elaborated account of civil religion, 'enforcement' emerges not as a crude despiritualized violence, but as the sacralized focus of a grandly articulated system of religious meaning in which denominational religion takes second place. Civil religion and denominational religion are not, in this view, equal partners uneasily at peace with one another. Denominational religion tells us about civil religion only indirectly.

To exemplify the way in which nationalism triumphs over sectarian claims, I choose Hart's discussion of the Rev. Billy Graham's views about Dwight Eisenhower. As commander of World War II Allied troops in Europe and twice president, Eisenhower stands as one of the revered holy fathers of 20th-century U.S. civil religion. In a recurring homily of the faith, citizens are reminded of his observation that government should be founded in religion, and he didn't care what religion it was.[6] As Hart has it, Graham, a lifelong ambassador from denominational to national religion, made much of the fact that only after Eisenhower became president did he join a church and receive baptism. But Graham misunderstood Eisenhower's gestures. In these acts the nation's highest religious officer cultivated diplomatic relations with persisting native faiths. The foundation of Eisenhower's civil devotion had been laid during his initiation as a West Point acolyte. He described this experience with the fervor of the spiritually transformed:

> My first day at West Point—June 14, 1911—had been rough. My classmates and I had been barked at and ordered by upperclassmen to do all sorts of ridiculous chores, on the double. All 285 of us were weary and resentful.
>
> Towards evening, however, we assembled outdoors and, with the American flag floating majestically above us, were sworn in as cadets of the United States Military Academy. It was an impressive ceremony. As I looked up at our national colors and swore my allegiance, I realized humbly that *now I belonged to the flag*. It is a moment I have never forgotten.[7]

Religion is not rhetoric. A religion constituted by rhetoric alone, as Hart argues in *The Political Pulpit*, doesn't do anything.[8] But U.S. civil religion does do things. It kills. It commands sacrifice. It transforms infants, non-believers, and converts from other national faiths into Americans. It even mobilizes churches, synagogues, and mosques. It offers patriotic instruction in efficacious spells and rituals that believers will put to work when crisis comes. This is why Eisenhower could say that government should be founded in religion and never mind which one. He believed that in the moment of group truth, all citizens would gather under the single tent of American sacrificial authority. The moral and physical continuation of the nation would depend on it.

Chapter 9

Rhetoric, Religion and Government
at the Turn of the Twenty-first Century

Robert V. Friedenberg

This essay is occasioned by the twenty-fifth anniversary of the publication of Rod Hart's *The Political Pulpit.* I wish to address three topics. First, does the contract between organized religion and the United States government, which Hart first posited in 1977, still make sense today?[1] Second, Hart claimed that the "primary contribution" that his study made was "an examination of the generically distinctive qualities of religio-political speechmaking."[2] Hence, I wish to revisit two of the qualities of religio-political speechmaking that Hart identified in 1977, with an eye toward determining whether they still seem valid. Finally, I wish to briefly speculate on the role of rhetoric in future relationships between religion and government in the United States.

Hart's Contract and America at the Turn of the 21st Century

Hart offers the metaphor of a contract to help explain the relationship between government and religion. That contract between the first party, government, and the second party, religion, features four key agreements between mainstream religion and the government. First, that "the guise of complete separation between the first party and the second party will be maintained by both parties."[3] As the twenty-first century opens, this element of the contract continues to make good sense.

At the founding of the nation and throughout its early years, organized religion essentially meant Christianity. Excluding the many Christian faiths that were present in colonial America, virtually the only other organized faith present in the colonies was Judaism. In 1654, twenty-three Dutch Jews fled Brazil when it fell to a Portuguese army, settling in the Dutch colony of New Amsterdam that became New York. But those twenty-three pioneers were not joined by large numbers of their coreligionists. It was not until 1730 that the first synagogue building was established in New York. On the eve of the American Revolution, the total Jewish population of the colonies numbered only about 2,500.[4]

Thus, the young nation was populated by individuals of many Christian denominations. As the country evolved, Hart argues, "the government of the United States and America's organized religious bodies entered into a very practical compact rooted in an understanding of the role public rhetoric plays in the minds of its citizens and the stabilizing effect public messages can have on their lives."[5] Hence, to use Hart's language, "the guise of complete separation between the first party and the second party" were maintained. There is no official state religion in the United States. The government does not show obvious preference or hostility to any single faith. Nevertheless, the separation is a guise insofar as organized religion supports the government, particularly at moments of crisis.

This "guise" seems to be in effect in 2002 as well as it was when Hart wrote in 1977. The mainstream faiths have, for example, been almost uniformly supportive of our recent war on terrorism. Moreover, government leaders have consistently acknowledged the importance of religion and religious principles as they have attempted to rally the nation. President George W. Bush's first major address, delivered three days after the terrorist attack, was the centerpiece of an elaborate interdenominational religious service at Washington's National Cathedral. It was the focal point of a national day of prayer and remembrance. Bush spoke of "God's signs," "prayers that yield our will to a will greater than our own," and "this world He created." Bush spoke of the unity that the country was experiencing in the aftermath of the terrorist attacks and observed, "this is a unity of every faith." He concluded, as he has concluded many of his major addresses in the weeks after the terrorist attacks, by asking that "God Bless America."[6]

Moreover, as leaders such as the President expressed their reverence and faith in God to help us through this crisis, religious leaders of all denominations expressed their support of the nation, and like Bush, called for God's blessings in the current crisis. The service in which Bush took part involved Christian, Jewish, and Islamic religious leaders. It was one of countless services held throughout the country as religious leaders of all denominations led their flocks in observing the national day of prayer and remembrance. A Pew Research Center poll found that "the September 11 terrorist attacks unleashed an unprecedented awareness of the role of religion in public life." That poll went on to find that after an initial surge in attendance at religious services, within a few weeks attendance at services had returned to near-normal.[7]

In September 2001, at a moment of crisis, the government sought the widespread support of America's mainstream religions for what would likely be a long and protracted war. It would appear that Hart's contract, which provides for the guise of complete separation between the government and organized religion, continues to hold. On the surface there is complete separation between religion and government. But, particularly at moments of crisis, the government seeks and typically obtains, the rhetorical support of America's religious communities.

Moreover, at such moments, government leaders typically acknowledge the supremacy of God and the importance of religion in the conduct of the lives of individuals and nations.

The second key agreement in the contractual metaphor between religion and government that Hart first posited in 1977 is that "the guise of existential equality between the first party (government) and the second party (religion) will be maintained by both parties, but the second party's realm shall be solely that of the rhetorical."[8] When Hart first wrote in 1977, a born-again Christian, Jimmy Carter, was just starting his presidency. Carter was followed by Ronald Reagan, George H. W. Bush, William Jefferson Clinton, and George W. Bush. All of these presidents professed, and often gave evidence of, sincere and deep religious conviction. Yet, organized religion seems to have had relatively little impact on the policies of our national government during these years.

Perhaps one of the reasons that religion's realm is largely rhetorical in a nation such as the United States becomes evident in a re-examination of Robert Bellah's classic article, "Civil Religion in America." Bellah's case that there is a civil religion in America is based upon his examination of presidential inaugural addresses. The inaugural address that receives the most attention from Bellah is that of John F. Kennedy. For Bellah, Kennedy's inaugural address exemplifies this genre of presidential speaking. Kennedy's whole address, claims Bellah, "can be understood as only the most recent statement of a theme that lies very deep in the American tradition, namely the obligation, both collective and individual, to carry out God's will on earth. This was the motivating spirit of those who founded America, and it has been present in every generation since."[9]

If Bellah is correct in observing that those who founded America felt an obligation to carry out God's will on earth and that obligation has been present in every generation since, and I suspect that in the main he is, we need only to look to the founding generation to see why religion's realm is rhetoric. The American Revolution was fought by a religiously diverse group of colonies populated by an even more diverse group of citizens. At the time of the revolution the Puritan tradition remained strong in Massachusetts, but Anglican, and Baptist churches were also common. Baptists were strong in colonies such as Rhode Island, New Jersey, Pennsylvania, and Delaware. Yet, they existed side by side, especially in Pennsylvania, with Quakers, Mennonites, Moravians, Lutherans and Presbyterians, and in Rhode Island with approximately one-half of the Jewish population in the colonies.[10] The Presbyterians were also especially numerous in the western parts of Maryland, Virginia, North Carolina, and South Carolina. Though many Presbyterians lived in Maryland, the colony was founded in part as a haven for Catholics.[11] While other examples could be given, clearly the thirteen colonies that declared their independence in 1776 were a religiously diverse group. Even in the United States of 1776 it would have been difficult to know what "God's will on earth" was, much less to carry it out. In the years since, America has grown even more religiously diverse.

Hence, the guise of equality between church and state exists in part because for true equality America's religious establishment would have to speak with one voice. The multivoiced American religious establishment can rarely agree within itself, not only on what is God's will, but also on how God's will should be expressed in specific public policy. That situation existed in 1776 and has no doubt been exasperated in the years since with America's growing religious diversity. It is difficult to think of any major federal government policy in the last twenty-five years, since Hart wrote, that was brought about by the efforts of organized religion. Public policy is essentially the province of government. Though some religious organizations have strongly supported candidates, including several of our recent presidents, it is hard to see any tangible effect that organized religion has had on federal policy. Public policy, relative to two of the more controversial issues upon which many organized religious groups have taken positions—for example—prayer in the schools and abortion, remains largely unchanged since 1977. Hence, the second agreement that Hart advanced in 1977, that the guise of equality between government and religion be maintained but that the religious "realm shall be solely that of the rhetorical," seems to still hold up, twenty-five years later at the turn of the millennium. Moreover, the growing religious diversity of our population suggests that this agreement is likely to continue to characterize America well into the foreseeable future.

The third agreement between government and religion that Hart postulated in his contract metaphor was that the "first party [government] rhetoric will refrain from being overly religious and second party [religion] rhetoric will refrain from being overly political."[12] Once again, Hart's observations concerning the rhetorical relationship between government and religion appear, from the perspective of twenty-five years, to remain accurate. The religious rhetoric of government leaders is certainly not "overly religious." That rhetoric is not involved in the articulation of substantive positions. Rather, it is almost a decorative rhetoric. Like a decoration, everyone, even those who are not "true believers," can appreciate it for its sentiment and beauty. Given the religious diversity of the nation, this seems to be virtually the only choice that elected leaders have.

For a governmental leader to utilize "overly religious" rhetoric would likely mean that leader would have to use faith-specific rhetoric. But to do so would likely cause an immediate negative reaction from many citizens who were not of that faith. Hence, government leaders use religious rhetoric that is widely acceptable and inoffensive. When, for example, the term "crusade" was used in naming one of the military operations in the war on terror, a small furor erupted. The term was perceived by some to be offensive to Moslems and quickly dropped from usage.

One of the few, if not the only, American president to consciously think of himself as a religious leader, who referred to himself as a "preacher," was Theodore Roosevelt.[13] It is instructive to see what Theodore Roosevelt "preached" when he so famously used the White House as a "bully pulpit." Roosevelt's preaching well illustrates a government leader who does not use "overly religious" rhetoric. Elsewhere, I have characterized much of Theodore Roosevelt's speaking as "the rhetoric of militant decency."[14] That rhetoric centered around five *topoi* or themes that consistently appeared in his speeches. These *topoi* constitute the basis of Roosevelt's beliefs. None are overly religious. None is unique in any way to his Dutch Reform religion. All have been, to some degree, treated by all of our presidents since Hart first wrote in 1977. Roosevelt's rhetoric of militant decency revolved around the appropriate use of power, his concern for social order, the importance of work, the need for individuals and nations to exert social responsibility, and the importance of character for both individuals and nations.[15] All can be related to the religious teachings of virtually all faiths. None are overly religious. However, most importantly for our present purposes, though these are the central *topoi* of the president who served at the turn of the twentieth century, roughly seventy-five years before Hart wrote, they are constantly reflected in the public speeches of political leaders who are serving at the turn of the twenty-first century, a quarter of a century after Hart wrote.[16] Hart's observation that government rhetoric is not "overly religious" seems as true today as it was when he first wrote.

The second part of this agreement was that religious rhetoric "will refrain from being overly political." Once more, Hart's observations circa 1977 seem to remain accurate twenty-five years later. For religious rhetoric to be "overly political," presumably it would have to deal with specific candidates and policies. Though some religious organizations have supported specific public policies or candidates, such rhetoric is not the thrust of contemporary pulpit speaking on politics. Rather, that speaking is not overly political. One measure of the fact that religious rhetoric is not overly political can be seen in the prayer books of America's Jewish community. Like many faiths, the prayer books of American Judaism include a "prayer for our nation." This prayer is used in every Saturday morning service. It reads as follows:

> Our God and God of our ancestors: We ask Your blessings for our country, for its government, for its leader and advisors, and for all who exercise just and rightful authority. Teach them insights of Your Torah, that they may administer all affairs of state fairly, that peace and security, happiness and prosperity, justice and freedom may forever abide in our midst.
>
> Creator of all flesh, bless all the inhabitants of our country with Your spirit. May citizens of all races and creeds forge a common bond in true harmony to banish all hatred and bigotry and to safeguard the ideals and free institutions which are the pride and glory of our country.
>
> May this land under Your Providence be an influence for good throughout the world, uniting all people in peace and freedom and helping them to fulfill the vision of Your prophet:

"Nation shall not lift up sword against nation, neither
shall they experience war any more." And let us say: Amen.[17]

Clearly the preceding prayer is not overtly political. Rather it is worded in
generalities with which the vast majority of most Americans would agree. While
it is but one prayer, from one service, of one branch, of one faith, such prayers,
couched in broad generalities, are not unusual. As the twenty-first century opens,
religious rhetoric in this nation is not overtly political. Just as the rhetoric of political leaders would likely have to be faith-specific to be thought of as overtly
religious, so too, the rhetoric of religious leaders would likely have to be policy
and candidate specific to be thought of as overtly political. Though religious
leaders speak on behalf of policies and candidates, that speaking does not dominate their rhetoric. Moreover, the diversity of religious beliefs within the United
States makes it difficult, when religious leaders do choose to speak on a given
policy or candidate, to find them speaking with a strongly unified voice. However, when the nation faces a serious crisis, such as most wars, the nation's religious leaders do speak with one voice, and that voice is in support of government
policies. In sum, Hart's third agreement, that the rhetoric of the government not
be overly religious and that the rhetoric of religion not be overly political, seems
to have stood the test of time since he first wrote.

The final agreement that Hart posits in his contract is that neither the government nor mainstream religion, "in any fashion whatsoever, make known to
the general populace the exact terms of the contract contained herein."[18] This
agreement also seems to have stood the test of time since Hart first wrote. It has
done so largely because it is in the best interests of both parties that the nature of
the relationship between government and religion not be clear. Government continues to maintain coercive power over individual citizens including the power to
wage war and conscript citizens to die in those wars, the power to confiscate
property in the form of taxes, and the power to punish those who fail to abide by
government rules. Religion's role remains largely rhetorical. Though organized
religious groups can and on some occasions do address political issues, and
though clearly the government seeks and values such support, the government
has little to fear from religion. In a democracy it does not make sense for the
government to remind voters that one of the pillars of government support, organized religion, is powerless, and indeed is dependent on the government for
such things as tax breaks and other forms of financial support. Nor does it make
sense for organized religion to remind its adherents, in a nation where already
much of the population has opted out of organized religion, of its relative weak-
ness.

In sum, the contractual metaphor that animates Hart's *The Political Pulpit*
continues to make good sense today. That metaphor is built around four understandings or agreements between civil authorities and religious leaders. As we
have seen, those understandings are largely operative today, twenty-five years
after Hart first wrote.

Distinctive Qualities of Religio-Political Speechmaking

After presenting his contract metaphor as a means of helping us to understand the nature of American civil religion, Hart turns his attention to what he perceives to be the "generically distinctive qualities of religio-political speechmaking." Hart claimed that such rhetoric has four distinctive qualities. Space permits a consideration of only two of these qualities.

Hart called the first distinctive quality of religio-political speechmaking, "expedient complexity."[19] After searching for references to America's God(s) in the speeches of Richard Nixon, Hart concluded that "Nixon mentioned God selectively throughout his career, his choices apparently being dictated exclusively by the demands of the rhetorical situations he faced." Hart subsequently claims that Nixon's "rhetorical behavior was rather typical of his political predecessors and, conceivably, of his successors as well."[20] The expediency that Hart describes in Nixon's invoking of God across the last 36 years of his public career seems to be, as Hart anticipated, characteristic of at least one of his successors as well.

I have recently begun to examine a sample of George W. Bush's speaking in the two months following the terrorist attack of September 11, 2001. My examination suggests that like Nixon, Bush's choices are heavily dictated by the rhetorical situations he faced, or expediency. My examination was nowhere near as comprehensive as Hart's examination of Nixon. Nevertheless a similar pattern emerges.

I examined a total of 16 speeches delivered between September 11, 2001 and November 10, 2001. All of these speeches dealt in some fashion with the terrorist attack and our response to that attack. Bush made no reference to God in five of these speeches. He made references to God in six ceremonial speeches. He made references to God in five non-ceremonial addresses. More revealing is Bush's invoking of God. In these speeches he made references to God a total of 25 times. Two such references were in the speech introductions. Seven were in the body of the speech. Three of these seven were to Allah and were conscious attempts to adapt to his audience.[21] Sixteen of these references were in the conclusion. God was invoked by Bush most commonly in closing his speeches with the phrase "God Bless America." While my sample includes a far higher percentage of ceremonial addresses than did Hart's, the key point is that Bush called on God primarily in a ceremonial sense at the end of his speeches. Though few would question that Bush's religious beliefs seem more strongly held than those of Nixon, his rhetorical use of God seems to reflect much of the expediency that Hart found in Nixon.

The "complexity" component of Hart's "expedient complexity" characteristic of America's civil religion is based on Hart's claim that in his study of presidential inaugural addresses God is manifest in no less than five different ways. Hart finds that presidents have spoken of "God the Inscrutable Potentate, God the Witnessing Author, God the Wise and the Just, God the Philanthropist, and God the Object of Affection."[22] One could certainly read several of these meanings into the way Bush invokes God. Though Hart finds America's God is exceedingly complex, most importantly, Hart finds that "at least as presented rhetorically, America's God is an expedient God, one who watches over us as we set about our various national tasks."[23] It is primarily in this sense that Bush seems to repeatedly invoke God's blessing on the United States as he rhetorically led the nation in its first few months of war on terrorism.

The second principal quality of religio-political speaking that Hart found in his 1977 study was "non-existential content." Essentially, Hart argues that civil religious rhetoric does not deal in an active behavior oriented manner with the issues of the moment. Such rhetoric is the rhetoric of the political activist. Hart notes that Martin Luther King was a "curious case" and he was essentially a rhetorical figure whose rhetoric was the focal point of his civil right demonstrations.[24] When I first read Hart's work, years ago, I had more trouble with this claim than with most others. I still do. In the years since Hart wrote, America's churches, synagogues, and other houses of worship have certainly produced their share of social critics and government lobbyists. Hart may well still be right in claiming that these are primarily rhetorical activities, but such activities are also frequently accompanied by more tangible activist behavior. The religious institutions of virtually every community, for example, engage in active behavior to help feed, clothe and house the poor. Moreover, if President Bush has his way, it seems likely that organized religion may become even more activist. Though this is not the place to detail or argue the merits of Bush's faith-based proposals, it would seem that if they are ultimately adopted they will make organized religion more activist, at least in fighting poverty. The most controversial aspect of the president's proposals would allow religious groups to compete on an equal basis with secular agencies for federal government anti-poverty funds.[25]

Perhaps my difficulty with Hart's claim that the content of civil religious rhetoric is non-existential is one of degree. I suspect that I am reacting in part to the "non" part of "non-existential." My own view is that while Hart was largely correct in suggesting that religious proponents avoid embracing activist, policy-oriented themes, much less behavior, this avoidance is at least to some degree a function of topic. The less controversial the topic, the more likely that an activist behavioral concern for the tangible exigencies of the moment will be characteristic of such discourse. For example there are few who would deny the merit of helping the poor. Hence, most faiths engage in a wide variety of tangible activities on behalf of the poor. In contrast, recent advances in medical science have helped to generate considerable controversy over the merit of gene research and cloning. Few, if any, faiths engage in a wide variety of tangible activities on behalf of these medical practices.

Nevertheless, though I have some difficulty with one of the four characteristics of religio-political rhetoric that Hart advanced in 1977, on balance his characteristics continue to make perfectly good sense twenty-five years later.

Conclusions

As the preceding pages suggest, I admired Hart's work when it was first issued and find that his primary points are still largely valid. America will likely grow even more religiously diverse in the future than it is today, or was when the nation was founded. Yet, it is likely the nature of the relationships between religion and government will remain largely the same. Organized religion teaches private virtue. Regardless of the specific faith, virtually all organized religion subscribes to the Decalogue and the golden rule. Ultimately, democracies such as our own maintain order through the self-regulating behavior of citizens, not through authoritarian rule of force.

On November 26, 1789, nine months after the first presidential election, seven months after the creation of the Department of State, and two months after the creation of the Treasury and Justice Departments, Gershom Seixas, the outstanding Jewish preacher in the late colonial and early national period of our nation's history, preached a thanksgiving sermon to his Shearith Israel Congregation in New York City. In words that urged self-regulating behavior on the part of his congregants and that illustrate characteristics that Hart finds typical of the relationship between religion and government, Seixas claimed that among his congregant's duties:

> it is necessary that we, each of us in our respective situations behave in such a manner as to give strength and stability to the laws entered into by our representatives, to consider the burden imposed on those who are appointed to act in the executive department, to contribute as much as lays in our power, to support that government which is founded upon the strictest principles of equal liberty and justice.[26]

It is likely that messages such as this, consistent with Hart's analysis of the relationship between religion and government, will continue to be preached from American pulpits in the foreseeable future. Moreover, it is likely that the major points that Hart explicated in *The Political Pulpit* will largely hold true for the foreseeable future.

Chapter 10

President Clinton and
the White House Prayer Breakfast

Nneka Ifeoma Ofulue

In his 1992 nomination acceptance speech as the Democratic party's presidential candidate, William Jefferson Clinton revealed his vision of a *new covenant* between the American people and their government. And, in a manner that extends the religious allusion of "covenant" in his dialogue, President Clinton hosted clergy at yearly prayer breakfasts convened at the White House. No recent president has been less reticent about the role of religion in American civic life than has Clinton. Like many of his predecessors, Clinton used the annual National Day of Prayer Breakfast to perform the symbolic role of the President as king, prophet, and priest of the nation's civil religion. Unlike them, Clinton hosted prayer breakfasts to further bolster his ethos in this role.

Scholars of American political culture have long explored the relationship between the symbolic nature of the office of the Presidency and presidential discourse. Bellah for example, argued that the role of the President is cloaked in the tradition of American Civil Religion—a public piety that is part of the foundation of American Government.[1] Michael Novak argued that in addition to his administrative role, the President functions symbolically as the nation's king, prophet, and priest, the guardian of a national civil religion.[2] Other scholars have addressed the rhetorical nature of this *civic piety*[3] and of the role of discourse in crafting presidential persona and ethos.[4]

In the *Political Pulpit*, Hart explained that though they permitted no legal entanglement between Church and State, the nation's Founders left a legacy of symbolic connections between the religious and political dimensions of American culture, a union created and sustained through rhetoric. Hart also explained that, as symbolic king, prophet, and high priest, the President serves as guardian of the nation's civil religion, a role crafted and sustained through discourse. Clinton's prayer breakfasts seem to affirm this relationship between the tradition of civil religion and the American presidency. That is, the merging of symbols of secular government (the White House) and religious practice (prayer) seem to reflect a need for civic piety to once again be rearticulated in public exchange among government, the church and the people. Thus continued scholarship on the relationship between civic piety and presidential rhetoric might prove fruitful.

The insights Hart outlined twenty-five years ago on both the rhetorical and presidential nature of American civil religion serve as a point of departure for this analysis of one of Clinton's White House Prayer Breakfasts. Hart's conception of civic piety is useful because it illuminates the rhetorical strategies enabled by the religio-symbolical dimension of the American presidency. I argue that Clinton's annual gatherings with clergy provided an appropriate context for him to construct a presidential ethos grounded in the rhetoric of American civic piety. This ethos, however, was threatened in 1998, when Clinton was faced with impeachment as a result of his entanglement with Monica Lewinsky. In this essay, I trace Clinton's attempt to regain a moral voice befitting a king, priest, and prophet by speaking through the biblical persona of King David, the redeemed leader of ancient Judah. By doing so, Clinton redeemed for himself a persona as the leader of American civil religion after personal scandal with the young intern.

The Rhetorical Nature of American Civil Religion

Defined originally by Bellah as "a collection of beliefs, symbols, and rituals with respect to sacred things and institutionalized in a collectivity," American civil religion locates America within a metaphysical order.[5] Public holidays and ceremonies sustain American civil religion and, thereby the identity of the American people. In his exposition of the *rhetorical* dimensions of civic piety, Hart helps the reader understand the need for cooperation between government and religion and the means by which such cooperation is sustained. Primarily, the relationship between church and state legitimates government's power and purpose. Under the canopy of American civil religion, institutions and official leaders function as symbolic stewards of our God-given rights of life, liberty and the pursuit of happiness, and are thereby transformed into agents of a divine order.

Because of its power to awaken in people a reverence for the intangible, Hart argued that government has looked to religion as a resource through which to imbue political leadership and public policy with an otherworldly significance. As Hart wrote, "when religion shares the motivational cosmos with government, it becomes only a short emotional step from faith to patriotism and from God to country."[6] The cooperation of church and state which has stood since the nation's inception remains, by virtue of the ability of participant agents to navigate cultural changes.

The Presidency and Civil Religion

Perhaps what I find most useful in Hart's alternative interpretation of civic piety is the degree to which it foregrounds the religio-symbolic dimension of the Presidency. Having recast civil religion as essentially a symbolic "contract" between faith and national identity, Hart locates the Presidency at the center of civic religion. Within such a frame, the President is charged with sustaining this symbolic tie. Because the relationship between faith and the American people has grounded our national self-conception, it must regularly be affirmed through public engagement between the people and their official leaders. The President of the United States stands as the ultimate guardian of this civic tradition. Furthermore, the President must not simply mouth "God and country," but must appear to embody the piety she or he speaks of.

Given this need to demonstrate an ethos of piety, Hart's concept of civic piety invites critics to see how particular presidents grapple with this task. Other scholars, likewise, find the presidency of interest to American civil religion. For instance, Walter Fisher wrote that "the Presidency is an office and a role, an institution and a persona. . . . It is a focal point of national reason and rationality; and it is a barometer of public morality."[7] This moral dimension grounds the role of the Presidency in the tradition of American civil religion. As Hart aptly declared, ". . . when an American president is inaugurated, he is also ordained"; to earn and fulfill this calling, the President must reflect the virtues he or she would endeavor to preserve.[8] This person would, therefore, have to *be seen as* possessing a personal ethos justifying his or her ordination. Despite dramatic changes throughout the nation's history, the President, as a moral leader, is expected to embody and articulate national values. "No American president," Hart wrote, ". . . has the rhetorical option of refusing to pay sufficient and regular homage to such fundamental aspects of our civil religion or of not embellishing such themes."[9]

Given this, the person who occupies the role becomes equally important. Since the responsibility to guard American civil religion is invested in the office of the Presidency, its occupant becomes the symbolic intermediary between the people and the order of civil virtues. Though the duties of the office are outlined in the Constitution, the symbolic role of the President as "moral barometer" seems to emphasize the enactment of the *office* as well as an enactment of this religio-symbolic *ethos* that lies within. Hart's symbolic contract becomes a critical lens through which one can examine the ways individual presidents appropriate the rhetoric of civic piety to craft a presidential ethos.

Public addresses are the primary means by which Presidents sustain the rhetorical tradition of civic piety, particularly when they present themselves to the people as the symbolic leader of the nation's civil religion. Likewise, as a significant element of rhetorical discourse, persona is an important dimension of presidential rhetoric. Understood as "a role or roles that a rhetor takes on for strategic purposes . . . persona is revealed in the language of the discourse . . . [and] influences an audience by creating or contributing to a rhetor's ethos or credibility."[10] Thus, rhetors can inter-textually construct their ethos by speaking through the voices of significant personae, simultaneously investing themselves with the innate character of the persona they embody and gain additional credibility.[11] I argue that through the voice of a culturally significant discourse and persona— the rhetoric of civic piety and the biblical persona of King David—President

Clinton constructed an ethos and enacted the religio-symbolic role of the President as the nation's high priest.

Presidential addresses become interesting in light of the mutually shaping relationship between the rhetoric of civic piety and presidential ethos. As Fisher argued, "ethos is [the] salient feature [of the presidency], whether considered as an office or a *role* to be enacted by specific persons."[12] Thus, in this examination of Clinton's prayer breakfast remarks I am interested in the connections between ethos, persona and civic piety. I examine them as rhetorical strategies by which this president overcame particular rhetorical obstacles and constructed a presidential ethos befitting the nature of his office.

Recovering Presidential Ethos

As host of the clerical breakfast, Clinton's opening remarks at the prayer breakfasts typically followed an invocation by a member of the clergy, after which Clinton affirmed the importance of the gatherings to his enduring leadership. In contrast to most of his speeches, Clinton's remarks were rather impromptu and brief. Nevertheless, three characteristic features appear in each of the remarks: the President always expressed the vision that framed his administration's policy agenda, he encouraged unity and cooperation between political and religious opponents, and he invited public and spiritual support from religious leaders and their faith-based organizations for the administration and its policies. Collectively, these three features reflect Clinton's effort to invest himself in the symbolic role of the President as priest and prophet of America's civil religion.

The prayer breakfasts at the White House offered Bill Clinton a unique opportunity to both affirm and undertake the symbolic responsibilities laid upon the office of the Presidency. First, the ecumenical nature of the gatherings transformed the White House into the symbolic temple of the nation's civil religion. Within this frame, President Clinton stood as the priestly king, embarking on each new year of his administration with the benediction of America's clergy. Secondly, through remarks affirming the role of faith in public policy, Clinton invited his audience to support their President in his endeavor to lead the nation as symbolic priest. In large part an effort to overcome religious political opposition he faced, Clinton's gathering transformed his clerical audience into national elders of America's civil religion. Ultimately, by locating himself at the center of this religio-symbolic orchestration, Clinton presented himself as national intermediary by interpreting the social, economic, and moral state of the Union, and affirming a national identity and shared promise of the American Dream. Subsequent gatherings reinforced the priestly role the President would play in the breach between the people and their collective destiny.

By the summer of 1998, President Clinton was faced with impeachment as a result of his entanglement with Monica Lewinsky. But more personally damaging to him was the loss of credibility and respect the clergy held for the President. Because of the rhetorical failure of Clinton's apology to the nation on August 17, 1998, he needed to display contrition for his misconduct again. Through previous

White House Prayer Breakfasts, he invested himself in the religio-symbolic dimension of the American Presidency as guardian of the nation's civil virtues. Clinton portrayed himself to the clergy as one who embodied national ideals, and who, with their support, would endeavor to lead the country to a common destiny. His indiscretion challenged this image and with it the authority granted him as President to interpret a national vision and to initiate public policies. To recover from the damage to his credibility, President Clinton reshaped his priestly persona into one that revealed him as a sinner, as the David-like "king" who by committing adultery had broken his oath to uphold Judaic law.

The primary source of Clinton's credibility problems was the discrepancy between his unequivocal denial of and his subsequent admission to an inappropriate relationship with Lewinsky. The public did not believe Clinton's statements about the affair were truthful, nor did they perceive him as genuinely remorseful.[13] Thus, the gathering of the President and the clergy took on more significance this particular year.

Because the prayer breakfasts had become routine, the media focused on how the scandal would shape the annual gathering. The question was how would Clinton use this occasion to navigate this crisis. As some critics suggested, President Clinton employed the prayer breakfast to demonstrate public contrition by confessing that he had sinned, asking forgiveness, and by submitting himself to the authority and accountability of religious leaders. Jodie Morse wrote "the recruitment of so many spiritual counselors to bear witness to Clinton's soul searching led politicos and pastors alike to wonder whether the White House in its darkest hour had settled on a new strategy: playing the God card."[14] She quoted a previous Clinton spiritual advisor, Robert Schuller, as saying "it would serve Clinton's cause well if it were made public. . . . It is very difficult to buy the genuineness of the repentance if it comes after the person has been caught, but it's easy for me to buy the sincerity of tears in private to a pastor." Clinton was thus faced with a difficult task: A public apology would be perceived as mere spectacle and, therefore, insincere, while a private apology, though more believable, would not be heard by the public. Because Bill Clinton was the President, he had to make redress publicly. As a public and religious event, the White House Prayer Breakfast offered Clinton an opportunity to present a more sincere public apology. Hence, to demonstrate contrition, redemption and purification, Bill Clinton appropriated the persona and voice of King David as he addressed the clergy at the White House Prayer Breakfast in September 1998.

King David was chosen by a sovereign God to lead the ancient Israelites to its destiny of prosperity and regional stability. Described by the prophet Samuel as "a man after [God's] own heart," David was ". . . sought and appointed . . . leader of [God's] people,"[15] as the embodiment of the traditions of Israel and a fitting mediator between the people and God. Like Clinton, who had garnered the support of diverse clergy, David benefited from the support of the clerical establishment in Judah. That support, however, was threatened by David's adultery and his conspiracy to cover it up. As his remarks at the ecumenical breakfast reveal, the story of David's sin, public humiliation, and spiritual redemption offered Clinton the rhetorical means to face the scrutiny of the symbolic national elders, demonstrate remorse and transformation, and to reclaim his presidential ethos.

During a period of war between Judah and the Ammonites, King David had a sexual liaison with Bathsheba, the wife of Uriah—one of his most dedicated soldiers. Having discovered that Bathsheba was pregnant, David recalled Uriah from battle. Twice, David tried to reunite the couple so that Bathsheba's pregnancy would be attributed to the soldier's reprieve from war. As a loyal warrior, however, Uriah was unwilling to indulge personal desires during a national crisis. David's efforts thus failed. Desperately, King David sent Uriah back to the battleground with a royal decree. In a letter Uriah delivered to his commanding officer, David gave orders to deploy Uriah to the front lines where he was sure to be killed. Upon Uriah's death, David then took Bathsheba as his bride, believing that his adultery and cover-up was hidden from all. Shortly afterwards, David was called to give an account of his sin by the prophet Nathan, from whom he had enjoyed the most support among the religious elders. Nathan rebuked David for his sins and his violation of Judaic law. Psalm 51 is credited as David's response to Nathan's confrontation, which reflects the fallen leader's journey from reproach to redemption.

Nathan's confrontation is recorded in the twelfth chapter of the second book of the prophet Samuel (2 Sam. 12: 7–9). In response to the charges levied against him, David declared, "I have sinned against the Lord" (2 Sam. 12: 13). In Psalm 51, recorded as his extended confession and repentance, David wrote "I know my transgressions, and my sin is always before me. Against you, you only, have I sinned and done what is evil in your sight, so that you are proved right when you speak and justified when you judge" (Ps. 51:3–4). The psalm ends with David's appeal to God for restoration of his salvation, righteousness, and his authority to lead: He wrote, "create in me a pure heart, O God. . . . Restore to me the joy of your salvation and grant me a willing spirit, to sustain me. Then I will teach transgressors your ways and sinners will turn back to you" (Ps 51:10–13). Thus the Bible outlines David's contrition and his redemption of his ethos before God and among his subjects. It also forms the basis of President Clinton's apology at the annual White House Prayer Breakfast.

One discerns at least three stages in David's psalm of repentance, each of which President Clinton reenacted. The first stage entailed acknowledgment and confession of one's sins; this was followed by demonstration of contrition and an appeal for spiritual cleansing, which would include submission to spiritual authority. The path of repentance concludes with the redemption of the contrite sinner *and* the restoration of the King's spiritual authority over Judah. Clinton's remarks to the clergy enact the first two stages. The President acknowledged his sin, submitted to clerical accountability, and appealed for forgiveness and cleansing. Enthymematically, then, the restoration of his authority should follow.

Early in his remarks at the breakfast, the President acknowledged and confessed his "sins" before the clergy gathered at the White House. Like David in

Psalm 51, it appeared that President Clinton's sin was "always before him." He stated emphatically, "I agree with those who have said that in my first statement after I testified I was not *contrite* enough. I don't think there is a fancy way to say that *I have sinned*."[16] He then acknowledged the damage his indiscretion caused, saying "it is important to me that everybody who has been hurt know that the sorrow I feel is genuine: first and most important, my family; also my friends, my staff, my Cabinet, Monica Lewinsky and her family, and the American people. I have asked all for their forgiveness."[17]

In explicit reference to the story of David, Clinton enacted the second stage of repentance, which entails a demonstration of contrition and an appeal for cleansing. He stated "that to be forgiven, more than sorry is required. . . . First, genuine repentance—a determination to change and to repair the breaches of my own making. *I have repented.* Second, what my bible calls *a 'broken spirit'*; an understanding that I must have God's help to be the person that I want to be."[18] The President reinforced his commitment to repentance by demonstrating the humility many argued was absent from his earlier apology to the nation: he spoke of "a willingness to give the very forgiveness I seek; a renunciation of the pride and the anger which cloud judgment, lead people to excuse and compare and to blame and complain."[19] In these words, Clinton evoked the image of contrition David demonstrated in his brokeness before the prophet Nathan. By letting go of *pride, anger, clouded judgment* and *excuses*, Clinton enacted the brokeness that follows "genuine repentance."

Furthermore, in a step that fortified this posture of contrition, President Clinton conceded to his need for accountability for his actions. However, it is to spiritual rather than legal accountability that he chose to heed, and announced that he had *submitted* himself to the authority of the clerical audience in general, and the counsel of notable evangelical pastors in particular. As he stated, "I will continue on the path of repentance, seeking pastoral support and that of other caring people so that they can hold me accountable for my own commitment."[20]

Psalm 51 reveals the final stage in the path of repentance, which forms the aim of Clinton's appeal to the clergy that day. By acknowledging and confessing his sins, and by submitting to accountability of the ministers, President Clinton endeavored to regain the religio-symbolic ethos invested in the office of the Presidency and, more personally, in him. Toward this end, Clinton said "I will intensify my efforts to lead our country and the world toward peace and freedom, prosperity and harmony, in the hope that with a broken spirit and a still strong heart I can be used for greater good. . . ."[21] Clinton seems to have been leading the way, rhetorically, toward his own restoration. Having acknowledged the support of those who want to heal the nation's rift, and reiterating his confession and contrition, Clinton concluded by presenting himself as a redeemed leader who has learned the lessons of falleness and redemption. As he said at the end of his remarks,

> I . . . sinned. And if my repentance is genuine and sustained,
> and if I can maintain both a broken spirit and a strong heart,
> then good can come of this for our country as well as for me

and my family. The children of this country can learn in a profound way that integrity is important and selfishness is wrong,
but God can change us and make us strong at the broken
places. I want to embody those lessons for the children of this
country.[22]

Finally, bringing his remarks and, thus, his public repentance to a close,
Clinton read from the Yom Kippur liturgy and from two other notable of King
David's psalms, appropriating their benedictive prayers and reinforcing his confession, contrition and redemption. Yom Kippur marks the annual day of atonement in the Judaic law. On Yom Kippur, God charged the priesthood to atone for
the nation's sins by purging their uncleanliness through blood sacrifice. (See Lev.
16: 1, 29–30, 34a). Thus, this liturgy implicitly referred to this act of personal
atonement: He prayed "Lord, help us to turn. . . . Revive our lives as at the beginning, and turn us toward each other."

Similarly, the President quoted widely known passages from Psalms 19 and
139, reaffirming his identification with religious traditions and the earnestness of
his repentance. In both chapters, David extolled God's Sovereignty and the justice of the Judaic Law, and surrendered himself to the purging hand of Yahweh.
In his conclusion, Clinton employed David's words to enact the same surrender
and commitment. David wrote, "O Lord, you have searched me and you know
me. You know when I sit and when I rise; you perceive my thoughts from afar. . .
. Search me, O God, and know my heart; test me and know my anxious thoughts.
See if there is any offensive way in me, and lead me in the way everlasting" (Ps.
139: 1 and 23–23); and (in Ps. 19: 14) "May the words of my mouth and the
meditation of my heart be pleasing in your sight, O Lord, my Rock and my Redeemer."

Clinton's version appealed to the clergy "to share my prayer that God will
search me and know my heart, try me and know my anxious thoughts, see if
there is any hurtfulness in me, and lead me toward the life everlasting. I ask that
God give me a clean heart, let me walk by faith and not by sight."[23] Most striking
however, are Clinton's final words at the breakfast, marking his most explicit
appeal for public restoration of his authority to lead. As the President said, "I ask
once again to be able to … be an instrument of God's peace; to let the words of
my mouth and meditations of my heart and, in the end, the work of my hands, be
pleasing. This is what I wanted to say to you today. Thank you. God bless you."[24]

A logical question arises about the effectiveness of Clinton's display of
"genuine repentance." If any evidence exists toward this evaluation, it lies in part
in the President's remarks at the gathering a year later. Clinton returned to the
1999 prayer breakfast ready to recover the priestly/kingly ethos and to proceed to
the task of initiating policy in the interest of the nation. By repeating his repentance and his commitment to accountability, Clinton affirmed the restoration of
the presidential ethos he had sought. He stated, "I have been profoundly moved,
as few people have, by the pure power of grace—unmerited forgiveness through
grace." Having been redeemed by God, and forgiven by family and others, the

President resumed the ethos of a leader and role model by embodying the biblical story of falleness and redemption. Thus, before the clergy in 1999, Clinton reported on his accountability and growth saying: "I'd like to say a special word of thanks to my good friend, Reverend Wogaman, and to Gordon MacDonald . . . and to Tony Campolo . . . who have kept their word to meet with me over the last year—both to help me and to hold me accountable. And I have kept my word to meet with them and to work with them."[25]

A year after the symbolic confrontation of the symbolic king with the nation's symbolic elders, Clinton enacted the persona of the restored leader before the annual gathering of clergy at the White House. On that day, the President proceeded with the symbolic charge of the office to interpret national vision and to initiate public policies toward that end. At the seventh annual White House Prayer Breakfast, Clinton recommitted himself to his "new covenant" vision of the symbolic relationship between the people and the government. He reaffirmed a common national purpose, the joint leadership of the church and state to steer the nation's path, and invested himself in the intermediary role as the symbolic President, Priest, and Prophet over America's civil religion. On this day, Clinton discussed youth violence and gun legislation, just as King David discussed new issues of the day, not his forgiveness and redeemed adultery.

Conclusion

In this chapter, I have chosen to examine the brief statements President Clinton delivered at annual breakfasts he hosted at the White House with diverse clergy, in order to understand the religio-symbolic dimension of the American Presidency. Specifically, I have examined how the tradition of civil religion, which grounds our political culture, places unique rhetorical constraints upon the office of the Presidency, as well as its occupant, and how President Clinton appropriated the discourse of civic piety to construct for himself an ethos befitting the symbolic dimension of the presidency. The significance of these breakfasts to the Clinton administration is attested in part by its priority on the President's annual calendar. For instance, though campaigning for re-election kept him from hosting a breakfast in 1996, Clinton promptly hosted a gathering of the nation's symbolic elders following his inauguration in January, 1997; he hosted another one eleven months later. Certainly, if in previous years the gatherings seemed unimportant, to the nation, the media, or political scholars in general, the moment for impeachment of the President in 1998 certainly bears testimony to the potential rhetorical impact of the Prayer Breakfasts on Clinton's ability to reclaim his ethos as the embodiment of American civic values.

As this analysis has demonstrated, these reflective moments in the White House with diverse clergy enabled Clinton to coalesce his role as Chief administrator with the symbolic role of the U.S. President as the guardian of civic piety. Through such rhetorical orchestration, Clinton thereby projected an image as the nation's civic high priest, effectively moderating obstacles that arose from his prior ethos and reputation, and from conservative political opposition. Furthermore, through the annual White House Prayer Breakfast, President Clinton sought to regain his presidential ethos after his involvement with Monica Lewinsky was exposed. By appropriating the biblical persona of King David, enacted through a public demonstration of contrition, purification and redemption, William Jefferson Clinton used the personae of prophet, priest, and king who had the support of the national elders and of the public, and thereby redeemed his own presidential ethos and image as the guardian of the tradition of American civil religion.

Chapter 11

American Evangelicalism, Democracy, and Civic Piety

A Computer-Based Analysis of Promise Keepers' Discourse

Michael E. Eidenmuller

> [In America there is] a form of Christianity which I cannot better describe than by styling it a democratic and republican religion . . . and from the beginning, politics and religion contracted an alliance which has never been dissolved.
>
> —Alexis de Tocqueville[1]

If politics and religion in the U.S. have often made strange bedfellows, they have, nonetheless, kept their sleeping arrangements. So argues Roderick P. Hart, whose *Political Pulpit* leads us to (re)consider both the nature of, and explanation for, their quixotic marriage on rhetorically constituted grounds.[2] Under the implicit terms and conditions of a contractual metaphor, Hart choreographs the tango of *civic piety* by prescribing and proscribing the range of rhetorical moves available to each partner. While religion occupies herself with domesticating the transcendent (and etherealizing the mundane), the state busies itself with practical affairs governing the collective public good. If and when the twain should meet on "official" business, religion is expected to perform her duty in servicing the state with her substantial symbolic resources. At its most benevolent, civic piety signifies that *chosen* public discourse used "to effect and maintain the delicate relationships shared by church and state," and by which, among other proverbial incantations, may "God bless America."[3]

Less palpable, perhaps, but no less important, are those cases in which "unofficial" religion makes implicit rhetorical demands upon the offices and obligations of the state. Promise Keepers (or PK), a Christian evangelical men's movement-organization whose revivalist rhetoric has reached millions, and whose conservative Protestant ideology is subscribed to by tens of millions, is of moment insofar as the interests of marriage, family, community, and society are held in common by both church and state. This essay, then, concerns the contract of civic piety from the vantage of mainstream religion. At issue is whether and to what extent the rhetoric of so-called unofficial religion is capable of negotiating successfully the rhetorical parameters of civic piety in religious-rhetorical situations of relatively public standing. More precisely, this essay considers the rhetorical prospects given American evangelicalism to coordinate publicly situated symbols in meeting civic piety's tenet not to be "overly political" while yet remaining true to its religious calling.

One way to gauge a body of rhetoric's politicality or religiosity is through the dimension of lexical or verbal style.[4] Politicians no less than priests make certain lexical choices, consciously or otherwise, at the expense of given alternatives. Such choices, when viewed across large amounts of rhetorical data, produce a kind of lexical map, as it were, in which certain stylistic tendencies may be charted and codified. Granting the validity of the measures involved, such maps may then be classified as relatively political or religious in lexical topography. This essay employs the construct of verbal style, and an attendant set of discriminating measures, to compare the lexical features of local and national (i.e., civically-situated) PK rhetoric, and argues that it is indeed possible for mainstream religion to negotiate successfully at least some of the demands of civic piety, while yet remaining consistent with its own ideological heritage. If my argument is successful, it follows that predictions concerning the demise of mainstream religion's tacit endorsement of civic piety's contractual obligations may be premature, if not mistaken.

My argument proceeds in four successive phases. I first divide PK rhetoric into two discrete rhetorical situations, one local, and the other national. I then provide an ideological context for understanding the rhetorical style of Promise Keepers, a context which will serve as an alternative (competing and complementary) explanatory construct to civic piety. Next, I discuss my argument's analytic methods. Here, I beg the reader's patience, as it is necessary to describe in some detail my methodology to make sense of the empirical results that constitute the "hard" rhetorical data of my argument. I then offer a comparative analysis of the stylistic features found in PK discourse across its two rhetorical situations and show how variations in these features may be accounted for partially by the contractual obligations of civic piety, and more generally by the rhetorical expectations issuing from PK's ideological heritage. Finally, on the basis of this analysis, I offer concluding remarks on the relationship between unofficial religion and civic piety, as that relationship was styled in the rhetoric of one organized body of mainstream religion near the turn of the twenty-first century.

Promise Keepers and the Tale of Two Rhetorical Situations

From January 10 to October 25 of 1997, Promise Keepers held twenty weekend conferences in stadiums and stadium-sized venues across the United States. In all, an estimated 638,297 attendees listened to 180 speeches delivered by many of evangelicalism's most celebrated rhetors. Included were Billy Graham and son Franklin, best-selling authors Gary Smalley and John Trent, Dallas Maverick's chaplain Tony Evans, Jack Hayford, the Reverend E.V. Hill, Bill Hybels, Greg Laurie, Crawford Lorritts, Max Lucado, and Luis Palau, among many other luminaries familiar to the culture of American evangelicalism. Topics ranged from family values and male friendship to racial reconciliation and financial integrity. The stadium events served at least two rhetorical aims: 1) to attract and recruit new members and 2) to stimulate or renew religiously-inspired solutions for a litany of perceived socio-cultural maladies related to marriage, family, and church community.

On October 4 of that year, approximately 900,000 followers gathered on the Washington Mall for a six-hour-long rhetorical offering styled *Stand in the Gap: A Sacred Assembly of Men* (or SITG) and dedicated themselves to corporate prayer and repentance. Broadcast live by various media, including C-SPAN, Odyssey, and FamilyNet, to a potential audience base of 173 million, SITG may well have been the single largest religious gathering of its kind in U.S. history.[5] SITG served to bring national attention to the problem—more properly a "crisis" for those subscribing to PK's mission and messages—of social alienation generally, and of religious fragmentation in particular. Compared with local PK stadium events, then, SITG was a public rhetorical affair, as evidenced by geopolitical setting, scope of production, audience size, and level of critical attention and exposure. It was the level of public-ness combined with a perceived socio-cultural crisis that brought PK SITG squarely into the domain of civic piety.

Promise Keepers and the Ideological Parameters of American Evangelicalism

PK's style of discourse flows from a rhetorical heritage that merges evangelical Christianity with American democracy. Its religious ideology, usefully codified by Bebbington, emphasizes 1) the necessity of personal salvation through Jesus-as-Christ *(conversionism)*; 2) the conviction that the Bible's content is the final authority governing Christian faith and practice *(biblicanism);* 3) the conviction that the individual believer is responsible for communicating the "good news" of Jesus to a lost and dying world *(activism)*; and 4) *crucicentrism*, the conviction that the redemptive work of Jesus-as-Christ, signified by death on a cross—perhaps more than the actual teachings of Jesus—constitutes the central theme of the Christian message.[6]

A second ideological stream feeding evangelicalism is found in the wider milieu of American democracy. According to historian Nathan Hatch, American democracy's unapologetic belief in the innate value of the common individual led to evangelicalism's shift from the esoteric theology of the elite to a simple, yet forceful, rhetoric of the masses.[7] The democratic ideal that privileged individual autonomy and the free exercise of thought found its evangelical analogue in the call for individuals to interpret religious truth for themselves.[8] As a result, evangelicalism shifted from a content-orientation to an audience-orientation. All that

was required was a rhetoric capable of appealing directly and powerfully to democratic sensibilities.[9] Much earlier Tocqueville had characterized the (democratic) style of American Christianity as audience-centered, intellectually open to
all, pluralistic and innovative.[10] Considered rhetorically, the ideological currents
running through evangelicalism have created rhetorical opportunities, tensions,
and constraints teeming with populist sentiment to which its discourse has adapted
with phenomenal cultural success.[11]

   The rhetorical character of PK also has been shaped by the democratic exigence of opposition.[12] In the years and months leading up to SITG, PK garnered
a curious, if not altogether unpredictable, range of critical commentary. Then
National Organization for Women president Patricia Ireland and others accused
PK of endorsing an anachronistically patriarchal vision of society bent toward the
systematic subordination of women—a well-marketed agent of the political
right.[13] On the other hand, feminist journalist Donna Minkowitz, who attended a
Florida PK stadium event disguised as a teen-aged boy, wrote in somewhat ar-
dent tones about how close PK seemed to the ideals of feminism.[14] The prox-
imity was not lost on separatist evangelicals who chastised PK for irrationally
adopting a psychological model of relationships that "feminized" the church by
"making the model normative for men."[15] And while other evangelicals excori-
ated PK for a politics of theology that fell nothing short of heretical ecumenicalism,[16] the official doctrinal position of the "Government Incarnate," as delivered
by its Chief Executor on the day of the D.C. rally, had it that

> No one can question the sincerity of the hundreds of thousands
> of men who have filled football stadiums across our country and
> who are willing to reassume their responsibilities to the families
> and to their children and therefore to our future.[17]

   Scholar of evangelicalism Randy Balmer captured the variegated public
opinion by calling PK a veritable "Rorschach test for the 1990's."[18] Although
assiduously affirming its apolitical character, PK, as well as avowedly political
interest groups, shares at least one rhetorical reality: Each is, in part, a "spectator
sport on which [one] can project [one's] desires, fears, and . . . wishes."[19] To that
end, religion and politics have a storied penchant for making both spectator and
spectacle of participating audiences.

   To sum my argument at this juncture, PK produced a sizeable body of rhetoric in 1997 that may be divided along local and national (i.e., civic) situational
lines. Both situations were shaped by the ideological requirements of a populist
religious tradition. What remains to be seen is whether the rhetoric of PK varied
between the two events, and if so, to what extent this variation may be accounted
for by the contractual obligations of civic piety.

   The next phase of my argument entails a description of the methods used to
discern the stylistic features of PK discourse and is followed by a stylistic analysis of those features within and across both of PK's rhetorical situations.

DICTION 5.0

Descriptive and comparative stylistic analyses were performed by the computer software program DICTION 5.0.[20] DICTION is a collection of thirty-one word lists (or dictionaries) that measure a discourse's *verbal style.* DICTION's analytic features are constructed from a cross-section of some 12,000 rhetorical artifacts, including Christian sermons. Individual word lists vary in size (10–745 words) and are organized according to theoretical type and/or rhetorical function.[21] The dictionary labeled "familiarity," for instance, contains forty-four "operation" terms calculated by C. K. Ogden to be the most commonly found words in the English language.[22] Included among these terms are demonstrative and interrogative pronouns (e.g., "this," "that"—"who," "what"), prepositions (e.g., "between," "on," "through"), and various conjunctions, particles, and connectives.[23] All told, DICTION contains some 10,000 individual words in its lexical corpus.

In its perfunctory operations, DICTION scans discrete 500-word segments of a text for instances of each term in its lexicon and produces numerical output in the form of raw frequency counts and standardized (z) scores. Importantly, DICTION provides a statistical basis for comparing raw frequency scores for any given dictionary across different types or classes of discourse, including political and religious discourses. This is accomplished by assigning each dictionary a "normative parameter," an upper and lower score range representing +/–1 standard deviations from the mean.[24] Parameters vary by discourse class and are based on a 20,000-item comparative sample of discourse delivered mainly in the U.S. between 1945 and 1998. For example, the normative parameter for religious sermon discourse is 123.05–149.50 on the dictionary named *familiarity.* Any 500-word discourse segment found to contain more or fewer *familiar* words than this score range exhibits a lexical style significantly different from the expected (generic) range for religious sermons. For text segments of less than 500 words (e.g., at the end of a speech), DICTION extrapolates the raw scores to a 500-word norm.

Noting PK's stylistic tendencies would not mean much if there were no comparative basis by which those tendencies could be measured. Consequently, I chose two comparative classes of discourse, as operationalized by DICTION's normative parameters, that seemed most obviously related to civic piety's two-party contract: political campaign addresses and religious sermons. Normative parameters for campaign addresses are derived from a sample (n = 2357) of major and third-party presidential candidates' speeches delivered between 1948 and 1996.[25] According to Hart, distinctive lexical features of campaign discourse include high levels of *self-reference* (e.g., "I," "me," "mine"), *present concern* (present-tense verb terms denoting general physical activity and task performance such as "keeps," "makes," "needs," "provides," "uses," "wants"), and *motion* terms denoting human movement such as "go," "ran," "travel," "walks." The co-presence of these terms, among the most generically distinctive to political campaigns, infuses its discourse with a distinctive tone of "unmistakable energy and immediacy."[26]

Normative parameters for religious sermons are calculated from a sample of 198 sermons delivered by a variety of denominational speakers in the U.S. between 1935 and 1996.[27] Mainline denominations including Episcopalians, Catholics, and Methodists are represented. Topics include doctrinal disputes, biblical exegesis, and social and moral concerns.[28] Religious sermons are comparatively high in the language of *satisfaction* (e.g., "happiness," "thanks," "celebrating," "encourage") and *inspiration* (e.g., "faith" "courage," "dedication," "wisdom"). In contrast to campaign discourse, religious sermons make comparatively little use of *self-reference, present concern,* and *motion* language.

Finally, two custom dictionaries were employed to further assess the relative degree of religiosity occupying PK discourse. The dictionary *religious* contained terms such as "believer," "Bible," "born-again," "Christ," "Christian," "church," "faith," "God," "holy," "Jesus," "prayer," "saints," "scripture," and "worship." The dictionary *irreligious* included, among other terms, "devil," "evil," "hell," "idol," "immorality," "Satan," "satanic," "secular," "sin(s)," "sinful," "ungodly," and "unsaved."[29]

Rhetorical Properties of Civic Piety: "Optimism" and "Expedient Complexity"

Hart argued that "optimism" is an essential feature of civic piety.[30] Verbal *optimism*, a concatenated dictionary (or variable) in DICTION, is conceptualized as "language endorsing some person, group, concept or event or highlighting their positive entailments."[31] Following Hart, I operationalized verbal *optimism* as a function of the individual scores on DICTION's word lists *satisfaction, inspiration,* and *praise.*[32] Thus, if the discourse of SITG is found to contain a significantly higher frequency scores for these variables (i.e., higher use of *satisfaction, inspiration,* and *praise* words) than is found in its local discourse, we may conclude that at least part of PK's rhetoric was negotiated in ways favorable to the contractual obligations of civic piety.

A second feature of civic piety, "expedient complexity," was measured by comparing and contrasting the God(s) of SITG with the "pantheon of Gods" found in civic piety.[33] To construct rhetorically the God(s) of SITG, discursive moments were selected in which "God" and other religious terms were highly concentrated. General God-themes were abstracted from these moments, further organized into higher-order God-types, and subsequently compared with the God-types discovered by Hart.[34]

I conclude this section with a summary of this phase of my argument. If civic piety is to have any explanatory value in accounting for the rhetorical character of unofficial religion's intersection with American civil-religion, we might expect a demonstrable change to occur between PK's local and national rhetoric. If the prediction that civic piety's contract will be honored with less zeal is correct—and in view of this essay's measures—we might expect PK's rhetoric to be more religiously styled at the local level and more politically styled at the national level. To the former expectation, we shall see that such a change did occur.

To the latter expectation, as we shall see, something quite to the contrary obtained, a finding that bears well for mainstream religion's rhetorical capacity to adapt to the contractual obligations of civic piety, while not violating the norms of its own ideological heritage.

Data Profile Summary

This essay processed raw lexical frequency scores for 151 stadium event speeches (1,585 discourse segments of 500 words) and the entire population of SITG discourse (76 discourse segments of 500 words).[35] A total of 798,535 words were processed. Mean scores for each of the aforementioned stylistic variables (e.g., *self-reference*) were calculated across all discourse segments for PK local (stadium event) and national (SITG) discourses respectively.

PK Style at Local Stadium Events

An analysis of PK stadium event rhetoric exhibits lexical tendencies that seem more typical of political campaigns than of religious sermons. A conspicuous lexical feature of PK local discourse is the relatively high levels of *self-reference* language (mean = 21.3 per discourse segment). This finding compares far more favorably with the language of political campaigns (normative parameters = 3.74–20.70) than with religious sermons (normative parameters = 0.0–13.41). PK stadium event style is also marked by relatively high levels of *motion* (mean = 5.52) and *present concern* language (mean = 17.56) that also compare more favorably with political campaigns (*motion* = 0.54–6.40; *present concern* = 8.45–20.28) than with religious sermons (*motion* = 0.35–4.21; *present concern* = 6.17–15.95). A brief view in context illuminates how PK's use of *present concern* and *motion* language gives its discourse that sense of urgency so typical of political campaign rhetoric:

> Listen, I *want* you to *take* baby steps . . . Wake up, *get* up, and
> *go* up. Say it again. Wake up, *get* up, and *go* up . . . You *need*
> to *get* up off the couch and *walk* away. *Walk* away from the
> TV . . . You *need* to *go* up to the mountain . . . It's time to
> *move* past the crowds of people.[36]

There is no argument here. Paved with imperatives, this rhetorical road directs immediate ("get," "need," "take," "want") human action ("go," "walk," "move"). It is a discourse styled in the here and now, ever leading travelers from some place to somewhere better. It is true, of course, that religious discourse labors hard under the imperative, not infrequently through negating terms—the "thou shalt nots" of language. It is PK's insistent styling of the imperative in terms of a positive, action-inundated present that gives this discourse the lexical flavor of political campaigns.

While PK's use of *self-reference* language is consistent with the discourse of political campaigns, it should also be noted that such language serves notice of evangelicalism's emphasis on the personalization of religious faith. Typically, self-references serve as a lexical modality for self-confession. When tightly strung together, such terms operate as narrative markers of identification under-scoring the rhetor's status as a religious insider among like-minded believers, as well as incessant linguistic reminders of the self's appointed and democratic right to speak to and for God. Franklin Graham, an insider's insider within evangeli-calism, whose mean *self-reference* score of 21.43 (across 21 discourse segments) approximates the PK stadium mean on this stylistic variable illustrates:

> *I'm* here to tell you fellows, *I'm* a sinner and *I* don't care who *my* [parents are]... You see, *I* had, one day, *I* had to get on *my* knees and *I* had to say to God *I* have sinned against you. *I'm* a sinner. *I* had to tell him that. *I* went through *my* teenage years... into *my* twenty's... *I* wanted to get involved in all the things that *I* could ... because *I*... wanted to please *my-self*.[37]

Hart avers that recent political campaigns "display the psychological talis-man of their age" in the frequent use of self-references.[38] If so, PK stadium style discourse may have fallen under a similar spell, as evidenced by popular Chris-tian psychologist and author Gary Smalley's comparatively pathological levels of self-reference language (40 discourse segments; mean = 39.84). As Smalley's self-referentiality crosses lexical paths with the terministic talisman of sex, satis-faction, and fulfillment, and cohabitates with the language of religion, the joint effect produces a kind of psychologized religious discourse, perhaps not unlike that which PK's evangelical critics find so troubling. Indeed, from a purely lexi-cal point of view, it is exceedingly difficult at times to distinguish the religious wheat from the psychological tares:

> I was no longer being satisfied sexually. And I was only mar-ried for two years. And I was frustrated. I thought to my-self... "I can't get turned on to the place where I get ful-filled?" I was so loaded up with drive sexually. But she wasn't satisfying; so I was sick in my heart over that. I was pretty in-sensitive and stupid... But I figured if I discussed this idea with her, who knows what this will lead to? So I didn't say anything. I was the most self-centered person I knew. I was so controlling   and   so   self-fulfilling   ...and   self-satisfying... Yet... the life that I now live I live by faith in the son of God who loved me and gave himself for me.[39]

Whatever substantive religious changes may have occurred, Smalley's life re-mains styled in the language of self-reference.

Graham notwithstanding, PK local stadium language is relatively free of "sin" (*irreligious* language). "God" and his terministic allies appear with much greater frequency (13:1) than do his lexical enemies.[40] This helps, perhaps, to explain the reactions of PK's religious detractors, whose separatist inclinations are grounded in a more conspicuous and frequently distributed lexicon of evil.

What religion may do spiritually, PK accomplishes stylistically. If God's love is the salvation of the Church, and God's mercy means her separation from sin, perhaps there is some rhetorical redemption in the lexical absence (and hence separation) of the terms for "sin" from the terms for "God." In the discourse of local evangelical ecumenicalism, it would appear that mitigated evil and bountiful good share a style of their own.

The emergence of the distinctive stylistic features of *self-reference, present concern,* and *motion* suggests that PK stadium discourse shares more in common with the discourse of political campaigns than with religious sermons. These particular stylistic traits, among the most pervasive in political campaigns, are of comparatively little importance in religious sermons. Other than the use of *religious* terms, for which no normative data are available, there is little lexical evidence to support a claim favorably comparing PK discourse with religious sermons. I conclude, therefore, that PK's local rhetoric is relatively political in style, a style that may be characterized as democratically-charged and psychologically-nurtured, and whose stylistic features may be explained by recourse to a populist ideological heritage.

PK Style at SITG

Having identified the stylistic character of PK's local discourse, I now move to ascertain whether any changes in discursive religiosity and politicality occurred in PK's nationally-situated discourse and, if so, whether the construct of civic piety offers a useful account of those changes. A second analysis performed on the discourse of SITG reveals something of a reversal of PK's local stylistic trends. A dramatic decline in *self-reference* language (from 21.3 to 13.2 per discourse segment) was accompanied by significant decreases in *present concern* (from 17.56 to 16.56*)*, and *motion* terms (from 5.52 to 3.06). Decreases in these measures of politicality were accompanied by a surge in *religious* terms (from 12.5 to 24.2). *Irreligious* terms increased very slightly (1.06 to 1.71). By these measures, then, the verbal style of SITG was both less political and more religious than PK local discourse.

To assess whether civic piety's rhetorical property of "optimism" played any role at PK SITG, individual lexical scores on *praise, inspiration, satisfaction* were examined. Each of these measures of *optimism* increased significantly from PK's local events: *Satisfaction* (5.06 to 6.44), *inspiration* (4.58 to 8.16), and *praise* (5.51 to 7.37). The rise in *inspiration* language was particularly acute. Consequently, the cumulative changes in six discrete indicators of discursive politicality and religiosity provide no evidence that PK's national discourse was "overly political." To the contrary, the evidence suggests that PK specifically toned down its politicality in favor of a verbal style directed toward religious optimism.

An analysis of "expedient complexity" at SITG revealed the presence of distinct God-types whose rhetorical attributes were favorable both to unofficial religion (i.e., American evangelicalism) *and* civic piety.[41] Thus, as "Our Creator

God looks upon this great gathering, He will see mankind, men of every tongue and tribe, men of every color, on their knees in humility of their hearts before Him."[42] Here is, in part, "God the Witnessing Author," but one particularly observant of a multi-racial gathering of men willing to transcend their domestic divisions on his behalf.[43] There are few traces of "God the Inscrutable Potentate" who works "oftentimes, but mysteriously, directly intervenes in the affairs of men."[44] In his stead, is a one-shot, now-is-your-time God who openly co-participates in the desires of "the people." This God, available to all, is especially apologetic to "abused sons and daughters," abandoned families, ill-treated spouses, and victims of "racism and discrimination."[45] Less like "God the Wise and the Just," who can be a "rather reluctant wellspring of justice,"[46] this God, on more than one occasion, thunders with holy abandon at the purveyors of a vitiated faith who claim democracy's privilege, but fail its charge.[47] In short, this is *God the Indefatigable Democratist*, forging ideological unity from cultural diversity, "ready to work in each of us" as individuals and individual interest groups "to make us one."[48] Compared with other SITG personages, this God is the most useful in negotiating the tensions between church and state, insofar as religion's duty to individual moral accountability and the state's interest in the collective public welfare are concerned.

In contrast to an occasional showing among civic piety's pantheon, "God the Object of Affection" is present at most every rhetorical turn at SITG.[49] This God is, by lexical degrees, "holy" (N= 75), "mighty" (N=55), "great" (N=48), "praise [worthy]" (N=37), "[full of] mercy" (N=37), "extraordinary" (N=34), and by fewer degrees "righteous," "powerful," and "loving"—a "great Promise Keeper."[50] In communion with *God the Indefatigable Democratist*, *God the Object of Affection* knowingly accepts multicultural offerings of praise. Particularly privileged are native Americans willing to credit him as their "Great Chief" and "conquering victorious warrior."[51] More typically, this God is the object of democratically-styled affection, reveling among the populist pronouns "we," "our," and "us"—"the God whom *we* love and care for so much," "*our* mighty fortress" who furnishes "the grace . . . that brings *us* together."[52]

Unlike the Gods of civic piety, the God of SITG requires uncompromising pledges of allegiance to his only Son. At his most benevolent, this is *God the Conditional Inclusivist*, granting visitation rights to all, but declaring with intransigent fortitude no special pleading:

> Jesus Christ is God's only son. Therefore, Jesus Christ is man's only savior. Christ is not one of many ways. . . . Nor is he the best of many ways. He is the only way. There is no other name under heaven given among men whereby we must be saved.[53]

This God, lying at the center of evangelicalism's ideological core, is absent among the childless gods of civic piety. He neither dines at civic piety's rhetorical table nor is invited to do so. Among other SITG personages, *God the Conditional Inclusivist* is perhaps the least civil and most certainly the least officially-styled. To all present lexical appearances, he is likely to remain so.

This, then, is the simple, triune God of SITG: *God the Indefatigable Democratist*, *God the Object of Affection*, and *God the Conditional Inclusivist*. Although rhetorically coherent, he is only marginally suited to the demands of civic piety, lacking, in particular, the requisite expedient complexity. Yet, if the God of SITG is perpetually excluded from civic piety's official ceremonies, there may be comfort in the recognition that it was he to whom "Madam Religion" turned in an hour of need to set her own rhetorical affairs in order.

Conclusion

This essay questioned whether mainstream, unofficial religion is rhetorically capable of meeting the contractual obligations of civic piety, while yet remaining consistent with its ideological heritage. In pursuit of this question, a macrostylistic analysis was used to characterize the relative degree of politicality and religiosity of Promise Keepers' rhetoric across local and national rhetorical situations. Findings from local PK events reveal that PK was more political than religious in verbal style.[54] As with political campaigns, PK packaged its local discourse in immediate, urgent tones and wrapped them plainly in the colors of democratic populism. The lexical irony would not have been lost on Tocqueville who was "altogether surprised . . . to find the political" where he thought he would "see only the religious."[55]

At the national level, however, PK SITG painted a different stylistic picture. In coordinating publicly situated symbols within a comparatively civic context, PK jettisoned those stylistic features which uniquely contributed to its local stylistic identity. In its place was a rhetoric relatively free of political tonalities, styled in the language of optimistic religion. Also found was the pervasive presence of *God the Object of Affection*. Their rhetorical combination suggests that civic piety played a positive, though limited, role in PK's stylistic crossover.

On the other hand, PK's national rhetoric also exhibited stylistic tendencies favorable to the expectations of a democratically-charged, evangelical Christian ideology. This is evidenced in God *the Indefatigable Democratist*, and *God the Conditional Inclusivist*, coupled with the dramatic rise in religious language. PK's democratic ideals also explain the precipitous decline in self-referentiality. Sensitized to feminist criticism and careful of its witness among the "great cloud," PK moved away from a self-oriented, masculine "I"—even for confessional purposes. By denying in no small measure the *self* its own language, SITG negotiated stylistically the democratic exigence of opposition, and, at the same time, enhanced a populist character in cooperation with the salvific, activist, and crucicentric ideals of its ideological heritage. The co-presence of these features served to check the balance of rhetorical power otherwise exerted by the executive civic piety.

As a consequence, the rhetoric of SITG failed the test for ordination as an "official religion." Its stylistic nature was too religiously exclusive for the comparatively mundane requirements of civic piety. This is not to say that PK breached civic piety's contractual obligations. Indeed, the singular accomplishment of SITG was an implicit endorsement of the idea that if religion wants to cultivate a legitimate voice in the public square, she must first put her own rhetorical house in order:

> I have a request for those of you who . . . may have come here to voice your opinions on specific political issues. We have dedicated this as a sacred assembly. Would you suspend today your appeal . . . and would you unite with us in appealing in prayer before a righteous and just God?[56]

From the vantage point of this essay, Stephen Carter is quite right to distinguish the religious campaigning of PK from the religiously-motivated, political campaigns of organizations such as the Christian Coalition and Liberty Lobby.[57] Moreover, if it is elsewhere or otherwise true that the contract of civic piety will be "honored with less zeal in the future," SITG offers hope for a brighter rhetorical tomorrow.[58] That hope lies in the mediating capacity of religion to invest the civic sphere with a prayerful rhetorical tone capable of bringing audiences otherwise divided into substantial communion.[59] It was precisely to this hope that Ben Franklin, amid much sparring division, made his seminal appeal on behalf of civic piety at the Constitutional Convention of 1787.[60] As SITG demonstrates, there is a rhetorical style to that civil-religious hope.

Implications

This analysis suggests that any unofficial religious body's attempt to negotiate rhetorically the delicate balance between church and state will require some stylistic crossover. Such negotiation must necessarily be achieved by relinquishing some of the very lexical features that constitute local rhetorical identity. This is, in part, what a rhetoric of civic piety predicts, provided that religion lives up to her end of the agreement. By promoting those stylistic traits favorable to both civic piety and unofficial religion, the rhetoric of SITG serves notice of evangelicalism's enduring ability to adapt to the contractual and ideological obligations of different rhetorical environments, rising perhaps to an uncharacteristic level of rhetorical sainthood, even if she elsewhere plays the harlot in political beds of her religious undoing.

Finally, the rhetoric of power in American democracy has long rested in populist appeal. To the extent that democratic populism cannot be isolated from lexical style, we may expect rival interest groups to employ its language to gain a rhetorical upper hand. From this perspective, we can view feminist and evangelical separatist reactions to PK not merely as a contest of ideas, but as a struggle over the very *terms* of power and authority to which those ideas are wed. In the case of Promise Keepers, unofficial religious discourse styled in the language of optimistic religion and democratic populism may be seen as an attempt to gainsay less civilly-styled rivals, even if it is itself disenfranchised by the contractual obligations of civic piety. In this way, the exclusive nature of unofficial religion is styled more inclusively democratic, engendering a paradox between rhetorical style and ideological substance whose tensions may understandably give rise to the Rorschachian reactions ascribed to it. In the main, however, and among ideologically similar audiences, the rhetorical style of American evangelicalism remains a testament to the unifying power of democracy and religion in America.

Chapter 12

Forging a Civil-Religious Construct for the Twenty-first Century
Should Hart's "Contract" Be Renewed?

Martin J. Medhurst

Jimmy Carter was in the White House. G. Gordon Liddy was in prison. No one had ever heard of the Moral Majority, much less the Christian Coalition. Inflation was still a problem—despite Jerry Ford's WIN campaign—which stood for Whip Inflation Now. The stock market hovered around 1450. The Soviet Union still existed, but it was the age of detente, at least for a little while. Cable television was beginning to change American viewing habits. But CNN was still a twinkle in Ted Turner's eye. Very few people could find Afghanistan on a map. Few people had reason to. This was the world of 1977.

Into this world came a small book titled *The Political Pulpit*. It was the first scholarly book by an already-prominent associate professor at Purdue University, Roderick P. Hart. Professor Hart had become prominent by doing all those things that assistant professors were supposed to do in what was then called the field of Speech Communication (a decade earlier when Hart began his graduate studies at Penn State the field was simply called Speech). He had published early and often and had placed some of those publications in *The Quarterly Journal of Speech* and *Speech Monographs*—two of only three national journals then published by the Speech Communication Association.

In the spring and fall of 1977, I was a graduate student at Penn State, taking courses from Carroll Arnold, Richard Gregg, and Conrad Cherry—all of whom were specifically recognized in *The Political Pulpit* as intellectual influences on Hart. That same year, I published my first major study in a speech journal—the *Central States Speech Journal* to be precise—titled "American Cosmology and the Rhetoric of Inaugural Prayer."[1] It was an exploration of one kind of American civil-religious discourse or, what in his book Hart prefers to call the rhetoric of civic piety. I later completed my dissertation on the same topic.[2]

I start with these observations to make a simple point: 1977 was a long time ago. Indeed, many aspects of that world no longer exist. Those that do still exist have been, in many instances, radically transformed. It hardly seems fair, therefore, to expect that a "contract" published so long ago should be expected to remain in full force some 25 years later. Indeed, I shall argue that several parts of the contract have long since been breached and that a new construct, not a new contract, is needed for the twenty-first century.

First, I will comment on the three main parties to Hart's contract—the United States government, organized religion, and the American citizenry—and attempt to clarify some of the interrelationships between and among these terms, relationships that may bear more than one interpretation. Second, I will analyze some contemporary instances of civil-religion and civil-religious discourses as manifested in the talk of those parties identified by Hart as "official" civil-religionists, particularly presidents and clergy who perform civil-religious functions. Finally, I will try to redraw the boundaries of the contract for the twenty-first century.

The Parties to the "Contract"

Hart identifies the three main parties to the contract as the U.S. government, organized religion, and the American citizenry.[3] Part of the problem with the contract—indeed, any contract—is that the terms refuse to stand still. What is part of organized religion or the private realm of the solitary citizen one day may become, the next day, part of the governmental structure. Indeed, the history of these now firmly United States can be told as the story of ever-increasing centralization of government and ever-expanding realms over which government claims authority.

Today we take for granted the separation of church and state, even though that precise language is found nowhere in the Constitution. As Michael J. Sandel reminds us, "It is striking to recall that, for all its familiarity, the requirement that government be neutral on matters of religion is not a longstanding principle of constitutional law, but a recent arrival, a development of the last [fifty-five] years. Not until 1947 did the Supreme Court hold that government must be neutral toward religion."[4] We also presume that the Constitution "disestablished" religion when, in fact, there was never a federal religion to be disestablished in the United States and the Bill of Rights—the first ten amendments to the Constitution—did not, as originally drafted and implemented, apply to the states. Indeed, as Sandel notes:

> Some states did not disestablish religion until well into the nineteenth century. Connecticut continued tax support for religion until 1818, Massachusetts until 1833. New Jersey restricted full civil rights to Protestants until 1844, and Maryland required belief in God as a condition of public office until the

U.S. Supreme Court struck it down in 1961. Even in states without establishments, some nineteenth-century courts held Christianity to be part of the common law.[5]

My point is not to try to re-establish religion, but to underscore the fact that what counts as "religion" versus what counts as "government" has continuously evolved throughout the American experience—and is still evolving today. Take, for example, the issue of abortion. In 1972, abortion was still considered to be primarily a moral issue involving moral theology ("religion") and the conscience of the individual ("citizenry"). There were, of course, laws against it, some states being more restrictive than others. Then came *Roe v. Wade* (1973) and the law ("government") moved from abortion opponent to abortion defender. What had previously been primarily a moral and religious issue was now, we were told, primarily a legal one. Interestingly, writing in 1977, Hart makes no mention of abortion, even though it was fast becoming the definitional issue that would separate millions of Roman Catholics from the Democratic Party and awaken the somnambulant giant of American Evangelicalism.

Indeed, the case can be made, I believe, that at the precise moment Rod Hart was articulating his contract, the very terms of the contract were in the process of changing. The reason for this is simple: Hart's contract looks backward in time and reflects the America that existed from roughly 1925 to 1975—from the humiliation of William Jennings Bryan at Dayton, Tennessee to the re-entry of American Evangelicals into the political process, spurred, in large measure, by the abortion license. As a picture of America at mid-century it was a reasonable facsimile of the way that civic and religious matters were often reconciled. It was not, however, an accurate picture of the relations before 1925 nor was it an accurate rendition of relations in the new world that was coming into existence.

One of Hart's central points is that "civic piety is the rhetorical cognate of disestablishment."[6] Yet, we know that the rhetoric of civic piety predated formal disestablishment by at least 150 years. America imaged as "God's New Israel," as a "city set upon a hill," as the "redeemer nation" who had been "chosen" by God to make an "errand into the wilderness" is language that dates from 1630 forward.[7] The Puritan jeremiad was a rhetorical form that specifically linked the behavior of the civic realm with the blessings and/or curses of the spiritual or religious realm. What started as a purely religious rhetorical form in the Hebrew Scriptures became a civil-religious form in the hands of the American Puritans and their descendants.[8] Even today, American politicians often use what Kurt Ritter calls the "secular jeremiad" to accomplish their purely political purposes.[9] So, precisely in what sense civic piety is a "rhetorical cognate" of disestablishment is unclear.

Perhaps what Hart means is that civic piety parallels in the rhetorical realm what disestablishment accomplished in the legal realm. Or, perhaps he means that civic piety became the *lingua franca* of disestablishment. Whatever his precise intent, it is clear that the rhetoric of civic piety continued, unabated, after formal disestablishment. Was it the only kind of language used to figure relations between religion and government? No. Many religionists continued to use the purely theological/moral language of biblical revelation without resort to civic pieties. Indeed, it is widely recognized that the American polity of the nineteenth century was dominated by a Protestant ethos, an ethos expressed both in the language of religion and the language of civil-religion.[10]

But just as the "government" was an ever-changing entity, so, too, was "religion." What started at the beginning of the nineteenth century as an overwhelmingly Protestant ethos had become, by the beginning of the twentieth century, a Protestant-Catholic ethos and by 1925 a Protestant-Catholic-Jew ethos. It is this tripartite division of Protestant-Catholic-Jew that Hart seems to presume in his book. He calls it "mainline religion." This was the "official" religion of the Republic as it emerged from World War I. This ethos so dominated American culture in the mid-twentieth century that Will Herberg, writing in 1955, could identify it with "the American Way of Life."[11] Of course, that "Way" was never quite as pluralistic as its terms seemed to imply. Protestant meant the mainline, liberal Protestant establishment as represented, for example, by the National Council of Churches. Evangelical protestants, who were not part of the National Council, were excluded from the formula. Catholic meant the American Bishops and their political stances. Blue-collar, ethnic Catholics, especially those who tried to retain their cultural heritage and traditions, were not part of the equation. And Jew meant mostly Reform Judaism, with an occasional nod to Conservative Jews. Orthodox Jews were never included in what passed as establishment religion.

But all of that began to change in the 1970s. Evangelicals and Fundamentalists, who had largely abandoned the public square following the Scopes Trial, began to reconsider their estrangement from American culture and politics. Ironically, the vehicle of their return to national politics was that born-again Baptist Democrat, Jimmy Carter. At the same time, blue-collar Catholics were coming to the realization that neither the Bishops nor the labor unions necessarily represented their views. Likewise, Orthodox Jews began to sense an estrangement of their own from an American culture that seemed to worship the self, oppose various forms of private, religion-based education, and bask in the abortion license. All of these forces came together, in 1980, to elect Ronald Reagan and neither the religious nor the political map has ever been the same.[12]

So, when Professor Hart issued *The Political Pulpit* in 1977, he was on the cusp of a major revolution in religion-government relations. Indeed, the revolution had already begun, but neither its existence nor its implications were acknowledged in the book. According to Hart, the "contract" between the parties was this: religion agrees to stay out of electoral politics and governance in exchange for the right to display the rhetoric of civic piety on ritualized occasions of state such as inaugurations, Fourth of July celebrations, bicentennial events, presidential prayer breakfasts, and the like. Religion's role is symbolic and rhetorical only, and when it dares to speak its name outside of these carefully circumscribed boundaries, it is to be met with disdain, umbrage, and, ultimately, rejection.

Reading that last sentence in 2002 simply underscores my thesis that much has changed. Between the time that Hart issued his book and today, we've had the Religious Roundtable, The Christian Voice, The Moral Majority, Concerned Women for America, The American Family Association, The Family Research Council and, of course, the Christian Coalition. All of these groups—and many others on both the Left and the Right—have sought to bring religious and moral values to bear on questions of public policy and governance. They have sought to do so not, for the most part, through the church or synagogue as an institution, but rather as citizens joining together in political compacts or associations that draw from the church and synagogue but which have a corporate existence quite apart from those institutions. This poses two related difficulties for Hart's contractual approach.

First, Hart's contract involves "organized religion" as a main party. But the Christian Coalition is not an organized religion in any meaningful sense of that term. It is a political organization made up of citizens with common moral and ethical values who come from a fairly wide range of institutional religious backgrounds and who act not in the name of the church or religion, but in the name of themselves as citizens who have made common cause to affect the socio-political landscape.[13]

This leads directly to the second problem with Hart's formulation. His "citizenry" party to the contract appears to have no structural relationship to the "organized religion" part of the agreement. It's almost as though the three parties are conceived as being totally separate from one another, with little or no overlap. Obviously this is not the case. People who are members of organized religions can, in their capacities as citizens, act out their personal moral and ethical agendas in the political arena. To the extent that their fellow citizens agree with or support those beliefs, they may be able to enact that agenda as public policy.

So, just as "government" and "organized religion" have changed over time, so, too, has the nature of "citizenship."[14] We are all familiar with the limitations placed on citizenship at the time the Constitution was drafted. And we are familiar with the progressive enfranchisement of various groups, particularly African Americans and women. Yet, it is only recently that we have become aware of the enfranchisement or empowerment of another group—Americans with deeply held religious values, most of which have their source in the Bible, as interpreted by those Americans. It is not that this "group" was ever specifically disenfranchised (although there are specific cases where some were); rather, it is that they disenfranchised themselves in the 1920s by intentionally withdrawing from the larger society and specifically from such "worldly" preoccupations as politics.

It was the "discovery" of this values-based group that led pollster Richard Wirthlin to formulate the strategy—based on an appeal to "family, work, neighborhood, peace, and freedom"—that led to the election of Ronald Reagan in 1980.[15] It is a different kind of demographic than race or gender, but it is a demographic nonetheless—and one with powerful predictive value, according to Wirthlin and others.[16] Of course, what Wirthlin discovered had always been there, but it had not always been socially or politically engaged. Once engaged, however, it proved to be a powerful force for change. The old formula of Protestant-Catholic-Jew would suffice no longer.

Talking Religion in the Civic Realm

One result of this revolution in the relationship between religion and government has been a marked change in the kind of language used both by politicians and by religiously motivated clergy and laypeople. This change has happened alongside of the traditional rhetoric of civic piety, not in place of it. One can still find the traditional civil-religious formulas at play on ritualized occasions of state. But alongside of these formulas one also finds a new, more personalized, more religion-specific language being used. If space permitted, I believe I could illustrate a continuing trend toward more religion-specific language, starting in the mid-1970s and progressing to the present. However, let me just point to some examples from the 2000 presidential election campaign to illustrate my point.

When asked to name his favorite philosopher during the primary campaign, George W. Bush answered, "Jesus Christ."[17] Alan Keyes, another of the Republican hopefuls, took Bush to task on the ground that "Jesus Christ is my God and Savior. He's not a philosopher."[18] At the Iowa Republican TV debate in December of 1999, George W. Bush told the audience: "When you turn your heart and your life over to Christ, when you accept Christ as the savior, it changes your heart and changes your life and that's what happened to me."[19] During the New Hampshire primary, Keyes noted that "At every stage of what we do in this campaign, we rely on prayer and we trust in God's will. We rely on our faith and we work in that fashion."[20]

Appearing on the TV magazine *60 Minutes*, Al Gore claimed to be a "born-again Christian" and endorsed "faith-based organizations" as conduits for distributing social services to the poor and needy.[21] "I believe in keeping my faith as the center of my life and everything I do," Gore told the *Catholic Digest*.[22] Speaking to the interracial congregation at the Potter's House in Dallas, Texas, Gore lashed out at the "cultural pollution" that has defaced American society, noting: "I believe that the purpose of life is to glorify God."[23] As one reporter noted, "In an 18-minute address, the vice president quoted Scripture four times, recited portions of a hymn and recounted two Bible stories."[24] On election day, Gore visited African American churches, urging the congregants to "take your souls to the polls."[25]

Democratic vice-presidential candidate Joe Lieberman was, perhaps, the most outspoken of all about the relationship of his faith to his politics. The first Jew to run on a major party ticket, Lieberman seemed to bask in the celebration of his faith. "[My family adheres] to a lot of the . . . values and the laws that come right out of Old Testament," he proclaimed.[26] He called for "a place for faith in America's public life" and told an audience at the University of Notre Dame: "Let us break through some of the inhibitions that have existed to talk together across the flimsy lines of separation of faith, to talk together, to study together, to pray together, and ultimately to sing together His Holy name."[27]

But it was not just politicians who spoke the language of particular religious convictions. So, too, did many clergy, both verbally and nonverbally. At the Allen African American Episcopal Church in New York City, the Reverend Floyd Flake endorsed Al Gore from the pulpit, then turned the pulpit over to the vice president for a political talk. In Detroit, the Reverend E.L. Branch of the Third New Hope Missionary Baptist Church urged his parishioners to vote for John McCain as a way of disrupting the Michigan primary vote and preventing a Bush win.[28]

The Christian Coalition was, of course, actively working on behalf of George W. Bush.[29] Also in Bush's corner was the Reverend Billy Graham. Just two days before the election, Bush arrived in Jacksonville, Florida, where he started the day at a prayer service attended by Dr. Graham. Emerging from the service, Graham noted: "I don't endorse candidates. But I've come as close to it, I guess, now as anytime in my life, because I think it's extremely important. We have in our state absentee voting. I've already voted. I'll just let you guess who I voted for."[30]

Whatever else one might say about this rhetoric, one thing is clear: this is not the rhetoric of civic piety or of traditional civil religion. This is not the religion of the Republic as described by scholars of American history nor is it the bland Deism of the Founders. Here we find no references to "Nature and Nature's God," or the hand of the "Creator," or the agency of "Divine Providence." Instead, we find particular beliefs, articulated within the framework of a campaign for public office, and offered as either the motivation for or the value structure underlying specific public policies such as funding of faith-based organizations, support for content restrictions in film, television, and popular culture, education vouchers, increased funding for education, support for tougher environmental standards, and a host of other public policy issues. Such rhetors are not playing by the unspoken rules or the implicit designs of Hart's contract, nor have they been doing so for the last 25 years. What is going on?

Toward a New Construct for the Twenty-first Century

What is going on—and has been going on for at least the last 25 years—is the reemergence of one segment of the electorate to full participation in the rhetorical barnyard that constitutes the "public square" in America. This segment is American Evangelicalism. Having earlier abandoned the public square in the 1920s, the Evangelicals, along with their Fundamentalist allies, returned in full force in the 1970s. Concurrent with this return of theologically conservative Protestants was the rhetorical awakening of millions of traditional Roman Catholics, an awakening brought about almost entirely by the Supreme Court's ruling in *Roe v. Wade* which, for the first time in American history, made abortion a legally protected right. By the end of the 1970s, Evangelicals, Fundamentalists, Catholics, and Orthodox Jews were joining together to reassert their right to participate *as equals* in American political life.

Part of the reemergence of these groups—the most public part—became manifested in organizations such as The Moral Majority, founded in 1979 by the

Reverend Jerry Falwell. Such organizations came into being for the explicit purpose of taking an active part in the political life of the nation—and trying to energize what was believed to be a huge electoral base by encouraging fellow believers to join with them. However, I believe that the more important development—at least for our purposes—was the intellectual revolt, led primarily by neoconservatives such as Richard John Neuhaus, Peter L. Berger, Michael Novak, and others, that both articulated a rationale for allowing religion to re-enter the public square and illustrated, through both scholarly and popular writing, the nature of the contribution that could be made by religiously motivated and informed public rhetors.[31]

Proceeding from a Tocquevillian perspective, Neuhaus and others argued that religion was not only one of the important mediating structures in a culture, but the most important one, and that by ignoring religion or trying to marginalize it, one risked the very possibility of a liberal polity. As Neuhaus puts it: "Our question can certainly not be the old one of whether religion and politics should be mixed. They inescapably do mix, like it or not. The question is whether we can devise forms for that interaction which can revive rather than destroy the liberal democracy that is required by a society that would be pluralistic and free."[32]

To build their case, the neo-conservatives began at the beginning, with the Founding of the Republic. Their argument was straightforward. At the beginning, and throughout most of American history, religious values were central to governance. As Harold J. Berman noted: "the role played by government in the social life of America in the 1780s (and for almost a century and a half thereafter) was openly and strongly influenced and directed by religion."[33] Far from there being hostility between government and religion, there was an amicable relationship between the democratic form of government and American religiosity. Since the Founders specifically noted that human rights were inalienable because they were grounded in the nature of God—that Americans had been "endowed by their Creator" with such rights—"religion and democratic self-rule were at the outset all but indissolubly linked."[34]

Having grounded their analysis in the American experience, these intellectuals then went about the task of formulating a theory of the public square. Their position was that the public square, by definition, can never be completely naked. That is, one can try to remove all religious influences from culture, society, and politics, but the meaning vacuum will still be filled by someone with something. In this case, it will be filled by the state with beliefs and values that are relative to the historical moment. As Neuhaus writes:

> The state is not waiting with a set of absolute values of its own
> or with a ready-made religion. Far from waiting with a package
> of absolutes, in a society where the remnants of procedural de
> mocracy survive the state may be absolutely committed only
> to the relativization of all values. In that instance, however,
> the relativity of all things becomes the absolute. Without the

counter-claims of "meaning-bestowing" institutions of religion, there is not an absence of religion but, rather, the triumph of the religion of relativity.[35]

Traditional religions and people of all religious faiths must, therefore, help to repopulate the public square with ideas, beliefs, values, and attitudes that can counter the march toward relativity. In so doing, such people, far from harming democracy, will actually be insuring its continuation since there exists "an inherent and necessary relationship between democracy and pluralism."[36] As Neuhaus explains: "Pluralism, in this connection, does not mean simply that there are many different kinds of people and institutions in societal play. More radically than that, it means that there are contenders striving with one another to define what the play is about—what are the rules and what the goal."[37] This, then, is the first step toward insuring the continued viability of liberal democracy—to make sure that all parties, including religious ones, have a voice in the ongoing dialogue. Religious voices and values must not be shut out or shunted off to the side as happens, for example, when people claim that religion is a—"private" matter that has no place at the table of political give and take.

As legal scholar Stephen L. Carter notes: "We do no credit to the idea of religious freedom when we talk as though religious belief is something of which public-spirited adults should be ashamed."[38] "What is needed," Carter holds,

> is not a requirement that the religiously devout choose a form of dialogue that liberalism accepts, but that liberalism develop a politics that accepts whatever form of dialogue a member of the public offers. Epistemic diversity, like diversity of other kinds, should be cherished, not ignored, and certainly not abolished. What is needed, then, is a willingness to *listen*, not because the speaker has *the right voice* but because the speaker has *the right to speak*. Moreover, the willingness to listen must hold out the possibility that the speaker is saying something worth listening to; to do less is to trivialize the forces that shape the moral convictions of tens of millions of Americans.[39]

And that, in the final analysis, is the answer to Hart's "contract." It is a contract that never should have been ratified in the first place because it makes of religiously inclined people second-class citizens. It presumes a wall of separation not only between Church and State, but also between religion, government, and the citizenry—a wall that should not be erected and cannot be sustained. What is needed is a construct, not a contract; a porous screen door, not an impregnable wall between citizens, their mediating structures, and their government. The construct should be that of civic—and civil—engagement. Such a construct would affirm all voices—whether religious, secular, or civil-religious—as legitimate participants in the conversation that is American democracy. Such a construct would judge the worth of the arguments, not their source or motivation. Such a construct would depend, exclusively, on the abilities of all parties to persuade others. In the final analysis, that is what democracy is all about.

Hart's "contract" is a good *description* of the implicit rules of the game between religion and government from 1925 to 1975. It must not become a *prescription* for the future. For my own part, I would much rather know that Al Gore considers himself to be a born-again Christian, that Dick Cheney believes religion to be a private matter, that George W. Bush has the endorsement of Billy Graham, and that Joe Lieberman is looking forward to the day when we may all sing with one voice. Until that day, I will be satisfied to know that while we may not all be singing off of the same page, at least we have all been issued a songbook and can freely join in the singing whenever the spirit, be it religious or secular, moves us.

Chapter 13

Official and Unofficial Civil Religious Discourse

Steven R. Goldzwig

> [W]e Americans are the peculiar, chosen people—the Is-
> rael of our time, we bear the ark of the liberties of the
> world.
>
> —Herman Melville[1]

Rod Hart's *The Political Pulpit* remains a landmark work in rhetorical studies.[2]
Hart's analysis of civil religion and his characterization of the rhetorical properties of American civic piety still have resonance some twenty-five years later.
Perhaps Hart's greatest contribution is the careful case he presents for the unique
contribution rhetoric (and a rhetorician) can make to the discussion and understanding of civil religion in America. In pursuing this goal, Hart added a dimension to American, political, and religious studies that had been largely ignored.
Like some other scholars at the time—and Robert Bellah was first among
them—Hart set about arguing the importance of American civil religion as a
heuristic metaphor and, going further, isolated its perdurable rhetorical features.
In specific terms, Hart's careful argument on Bellah's misappropriation of the
term "religion" as the larger umbrella term for the phenomenon under study was
and remains a significant contribution to the literature on civil religion.[3] The term
"civic piety" was effectively argued as a more felicitous nomenclature. Moreover, Hart, unlike Bellah, was able and willing to distinguish between "official"
and "unofficial" civil religion. However, the bulk of Hart's study focused on "official" or "mainstream" civil religious discourse. Those civil religious speakers,
groups, and organizations displaying sectarian, partisan, and overtly ideological
proclivities were largely beyond the scope of Hart's study.[4]

    Hart's alternative to Bellah's model was a rhetorical model: "Civic piety, in
America at least, emerges not so much from blind momentary passion, but from
a knowing, practiced, thoroughly pragmatic understanding of the suasory ara-

besques demanded when God and country kick up their heels rhetorically."[5] Part of the relationship described here is one of unstated contract between the political and religious establishments. Hart employs the contract metaphor as a heuristic device. That contract provides that each party adopt the "guise" of separation, that employment of mainstream religion by the politician will be mainly rhetorical, and that each party will refrain overtly overstepping its bounds rhetorically.[6] Rabid "public theologians" are prone to do violence to this contract. The contract is informed by three primary principles: "that religion can provide an ultimate meaning system for its adherents, that government is able to exert coercive influence on the affairs of its citizens, and that both government and religion wield considerable rhetorical power."[7] As Hart summarizes, "In short, religion gives us faith in faith. And when religion shares the motivational cosmos with government, it becomes only a short emotional step from faith to patriotism and from God to country—presuming, of course, that our political leaders have their rhetorical wits about them."[8] Thus, "the philosophical power of religion and the coercive influence of the state are buttressed equally by their ability to use *rhetoric* often and well" [emphasis added].[9]

Both religion and the state are sources of power. Yet they remain unequal partners. The state has coercive power while religion can only revert to symbolic influence. Thus, Hart argues, the state has existential jurisdiction over the citizenry and various institutions while the church has rhetorical jurisdiction over the American people. The rhetorical strategies of civic piety as gleaned from "official" sources—i.e., expedient complexity, nonexistential content, ritualistic presence, and prosaic animus, help ensure that the contract survives. In Hart's view Americans revel in talk and that symbolic state is the key to preserving the contract. As Hart notes, "should some far-sighted prelate or politician fail to notice the fine print imbedded in the civil-religious contract and . . . misperceive its rhetorical nature, the American people will come a-marching . . . [S]o let both clergyman and congressman be warned—civic piety, not civil religion, is the order of this and every day in these tenuously united states of ours."[10] These insights and conclusions, among others, represent a major contribution. Hart taught us how such discourse functions and why it is indeed a significantly powerful form of "talk" in the national religio-political and cultural lexicon.

Civil Religious Discourse and the Presidency

One need only consult traditional public sources to confirm that "official" civil religious discourse as described by Hart perseveres. Perhaps the most dominant public source of "official" civil religious discourse inheres in the national consciousness through the auspices of the presidency. Richard Pierard and Robert Linder maintain that, "historically speaking, the presidency has been intimately linked to civil religion, and this has bonded the presidency to religious Americans."[11] Whether encountered in a prophetic or priestly version, civil religion "represents an alliance between politics and religion at the national level, resting on a politicized ideological base: (1) there is a God; (2) his will can be known and fulfilled through democratic procedures; (3) America has been God's primary agent in modern history; and (4) the nation is the chief source of identity for Americans in both a political and religious sense. According to this outlook, Americans are God's chosen people, a New Israel which made the exodus to the promised Land across the sea and became a 'city on a hill,' a light to the nations, proclaiming the message of democracy as the salvific doctrine that will lead the human race to freedom, prosperity, and happiness."[12] The President is the "pontifex maximus" of American civil religion.[13] According to esteemed church historian Martin E. Marty, Ronald Reagan "politicized and exulted civil religion to its highest point in American history."[14] But all presidents have carried on the tradition of civil religious discourse.

In his inaugural address, George W. Bush, like his predecessors, resurrected obligatory "official" or "mainstream" civil religious discourse.[15] Bush identified God as the source of our national unity and indicated that God's work must truly be our own: "Our unity, our union, is the serious work of leaders and citizens in every generation. And this is my solemn pledge: I will work to build a single nation of justice and opportunity . . . I know this is in our reach because we are guided by a power larger than ourselves who creates us in His image." God's hand is upon this nation and guides its efforts: "Americans are generous and strong and decent, not because we believe in ourselves, but because we hold beliefs beyond ourselves. When this spirit of citizenship is missing, no government program can replace it. When this spirit is present, no wrong can stand against it." This is reinforced with biblical allusions: "And I can pledge our nation to a goal: When we see that wounded traveler on the road to Jericho, we will not pass to the other side."

God's hand in directing America and its cause is the same now as it was when our forefathers founded this nation: "After the Declaration of Independence was signed, Virginia statesman John Page wrote to Thomas Jefferson: 'We know the race is not to the swift nor the battle to the strong. Do you not think an angel rides in the whirlwind and directs this storm' . . . Much time has passed since Jefferson arrived for his inauguration. The years and changes accumulate. But the themes of this day he would know: our nation's grand story of courage and its simple dream of dignity . . . We are not this story's [A]uthor, who fills time and eternity with [H]is purpose. Yet [H]is purpose is achieved in our duty, and our duty is fulfilled in service to one another . . . The work continues, the story goes on. And an angel still rides in the whirlwind and directs this storm . . . God bless you all, and God bless America." Thus we have an amorphous God calling us to unity and purpose, self-sacrifice and mission, setting us upon a path of rebirth and renewal and a president, in highly recognizable form of symbolic summons, coaxing us to our better angels in the practice of republican virtues. There is classic symbolic inducement in the words and mythic construction in the interpretation.

George W. Bush also performed the priestly function often required by American civil religion in his moving call for a "National Day of Prayer" in his address at the National Cathedral on September 20, 2001.[16] Indeed, in times of national crisis and national shock, grief, and mourning, civil religious discourse provides a rhetorical call to recommit ourselves to national purpose and resolve: "America is a nation full of good fortune, with so much to be grateful for. But we are not spared from suffering. In every generation, the world has produced enemies of human freedom. They have attacked America, because we are freedom's home and defender. And the commitment of our fathers is now the calling of our time." And: "On this national day of prayer and remembrance, we ask almighty God to watch over our nation, and grant us patience and resolve in all that is to come. We pray that He will comfort and console those who now walk in sorrow. We thank Him for each life we must now mourn, and the promise of a life to come." Bush dutifully and fittingly performs his priestly function of national assurance and national blessing by concluding: "As we have been assured, neither death nor life, nor angels nor principalities nor powers, nor things present nor things to come, nor height nor depth, can separate us from God's love. May He bless the souls of the departed. May He comfort our own. And may He always guide our country . . . God bless America." Bush's words confirm the following claim offered by Pierard and Linder: "One must not forget that American society contains a significant religious component and civil religion plays a key role in establishing national unity by promoting a common religious faith."[17]

Having confirmed that civic piety as outlined by Hart and as described by Pierard and Linder is still fully alive and healthy in America, the question of why such discourse perseveres is open to dispute. So too, of course, are the judgments and evaluations regarding the proper interpretation of this discourse. Scholarship on civil religion has occasioned ongoing, often vexing disputes over the originality, definition, existence, and efficacy of such a concept. Given space constraints, I have neither the hope nor the intention of doing justice to this large body of scholarly work. In the remainder of this essay, I would like to direct my comments to three sets of innate tensions which inhere in civil religion and its narratives: (1) church and state, (2) republicanism and liberalism, and (3) pluralism and secularism.

Church and State

The dual obligations posed by religion and the state place the religiously inclined into a de facto dual citizenship. As individuals presumed under allegiance to the service of two masters, it is not surprising that there will be, at times, and under certain circumstances and situations, divided loyalties and inevitable conflicts. While some argue that church and state might work best if each acknowledges its own limitations and neither oversteps its proper boundaries and interests, it is a difficult terrain to navigate in a circumspect fashion.

Let the sacred serve the secular when it seems propitious, and the secular will defer by adumbrating a "hands off" approach to religious affairs, verbally promoting both separation of church and state and a concomitant advocacy of religious freedom. But in any particular era, this "silent agreement" sometimes seems strained; at times, the covenant can even seem "broken." At such times, scholarly attention to civil religious narratives is even more necessary and our critical interpretations are perhaps more immediately relevant. When civil law conflicts with religious conscience and the rhetorics of the state are at loggerheads with the rhetorics of religion, the more unsavory, hard to navigate undercurrents of civil religion are sometimes laid bare. The teeming contradictions, inconsistencies, and sometimes, downright unparallel universes can be exposed like live wires whipping in a virulent thunderstorm.

My own take on developing a useful method of accounting for civil religious discourse is to investigate the ways and means the state and/or its surrogates appropriate and employ religious symbols as a means of pursuing particular interests. In turn, we also must address how religious sects, groups, or individuals try to influence the state. Thus, part of the task of exploring the rhetoric of civil religion in general is to characterize and catalogue state-inspired-and-led references to God and godly-values that imbue the state with transcendent appeal *as well as* religious-inspired-and-led references to God and godly values that either bless or challenge the political status quo. I believe these discursive activities vitally affect our interpretations of civil religion in any particular era and they have significant implications for church-state relations.

It is probably important to point out the obvious in this context. Some strains of what Hart might label "unofficial" civil religion take on a decidedly liberal or conservative character in aim or goal, if not tone. Certainly the civil religious discourse of Martin Luther King, Jr. and Jesse Jackson, for example, differs markedly in its goals than that of the Reverend Jerry Falwell and Pat Robertson. The Southern Christian Leadership Conference is not the Christian Coalition. Having pointed out the obvious, it does seem to me a potentially useful scholarly enterprise to examine the inherent similarities and differences that might append here. At a minimum, detecting and accounting for the differences between the prophetic and priestly voices reverberating in these liberal and conservative strands of discourse may contribute to a further understanding of the phenomenon discussed in these pages. In addition, rhetorics of "rights" and "virtues" both potentially contribute to "national moral character" and thus are *both* worthy of further investigation. Moreover, whether the unofficial strain is "liberal" or "conservative," the discourse and the actions of the interlocutors involved may at times impel the state into coercive action. That is, when pressed, the state has few qualms about suppressing religion when necessary. As Thomas Jefferson remarked, "it is time enough for the rightful purposes of civil government for its officers to interfere when principles break out into overt acts against peace and good order."[18]

Reference to the coercive power of the state occasions another vexing thought. It seems that not all forms of "official" civil religion promote benign republican virtues, nor do all "serve the people." Some have proposed that this is also true of civil religious discourse in the United States. Even those who firmly believe that civil religion is a harmless piece of manipulative stitchery that helps attach delicate patches to the intricate mosaic of the national quilt must admit that there is no inviolate guarantee that this will always be the case. What seems beyond dispute is that civil religious discourse can be employed by the state to mask and sometimes advance raw power. Rather than being "amicably divorced" from political society, civil religion might be integral to advancing the aims of repressive regimes. Marcela Cristi cites such cases in Spain, Malaysia, Chile, and China.[19]

Republicanism and Liberalism

Susan Okin, in a review of Michael Sandel's *Democracy's Discontent*,[20] notes that in America, historians have bemoaned the eclipse of community by individualism at least since 1650.[21] Okin argues that Sandel approaches the latter part of the twentieth century as demonstration of the failure of individualism. More precisely, Sandel contrasts republicans with liberals. Sandel valorizes republicans, who through the practice of civic virtue, come to understand the importance of self-government as a means of serving the common good. Republicans thus are portrayed as focused on character and civic virtue. Republican virtue comes from the distinct understanding that citizens are "obligated to fulfill ends we have not chosen."[22] This view adumbrates the concept of the "encumbered" self, i.e., the creation and implementation of a self that recognizes and enacts innate fundamental duties to others.

For Sandel, liberals value and defend "free and independent selves, unencumbered by moral or civic ties they have not chosen."[23] Here individual rights are said to have precedence over majority decisions. Okin asserts Sandel locates liberalism's "great error" in its failure to engage the great moral issues in political life. If Okin is correct (and I believe she states the case well), Sandel's polarized, manichaean account of "good" republicans and "bad" liberals, certainly can be related to the discussion of civil religion. It matters very much if "rights" discourse is *actually* trumping that of traditional "republican virtues." How this plays out and what difference it will make in the twenty-first century version of the American dream is, to my mind, quite consequential. Nevertheless, as Okin rightly observes, the fact of the matter is "there have always been strong liberal and republican currents in U.S. political discourse . . . and . . . these currents often coexist in the beliefs of the same thinker."[24] Okin poses the following question: "What civic virtues matter here and now?" Another "tough question" is: Can "the independence required of republican citizens . . . co-exist with capitalism on any scale at all [?]."[25] One might also add that increasing globalization will impact the concept and the conduct of nationhood. The unique forms of civil religion in the United States and those of other nations in the international community need to be monitored, analyzed, and evaluated, especially for major changes in both the strength and contour of civil religious discourse. Transnational developments in civil religious discourse may affect the U.S. of the future.

A Note on the Future

The future, of course, is filled with new challenges. In the aftermath of September 11, Americans are discovering that the traditional three-faith system (Protestant-Catholic-Jew) identified by Will Herberg may have to be revised.[26] The traditions of Islam have become important, not just because Americans are newly curious after having experienced immense tragedy, but also because there is now a significant portion of American citizens who identify with and practice Islam. There are now over 7 million Muslims in the United States. Many experts believe that the increasing Muslim numbers are eclipsing that of the U.S. Jewish population. In the process of opening up to the changed religio-cultural terrain and in response to the terrible events of September 11, Americans from the comfortable traditions of the three-faith system have also had to confront their own limited understanding of the religious tenets and cultural practices of American citizens who are simultaneously practicing Muslims, Buddhists, Hindus, and Sikhs. While a religion like Islam may be able to comfortably engage "official" forms of civic piety, it is unclear how well it can or will live with "unofficial" sources of civil religious discourse, especially the more virulent strains. In any event, the increasing presence of differing religious confessions is likely to affect, if not alter, certain interpretations and audience reactions—and, therefore, has the potential to alter rhetorical pronouncements. How this takes place and how we as a nation reinterpret civil religious discourse in the face of these changes, of course, remains an open question.

Pluralism and Secularism

One likely place where changes in religious lexicons might be detected is in the dispute over the integrative and legitimation functions of American civil religious discourse as handed down by tradition. Two very large trends could tend to further mitigate or vitiate those functions: the increased internal religious and cultural pluralism alluded to above and increased secularism. While Americans are overwhelmingly religious, they are also increasingly wooed by the secular culture and its material enticements. Brief examples will have to suffice in this context. Increasing pluralism, on its face, can be viewed as a force in mitigating the purported integrative and legitmation functions of civil religion. As Cristi points out, the "positive" attributes of American civil religion, including its alleged role in "nation-building, moral order, national identity and solidarity, and its purported function in building and sustaining community have yet to be empirically verified."[27] Perhaps, Cristi theorizes, civil religion plays such a role with elites, but the jury is still out on how powerful and effective civil religious discourse is with marginalized peoples both in the United States and elsewhere. Peoples of color and those in underresourced communities may have very different interpretations of civil religious discourse. Rhetoricians need to take notice of and document such differences. One thinks of the patriotic tunes "My Country 'Tis of Thee" and "God Bless America" as ultimate expressions of civil religion. Yet those songs have not produced totalizing identifications. In America, we still have the ongoing phenomenon of the African American "national anthem," the perennial song sung at many Martin Luther King, Jr. Day celebrations across this nation, "Lift Every Voice."

Acceptance of civil religious discourse as a viable American discursive practice seems to require a faith that people find assurance in appeals to the sacred in
promotion of the secular. In giving ourselves over to the rhetoric of civic piety,
for example, we are somehow involved in both condoning and promoting a
community of values important to a democratic state, important, in particular, to
a uniquely American vision and set of values—liberty, freedom, equality, justice,
and fair play. As previously discussed, it is assumed that religion-inspired virtues
can sustain democratic republics. The values associated with civil religion, however, compete with other important value clusters and they often compete inter-
nally as well. Indeed, secular values have played a key role in competing against,
if not diminishing republican virtues. As Richard Fenn has made clear,[28] consensus in America may as easily be forged on efficiency, rule of the experts, and the
demands of the market.[29] While George W. Bush has played a key role as inter-
preter-in-chief of the new American civil religion of the twenty-first century, that
role was occasioned by the crisis of 9/11. As Cristi observes, civil religion "may
be something that varies with particular historical or national circumstances.
Consequently civil religious themes would tend to emerge or become more visible in periods of national or international crises."[30] But even here Bush's "value
message" was mixed. One method Bush recommended for helping America "get
back to normal" was for each American to resume his or her role as a consumer
as an antidote to the damage done by September 11 and a flagging economy.
While his recent calls for self-sacrifice through a two-year pledge of public service (utilizing the existing Peace Corp and Americorp) are in line with republican
virtues, the former call seemed geared toward "individualism" and free enterprise. Thus, selfish motives seem destined to compete with the selfless in the new
world order of civil religion.

According to Ronald F. Theimann, "The greatest challenge facing American
democracy today is to develop 'pluralist citizens,' people capable of living in a
variety of different and sometimes conflicting worlds of meaning while still
maintaining a robust sense of personal and communal identity."[31] How far present and future forms of civil religious discourse will go in helping Americans
meet this challenge remains an open question. It is a question, however, that
rhetoricians, following Rod Hart's legacy, still seem well-positioned to answer.

Chapter 14

Broken Covenants and the American Pantheon
Church and State 25 Years after *The Political Pulpit*

Mark A. Gring

> Every social order rests on a creed, on a concept of life
> and law, and represents a religion in action. Culture is a
> religion externalized.
>
> —Rushdoony[1]

> The simple and private association is a society and sym-
> biosis initiated by a special covenant (*pactum*) among the
> members for the purpose of bringing together and holding
> in common a particular interest (*quid peculiare*). . . . Such
> an association can rightly be called primary and all other
> derivative from it.
>
> —Althusius[2]

The Roman emperor Tiberius received information from Palestine that showed
the truth of Christ's divinity, claims Tertullian, and thus proposed that an image
of Jesus Christ be placed in the Roman Pantheon (V.xxii).[3] This suggestion, re-
buffed by the Roman Senate, could be perceived as an astute attempt by Tiberius
to integrate the Christians into the Roman culture. The Christians, if they had
been asked, would have rejected this offer because they claimed an exclusive
position for Jesus Christ as God and they refused to worship any other deity. This
exclusionist attitude enraged the polytheistic Romans who charged them with
crimes claiming they were atheists, subversive to the government, and sexually
permissive.[4] Tacitus reminds us that the Christians were executed not because of
any penchant to burn Rome but because of their "antisocial tendencies."[5] The
charge of being antisocial may once again be leveled against Christians who op-

pose the theistic pluralism that characterizes our statist religion and who seek, instead, to influence all dimensions of life by their Christian world-and-life-view.

The question that drives this essay is what is the current relationship between church and state in the U.S. and how does rhetoric fit into that relationship? In addition to the overarching question are the following questions. Does Rod Hart's rhetorical contract still exist?[6] If it exists, in what form does it exist? If it does not, then why not? The contention of this essay is that the current church and state relationship exists in an ever-increasing tension because the previous assumption of a covenantal relationship between God, Church, government, and society was discarded; the covenantal paradigm was not replaced with a secular paradigm but with a different religious paradigm, the American Pantheon with its own creed, dogmas, myths and heroes. I contend that Hart's social-rhetorical contract never existed; there never was a mutually agreed upon *quid pro quo* arrangement between church and state. What Hart discovered was the discourse of the American civic religion—the new statist religion.

The discarded covenantal relationship was that which many religious Americans believe was formulated in Israel, passed down through the discourse of the early church, rediscovered by the Reformation and introduced to the New World by the Pilgrims and Puritans. The result of discarding the presumed covenant with God is that our discourse now resides in the newly dedicated American Pantheon, which was initiated long ago but has been consecrated by the blood of the 9/11 (2001) martyrs. Though it is not yet the sole religion, the American civic religion is the controlling religious hegemony that claims to be inclusive of all spiritual standpoints but excludes those religious perspectives deemed intolerant and dogmatic. Historic Christianity, with its exclusionist claims, is now the counter hegemony; it is a competing movement, sparked by the fervor of the Reformation and the American Puritans that attempts a gradual transformation of society based upon God's laws. Fueled by this polarity we are now situated at the precipice of heightened cultural disagreements and religious warfare. This sociopolitical warfare pits the discursive practices of the statist religion, currently defined by American civic religion, against those who contend for the sovereignty of Christ and the supremacy of God's laws over all areas of life.[7]

Roderick P. Hart's *Political Pulpit* presents a description of the late twentieth century developments of this statist religion, which he labeled the rhetorical contract. Hart dismisses the theological implications of this contract and accords it accolades because of its pluralistic tolerance, its potential for creating a perception of unity, and its ability to reduce apparent exigencies during times of crises.[8] Hart's perspective dismisses the assertion that every social order rests on a creed (or covenant—as per Althusius) that is the embodiment of its religion. Thus, in 1977 Hart was unable to recognize that his "rhetorical contract" embodied the hegemonic characteristics of the statist religion that was challenging the position historic Christianity had occupied previously in the United States. In essence, Hart ignores the effects of the Protestant Reformation on American sociopolitical formations, the essential religious nature of humanity, and the degree to which the discursive practices of the American statist religion was replacing the discursive practices based on the Biblical-covenantal relationship for church and state.

In an attempt to avoid a similar myopia, this essay will consider key ideas from the Reformation in order to present a more complete description and analysis of the current church and state relationship. The essay begins with the limitations of Hart's analysis, argues for the central role of covenant in Judeo-Christian religious discourse and early American Church-state discourse, and then presents examples from two competing religious paradigms that comprise the current church and state relationship.

Hart's Analysis Is Incomplete

Hart's description of the rhetorical contract, as apt as it is, fails to show us the degree to which we have abandoned our previous understandings of the covenantal relationships and obligations. I do not deny the accuracy of his description; I agree with it. Hart's rhetorical contract, though, is merely the discursive residue of the covenantal relationship that comprised church and state relations before the introduction of the American civic religion. The substantive assumptions regarding the covenantal relationship have been discarded and what remains are discursive phrases about "God's favor on us" and/or our special status as "God's chosen people." This civic religious discourse switches our attention from a perspective that acknowledged a sovereign, personal God who directs all of creation, to a perspective that only allows faith in "*statements* about faith, faith-in-faith as rhetorically pronounced."[9]

Secondly, Hart presumes that religion is a symbolically constructed system of ultimate meaning-creation that is best left as a private matter. Augustine, the reformers, the Puritans and others who accept the tradition of historic Christianity would argue vehemently against this presumption. Religion, based on covenantal theology, is relational, social, and systemic. It is neither a subjectively based Gnosticism, that wraps itself in secret knowledge and otherworldly longings while despising the here-and-now, nor is it merely an individual system of ethical constructs. Covenantal theology professes both the transcendent and immanent, the spiritual and embodied, the longing for the not-yet while continually engaged in the present. Historically its tendency is to express itself through theology and praxis—engaging in sociopolitical action to change the contemporary situation. In H. Richard Niebuhr's terminology, it is a system that engages society in order to transform it.[10]

Third, Hart's dismissal of conventional and doctrinal preaching as the "null case" of the church-state rhetoric reveals a lack of understanding of the impact of doctrine.[11] Doctrinal assumptions about the nature of God, the nature of humanity, and the nature of God's interaction with humanity produce dramatic effects on how we organize and define our social institutions. Our system of checks and balances is based on the doctrinal teaching about the fallen nature of humanity. Likewise, the concern about giving too much power to the state, or to the church, or to any individual is based on the assumption that our fallen state makes us susceptible to acting corruptly when we have unchecked power.[12]

Finally, Hart describes a religious discursive system that is predominantly Judeo-Christian. This, too, has changed. The acceptable religious discourse has now become a vague "spirituality" that includes, in addition to mainstream western religions, Buddhism, B'hai, Confucianism, Sikh, Moslem, and neo-pagan practices. All of these groups affect the nature and scope of the statist religion. Though the religious power brokers are predominantly those of the Judeo-Christian heritage, the acceptable religious discourse is broader and more inclusive. As will be evidenced by our examination of the National Day of Prayer and Remembrance from September 14, 2001, the American pantheon has extended well beyond the Judeo-Christian boundaries. We now turn to an examination of the concept of covenant and its place in church-state discourse. We will examine its central position in Judeo-Christian religious discourse, its role in the Reformation's response to the divine ruler-divine state, and the archetypal role of covenant in early American church-state discourse.

Covenant Is Central to Religious Discourse

David Tukey contends that the concept of the covenant is central to religious rhetoric. "In short, the notion of covenant is fundamental to western monotheism and thus provides a key construct in any analysis of western, religious rhetoric."[13] Other authors, specifically theologians, go further and contend that religion and covenant are virtually identical.[14] This concept is especially significant in Judaism and historic Christianity.[15] The concept lost its central position when dispensationalist theology and evangelicalism became the dominant paradigm for Christianity in the United States.[16] Despite the contemporary change in emphasis, we cannot begin to understand the religious rhetoric that embodies church and state interaction without first understanding the concept of the covenant and how it affects religious discourse.

It is not the scope of this essay, nor is there space, to give an extensive treatise on the concept of covenant. Thus, a brief overview will have to suffice for the purpose of this analysis. Judaism and historic Christianity claim a certain religious uniqueness because of their covenantal understanding of God's interaction with humanity. Both Judeo-Christian theology and the social practices of the Assyrians, the Hittites, Israel, and the Syrians, though, influence our contemporary understanding of covenant making. In its ancient practice a covenant was "cut" when an animal(s) was cut into two pieces and then those who bound themselves in the covenantal relationship, or their representative, would walk between the halves of the animal(s). The traditional practice of covenant making included a physical, a symbolic, and a metaphysical dimension.

Definitions for *covenant* vary and there is little ability to draw a solid conclusion from the etymology of the word but there are some commonly agreed upon attributes and assumptions. "Covenants, in brief, are symbolic interactions that bind people together in relationship. They possess five distinct characteristics that include (1) relational bonds, (2) symbolic nature, (3) loose structure, (4) connection to an external reality, and (5) sanctions (or blessings and curses)."[17] A covenant was neither a contract nor a *quid pro quo* arrangement. It was a lifelong bond, administered through bloodletting, initiated by an oath, involved obligations and privileges, and the participants were released from it only upon death. For the purpose of this essay I will focus on the relational bonds and the symbolic nature of the covenant.

First, there is consistent agreement about a covenant as a "bond" or "relationship."[18] To begin with, persons are involved in making covenants, "it always involves a person, either God or man, who makes a covenant."[19] The purpose of a covenant is the establishment of a relationship between two or more previously unrelated individuals.

> [The word covenant] . . . signified the creation by word and rite of a *relationship* between two parties; the making of a covenant effected a "union of spheres" which had hitherto been separate, and so had the effect of creating the same solidarity between them as in the case of natural blood-relationship. The new community of interests or "union of spheres" thus created brought with it specific rights and duties which the relationship in itself made binding and inviolable.[20]

Ultimately, all covenant relationships are social and comprise a community. Often this community is based on the creation of a community even though the ritual of covenant making is enacted between two individuals. Thus, in the Abrahamic covenant and the suzerain-vassal treaties, single individuals act as federal representatives for a larger community. This makes the covenantal bond both personal and structural-institutional (communal). "[Martin Noth] established the view that the covenant is . . . an *institution* with a definable function in ancient Israelite society and religion."[21] Ronald Arnett reinforces the institutional component when he defines covenant as "more than a guide; it is a commitment to people, institutions and ideas."[23]

Secondly, the act of cutting a covenant is both symbolic and ritualistic. It is symbolic because of the exchange of oaths, cutting animals asunder, walking between the pieces, and often the sharing of a meal or some form of gift. The symbolism conveys the creation of a bond with its related blessings and conveys that the covenant breaker will be liable for sanctions–being cut into as many pieces. It is also ritualistic in that it conveys a metaphysical reality that extends beyond the moment of the act[24] and binds the non blood-related participants in a familial way.[25]

Luther, Calvin, and other leaders of the Protestant Reformation incorporated two significant doctrines from Augustine: covenantal theology and the doctrine of original sin. The reformers saw all of life subject to God's laws and that God entered into a covenantal relationship with the chosen people (Israel and the church):

> God's covenant with man [sic] may be defined as an administration of the kingdom of God. Covenant administration is kingdom administration. The treaties are the legal instruments

by which God's kingship is exercised over his creatures. Con-
genial to Reformed theology surely is the centrality of God,
the Great King of the covenant, in this definition. It is God's
lordship that is the core and constant of the covenant.[25]

Similarly, humans engage other humans through covenants that invoke
God's covenantal consistency with the chosen people. Secondly, the doctrine of
original sin shaped every aspect of sociopolitical life because it presumes a human proclivity for self-destruction and actions that violate God's laws. Left to
themselves, humans will destroy each other and it is only by God's grace that we
have life and order. This doctrine contends that humans must have a system of
checks and balances that help us guard against our self-destructive behaviors and
help us to maintain social control and social unity. We next see how this concept
affects church-state interactions.

The Reformation Response to the Divine Ruler-Divine State

Israel was the first and only theocratic form of government based upon a divine
covenant.[26] Genesis 15 tells the story of God "cutting the covenant" with Abraham that began an eternal relationship with his offspring. In this ritual Abraham
acted as the covenantal (federal) representative for his offspring and obligates
them to follow God's laws in fulfillment of their covenantal mandate. The emphasis for social order and unity for the resulting nation was based upon divine
covenantal relationship and divine laws.

Other great ancient cultures such as Mesopotamia, Egypt, Babylon and As-
syria attempted to solve the problems of social order and political unity by claiming
that their rulers were the embodiment of divinity. Disobedience to the ruler was
equated with being atheistic and rejecting the god(s). Similarly, Greek city-states
with their theistic pluralism and Rome with its pantheon of gods, were not theocratic. The gods, it was claimed, directed and sanctioned the actions of their hero-
leaders and imparted special knowledge to those of higher status and rank but the
gods remained distant, impersonal, and capricious. The Romans were unusual,
though, in that they made the state the embodiment of the divine.[27] The divinity of
the state still did not stop Roman rulers from proclaiming some form of divine
privilege or proclaiming their own divinity. The presumed divine right of rulers, (as
opposed to their divinity), continued long after Constantine declared Christianity
the state religion. The introduction of the Roman Catholic Church as the supreme
theological and political institution did not change the older Roman presumption of
the state-as-divine; the church now represented divinity and divine sanction was
given to those of royal pedigree who supported the church's claim to power. T. E.
Wilder supports this contention when he states "The two centralized bureaucratic
powers, Pope and King, appealed to top-down divinely granted and, at least in certain spheres, unlimited authority."[28] Here we see a change in emphasis from the
statism of the Roman system, and its offspring, to the argument for ruling by divine
right. Both of these systems, though, still equated the state and/or the ruler with

divinity. If they were not themselves divine, they at least were the mouthpieces for the divine.

The Protestant Reformation reinstated a Biblical-covenantal understanding of the relationship between church, state, and society (based on the family as the basic unit); thus, de-divinizing the state and the ruler and placing law, specifically God's law, as the supreme rule.[29]

> By de-divinizing the world, Christianity placed all created orders, including church and state, alike under God. By denying divinity to all, and by reserving divinity to the triune God, all created orders were freed from one another and made independent of each other and together interdependent in their dependence upon God. Church and state were alike required to be Christian, but neither was able to be total Christian order.[30]

John Calvin was a central figure in this argument with his rediscovery of the three spheres of influence: church, government, and society.[31] All three areas were equally subject to God's sovereign laws and each of the areas was responsible to help insure that the other two maintained their obedience to God's laws. Maintaining the balance between the three equal spheres, while existing under the preeminent sphere of God's law, was only possible through the theological concept of the covenant. It took a federal (covenantal) theology to establish and maintain a federal political system.[32]

Covenant Is Central to U.S. History

Calvin and Luther, among others of the Reformation, had a dramatic impact on those who settled in the United States. It was the Biblical concept of covenant and the Calvinist argument about the three spheres of sovereignty that exist under the control of God's law that provided the framework for the U.S. religious and political systems and justified the American revolution. As Wilder claims, "Reformed theology makes it [the covenant] central to the social order."[33] The equating of a covenantal order with a federal order (and vice versa) was fundamental to the theological and political writings of Heinrich Bullinger, Samuel Rutherford, Johannes Althusius and Thomas Hobbes.[34] These authors influenced later groups, among them the Pilgrims and the Puritans.

The Pilgrims and the Puritans established their sociopolitical orders upon the theology and philosophy of the Reformation. The Pilgrim Mayflower Compact, for example, is the embodiment of a covenant among and between a people and their God. The Puritans, who came nearly a decade later, were also thoroughgoing covenanters.

> For our purposes we can conceive of Puritan covenants as consisting essentially of two 'external' and one 'internal' compacts between God and man [*sic*]. The church covenant and the social covenant were 'external' agreements that God initiated with men [*sic*] as members of the visible church and

> of a Godly state. In return for man's [*sic*] walking as faithfully
> as he could in divine paths, God would bless both the church
> and the land itself.[35]

The "internal" covenant of grace, on the other hand, provided for individual salvation. It was understood to be a monergistic act of God that was evidenced by
one's ability to believe God. It was this internal covenant that helped to define
their identity as a chosen people "Fleeing the corrupt Old World and destined to
establish a 'shining city on a hill' for all the world to behold. Given the nature of
this mission, Americans possessed a special covenant with God, a guarantee of
success if they would only live up to its terms."[36]

The concept of the covenant was also central in justifying the American war
for independence. Though Calvin claimed that Christians had an obligation to
obey the government even when it was abusive, other later reformers, such as
John Knox, argued that a ruler who broke God's laws was also a covenant-
breaker and should be considered a tyrant. Knox successfully united the concept
of one's salvation with the obligation to overthrow tyrants who violated God's
law. "Basing his arguments on various biblical texts (especially Exodus 34) that
teach a covenant between God and the people (not just their leaders), Knox argues that to refuse to resist an idolatrous regime is to run the risk of losing one's
immortal soul."[37] Knox, then, became the firebrand who presented a religious
justification for Scottish and American revolutions against England.

The Biblical basis for the covenantal (federal) order was not maintained.
Though some would argue that the emphasis has changed from a Biblical perspective to a political perspective, I contend that a religious emphasis is still present, it is only the accepted religion that has changed. The decline of the Biblical
concept of covenant and its implications for society, government, and the church
began with the rise of revivalism and the influence of the enlightenment in the
United States.[38] Murphy states that the change from one religion to the next is
based on the American claim to be a chosen people.

As Richard Johannesen maintains, the tenets of the American civil religion
have replaced Puritan faith as the grounding for arguments.[39] Americans are a
special, chosen people. To maintain that status, they need to live up to the principles articulated in the Declaration of Independence and the Constitution. They
need to emulate the great American leaders of the past such as Washington, Jefferson, Lincoln, and, more recently, Franklin Delano Roosevelt. Departure from
these traditions results in decline and, eventually, catastrophe.[40]

This fundamental religious change has not gone unnoticed by long-
established denominations. One denomination in particular, the Reformed Church
of America (RCA), now called the Reformed Presbyterian Church of North
America, has dissented from the government's stance since the late 1700s. Soon
after its writing, these church members recognized that the US Constitution failed
to acknowledge three key ideas: the subordination of government to the sovereignty of Jesus Christ, the independence of the church and its sole subordination to
Jesus Christ, and the covenantal relationship that exists between all three.[41] These

and other "covenanters" started the National Reform Association that proposed an addition to the preamble of the Constitution that recognized the sovereignty of Christ over all of life.[42] When the proposed preamble was rejected, the RCA members decided that "the church member should swear no oath of allegiance, elect no public functionaries to office ('for, between the *elector* and the *elected*, there is a representative *oneness*'), accept no office, including serving on juries, nor engage in any service regulated by an immoral law, such as engaging in the militia."[43] This condition of membership did not change until the last fifty years. Even today, RPCNA members forswear any oaths of allegiance that compromises their allegiance to Christ:

> It is deemed sinful for a Christian to take an oath which com-
> promises his supreme allegiance to Jesus Christ. It is also
> deemed sinful to vote for officials who are required to take an
> oath that a Christian himself could not take in good con-
> science. Voting involves the voter in responsibility for any act
> required of the official as a condition of holding his office.[44]

Though the National Reform Association is no longer in existence, per se, the "covenanters" still exist as a collection of dissenting citizens who, in one form or another, are attempting to bring about this constitutional reform.

The change from a Biblical understanding of covenant to a civil understanding of covenant has not resulted in an irreligious culture, instead we are a culture that has faith in "*statements* about faith, faith-in-faith as rhetorically pronounced."[45] Here, Hart is at his descriptive best and it is a thorough indictment of the orthodox church. It was the church that abandoned its leading role in politics, education, science, care for the poor and sick, and sociopolitical change and chose, instead, a spiritualized job description of "saving souls."[46] Likewise, it was the church that was willingly co-opted by political organizations in order to enhance the political revenues and the "religious vote" for whatever party would toss it their rhetorical scraps. For this harlotry the church was given its just payment, religious sophistry during civic occasions and banal religious pleas to a "genial philanthropist God and/or the Object of Affection God" in times of crisis.[47] Every vacuum seeks to be filled, and just because a people have abandoned historic Judeo-Christianity does not mean that they cease being religious. Instead, Americanism, with its myths, heroes, sanctions, promises, spiritual pluralism, and emphasis on tolerant acceptance is now the dominant statist religion. We have exchanged discourse about a transcendent and personal God for discourse about a transcendent and impersonal state.

American Pantheon versus American Covenant Renewal

There is now the development of two religious paradigms. First, there are those who embraced what Hart described as the rhetorical contract and, taken it to its logical end, a statist religion. This religious discourse is based on an autonomous spirituality and emphasizes religious pluralism, tolerance and American myths.

Second, are those who seek to restore historic Christianity and its covenantal basis for society. I argue for these as paradigms because neither of these have flagship institutions, recognized movement leaders, or particular political parties. They are, however, easily recognized from our recent history.

The statist religion is epitomized by the National Day of Prayer and Remembrance that took place on September 14, 2002. Unlike the Roman pantheon in Tiberius' time, the American pantheon included gods from all corners of the earth. The service in the National Cathedral reinstated the American civic religion with all the pomp, circumstance, and dignitaries that befit its national status. The dominant power brokers at this service were still those from the Judeo-Christian heritage but they spoke as if they recognized that they were involved in something larger than their own "personal religion" and were thus willing to refrain from any claims to soteriological exclusivity. Prominent among these religious representatives was Billy Graham.

Hart ended *The Political Pulpit* by suggesting that Billy Graham's "brand of civic piety is probably as much a harbinger of the rhetorical future as it is an echo of the American experience."[48] True to form, during this service Graham spoke words of reassurance, eschewed theological controversies, and sought to maintain an acceptable religious posturing. Graham, recognizing the minor role of his God in this pantheon, was apologetic about mentioning the name of Christ, claimed God's special care for all Americans and did more to reminisce about his past than to call his audience to repentance before God. Graham's references to Jesus Christ were made only after he made the rhetorical apology that he was speaking "For the Christian, I'm speaking for the Christian now."[49] His references to Christ as the means of salvation were made as a statement of personal reflection and his own personal reassurance rather than as a direct proposition. "I've become an old man now and . . . the older I get the more I cling to that hope that I started with many years ago and proclaimed it in many languages to many parts of the world."[50] He ended his presentation by referencing a previous faith statement given by Ambassador Andrew Young and by reassuring his audience that "He [God] will never forsake us as we trust in Him [sic]. We also know that God is going to give wisdom and courage and strength to the President and those around him."[51]

The service in the National Cathedral, opened by the Right Reverend Jane Holmes Dixon, was deemed a place for "people of many faiths" including "Muslim, Jew, Christian, Sikh, Buddhist, Hindu, all people of faith."[52] True to its emphasis on religious pluralism, tolerance and individual spirituality, the participants in this statist religious service were neither accosted by exclusionist claims regarding salvation nor were they asked to examine their own evil intentions and behavior in light of God's holiness. There was no reference to any external transcendent measure by which we were to analyze ourselves or to judge our individual or national behavior. Instead, the service emphasized our pantheon of gods, America's special place in the world, and our beneficent and care giving god who assuredly was not angry with us and would continue to protect us from the evil that exists in others rather than in us.

The second, and now subordinate paradigm, is that which talks about a sovereign God who rules over the three spheres of society in a covenantal relationship. This covenantal understanding of society does not mean that the adherents of this trend seek a theocracy; they seek, instead, to transform culture under the supremacy of Christ and under God's laws.[53] This is the covenant renewal religious paradigm. Those who seek to restore the Decalogue as the basis for American jurisprudence, those who opt out of governmental schools in order to educate their children, and the intellectual leaders who seek to affect sociopolitical policy, epitomize the covenant renewal movement. The most visible member of the movement who argues for the Decalogue as the legal basis for American jurisprudence is Roy Moore. This Alabama Supreme Court Chief Justice has employed various legal and social-activist tactics to bring attention to his argument. His message is that we need to recognize, once again, God's laws as a legal code and the basis for our legal system.[54] The Christian school movement (whether at home or in a parochial school), has no single national leader. It, too, is a grassroots movement that contends that a statist religion is endorsed in "government schools" and seeks to alter the national landscape by reinstating the sovereignty of the family sphere and the covenantal obligation to educate children according to the family's religious and educational convictions.[55] Finally, are the more visible intellectual leaders who seek to affect policy decisions based upon God's laws. Time and space allow me to mention only one of several notable individuals, Marvin Olasky. His policy and cultural suggestions based upon God's laws and a covenantal perspective of church, state, and family (social) relations have achieved national and international recognition. Three areas of focus include his work on welfare reform, compassionate conservatism, and reforming journalism. Olasky's work on welfare reform was endorsed by Newt Gingrich and others in the U.S. House of Representatives,[56] his structure for compassionate conservatism was endorsed by a presidential candidate (now a sitting president),[57] and his work to reform journalism includes editing the news magazine *World* and leading numerous workshops that teach journalistic analysis based on a Christian worldview.[58] Time and space don't allow me to include the work of individuals such as Chuck Colson (reforming prison systems and seeking a covenantal understanding of justice), Doug Wilson (reforming education and the understanding of marriage), Michael Ferris (home schooling, Christian higher education and conservative politics), and James Dobson (supporting the family institution and related political concerns), among many others. Those who undertake the work of reforming culture do so in the spirit of the National Reform Association but the focus is now much broader and seeks to transform all areas of life based on a covenantal understanding of God and God's laws.

Conclusions

What is the state of church and state relations? In a sentence, church and state are engaged in a struggle that pits the statist religion against historic Judeo-Christianity. Once again the orthodox historic understanding is being challenged. What does the God-talk have to offer to our culture and how far are its adherents willing to go to defend their professions as Truth? The heat of this conflict will not necessarily be waged in the public arena or between believers and non-believers. The heat of this battle will take place between religious perspectives that are willing to acquiesce to the statist religious paradigm and those perspectives that refuse to subjugate themselves to that paradigm. The battle is about a substantive religious liberty versus the appearance of religious liberty.

Robert L. Dabney, an esteemed Southern educator, theologian, and Civil War veteran, before his death in 1898 conveyed his despair that religious liberty was being truncated. "You may deem it a strange prophecy, but I will predict that the time will come in this once free America when the battle for religious liberty will have to be fought over again, and will probably be lost, because the people are already ignorant of its true basis and conditions."[59] His concern was not that any foreign invader or any anti-Christian group would forcibly take away such freedoms but that the succeeding generations of those who had purchased the freedoms with their blood would deem the freedom inconsequential and would let it slip away. The current statist religious paradigm promises unity and the absence of controversy because the emphasis is on a non-doctrinal spirituality and each person must accept everyone else's spiritual path as merely another way to achieve the same end. Historic Judeo-Christianity offers, at best, an ongoing tension regarding the roles and boundaries of the Church, the State, and the family. If Americans value the *appearance* of unity over true liberty and if the Church values its presumed political power more than it does the Truth it proclaims, then we have sunk to the level described by Dabney. The battle predicted by Dabney may not be one of armed resistance but those who would be affected by the loss of religious liberty are ill prepared to wage even a war of words and ideas. Unless and until the Church regains the thoughtfulness and conviction of historic Christianity, it has little of substance to offer a culture that, because of its fears, flirts with totalitarianism. A statist religious perspective, added to our own fears of survival, could be deemed sufficient justification for the state to assume totalitarian control. A covenantal perspective, in spite of our fears, keeps the church, state and family in check.

Unit 4

Final Reflections

Chapter 15

God, Country, and a World of Words

Roderick P. Hart

Reflecting on something one has written twenty-five years ago produces a mixture of pleasure and pain. The pleasure comes from remembering how several years of research resulted in something tangible, how a publisher agreed to deliver one's ideas to a wider audience, and how the resulting book advanced one's career. There is a subtler and more important source of pleasure: remembering that *The Political Pulpit* took a distinctively rhetorical angle on politics and religion, bringing the communication discipline into a discussion then dominated by students of theology, history, and sociology. No matter what faults may now be discovered in *The Political Pulpit*, this latter satisfaction endures.

But there is pain as well. As I examine the book at this remove, I find an author too sure of himself and, as Ron Lee points out, too flippant as well. The author overstates his case from time to time, perhaps fearful that his argument could not stand on its own unadorned. Too, the book sometimes gives short shrift to the deeply felt beliefs brought into the public square by religious practitioners. While the book never dismisses those concerns, its author is far too self-satisfied. This is a book written by a young man. Shame on him for being young.

When agreeing to respond to these papers, therefore, I did so with mixed emotions. For one thing, I felt slightly embarrassed that eight fine scholars would take the time to re-read something I had written so many years ago. They flatter me with their attention. But I also felt rather out of my element because politics and religion no longer occupy a central place in my intellectual life. Since the time *The Political Pulpit* was written I have mostly studied the intersection of language, governance, and the mass media, trying to find cultural explanations for why American politics sounds like it sounds and feels like it feels. This journey has taken me away from the religion of American politics. As a result, I happily defer on technical matters to scholars more expert in this area than me.

I shall not be mute, however. In re-reading *The Political Pulpit,* I find several things that need changing but its basic argument seems sound. The contractual model still binds politicians and religionists quite tightly, I submit once again, and the "terms" of the contract still determine how those who wish to advance themselves politically must operate. Heads continue to roll in the U.S. when politicians become too confessional or preachers too ideological. The God of the American civil religion continues to be a retiring God, more likely witnessed on ceremonial occasions than when public policy is debated. Religion is still given an honorific place on the political stage but it has little bearing on who goes to war with whom, on which groups prosper economically, or on where roads are built or when welfare checks are written. Despite their repeated rhetorical intermingling, politics and religion have an unbalanced, and fractious, relationship in the U.S.

Do I overstate? Ask Jerry Falwell, who when speaking on Pat Robertson's *700 Club* on September 14, 2001, blamed the ACLU, pagans, abortionists, feminists, gays and lesbians for the terrorist attacks three days earlier. Not surprisingly, a firestorm erupted, just as it has always erupted when the incautious remarks of "unofficial" civil religionists are caught in the media's net. Or ask John Ashcroft, who renounced the Lord more than thrice during the Senate confirmation hearings for attorney general in January 2001. Or ask Billy Graham who in 2002 was reminded of remarks he had made to Richard Nixon some thirty years earlier in the not-quite-solitary confines of the Oval Office: "This [Jewish] stranglehold has got to be broken or this country's going down the drain." Or ask the growing number of pedophile priests who look, futilely, to the Church for help in avoiding prosecution for their misdeeds. Or ask committed Christian George W. Bush, who did handsprings after September 11 to assure the nation's Muslims they had nothing to worry about when practicing their religion. The rhetoric of civil religion may have changed a bit during the last twenty-five years but its enforcement mechanisms have not. Religion is still the third rail in American politics and it is respectfully regarded as such.

This is not to say that *The Political Pulpit* was perfectly prescient. The story of religion and politics continues to unfold, as we see in the set of papers prepared for this volume. In these papers I find three major questions being asked, questions that may well affect how that story is told in the future.

Is the Contractual Model of Church-State Relations Conceptually Convincing?

Two of the finest essays in Unit 3 of this book are those by Ronald Lee and Carolyn Marvin, who go directly to the book's core arguments. Ron Lee, for example, worries that the book ignores the transcendent nature of religious experience, focusing as it does on the practicalities of political compromise. "No one seems sincere in this book," says Lee, and "there is no place for genuine devotion." The book is centrist in the extreme, he also argues, palpably denying the powerful motivational forces that propel persons of faith into the political arena. In a thoughtful overview, Lee shows how forces-of-conscience made Martin Luther King's "Letter from a Birmingham Jail" compelling for so many. Similarly, he says that Dan Quayle used religious understandings to inject the issue of family values into the national dialogue and that Bill Clinton returned to his religious roots when apologizing for the Lewinsky affair, thereby affirming the power of religious transcendence.

These are fair charges fairly made and I shall continue to ponder them. Lee's great fear is that *The Political Pulpit* becomes so caught up in the language of civil religion that it fails to feature the emotional experiences of living, breathing, believing Americans who respond to that language each day. But, as Professor Lee suggests, I am a pragmatist, and pragmatists are notorious for wanting to know what works, when, and why. I, for one, do not know how to calculate soul-force. For me, the political genius of Martin Luther King lay in what he did *not* say. Yes, he used biblical imagery to accost politicians for ignoring the plight of African Americans but he never threw down the gauntlet completely. King's Jesus was, like King himself, accommodationistic when dealing with the forces of entrenched power. And when Jesus stopped accommodating, King continued to do so, cutting his deals with the Kennedy and Johnson administrations, parting company with Malcolm X and Stokley Carmichael, instinctively reflecting the promissory nature of the New Testament rather than the sterner kerygma of the Old Testament. In similar fashion, Dan Quayle's refrains on family values and Bill Clinton's on redemption were—whatever their theological value—the canny strategic moves of canny political actors.

Most fundamentally, I reject Lee's insistence that one must distinguish sharply between the soulful and the expedient. For me, politics is best when it works well, when it delivers goods and services to people in an efficient and democratic manner. Bill Clinton and Martin Luther King were brilliant politicians and that is enough for me. The latter kept the nation from tearing itself apart in the 1960s and the former supervised a robust economy that kept people employed and the nation at peace in the 1990s. This was first-rate work in my opinion and if religious refrains helped them accomplish it that is fine with me. As a British prime minister once said, politics is for getting things done; if you want transcendence go see your archbishop.

Although Lee and I disagree about some particulars, we share a common respect for the power of rhetoric to shape political realities. Carolyn Marvin refuses to climb aboard our train. She calls into question both the philosophical and epistemological understructure of *The Political Pulpit,* arguing that the book reifies politics and religion and, hence, distorts them. In a brilliant disquisition, Marvin roams across the intellectual countryside, asking whether the book becomes reductionistic when featuring the *discourse* of politics rather than its coercive nature. Politics is powerful, Marvin argues, because it gets people to make blood sacrifices for the nation-state. And religion is powerful, she adds, because it provides intellectual and emotional sanction for so doing. The combination of these forces—civil religion—is powerful, says Marvin, because it is "a pervasive and complex system of sacrificial and regenerative beliefs, gestures, artifacts, and words that bind the citizens of the United States into a community of moral obligation."

In essence, Marvin accuses me of dandifying civil religion, of focusing undue attention on its linguisticality. "The most moving rhetoric cannot by itself hold a society together," she notes. Instead, it takes "believers who so agree on what is fundamental . . . that they will offer their own lives and their children's to defend it." Yes, I respond, but death must have a language. That is, people almost never throw themselves on the parapets willy nilly. They do so when bidden to do so—by their preachers, by their political leaders. Winston Churchill called forth his people in this manner, as did Franklin Roosevelt, as do Ariel Sharon and Yasser Arafat. These four have given their people a story worth dying for. And even the dead must have a language. Eulogists are routinely asked to round-out a person's biography, to make a whole narrative out of the miscellaneous happenings constituting a life. Rhetoric is therefore an art for those addicted to meaning, which is to say, an art for all of us.

Marvin's basic charge is that *The Political Pulpit* underestimates the power of nationalism by focusing so relentlessly on its rhetorical character. In her model, religion is a pale rival to the nation-state and its denominational rivalries a quibble. The richer story, says Marvin, is that religious nationalism has taken hold in the United States, thereby giving it moral legitimacy. Marvin asks us to develop a new, deeper model of church-state relations to account for these moments of sacrifice. That seems a worthy goal. But one can't help but notice that human societies differ in their *abilities* to call forth these sacrifices. Some nations issue war-time calls and their people run to the jungles rather than enlist. In other societies—those with a powerful, historic, religious tradition—they march to the conscription offices on the morrow. Why these different national experiences? Might rhetoric be part of the answer?

Is the Contractual Model of Church-State Relations Empirically Accurate?

The contributors to Unit 3 are not of one mind on this question. Three of them—Robert Friedenberg, Nneka Ofulue, and Michael Eidenmuller—find it generally satisfactory, although each looks at the matter somewhat differently. One contributor—Martin Medhurst—says that the model may have been accurate at one point in time but, like its author, it has aged badly. Cosmetic surgery would presumably correct neither condition.

In his essay, Bob Friedenberg applies the model to events surrounding the September 11 attacks and notes that mainstream churches were "almost uniformly supportive of our recent war on terrorism," much as they were during most domestic and international crises since the Founding. Friedenberg asserts that the "multivoiced American religious establishment can rarely agree within itself, not only on what is God's will, but also on how God's will should be expressed in specific public policy" contexts. As a result, says Friedenberg, "it is hard to see any tangible effect that organized religion has had on federal policy" in recent memory.

The Political Pulpit found this to be true as well, which is why organized religion so often relegates itself to the sidelines when sensitive public policy matters are being debated. The churches are not completely reticent, of course, with some of them lobbying legislators about prayer in schools, tax exemptions for church properties, state aid to private schools, abortion-on-demand, etc. But two points must be made about such issues: (1) they are largely institutionally relevant matters and (2) the churches rarely speak univocally. Christian fundamentalists want prayer in the schools but Methodists and Presbyterians do not; Catholics are opposed to public funding of abortions while Episcopalians stoutly defend a woman's right to choose; Disciples of Christ want state aid to private schools while Baptists fear governmental intrusions into their curricula. Such internecine struggles have long been part of American life, but so too has been an institutional reluctance to take stands on extra-religious (which is not to say extra-moral) issues: Vietnam, Watergate, Iran-Contra, the Gulf War, the Lewinsky scandal. As Friedenberg says, this makes civic piety "almost a decorative rhetoric."

Thus it is not surprising that when examining President Bush's rhetoric after September 11, Friedenberg finds a largely ceremonial discourse, one devoid of *specific* ideological force. Nneka Ofulue finds much the same thing when examining Bill Clinton's rhetoric during the Lewinsky scandal. Even though "no recent president has been less reticent about the role of religion in American civic life than Clinton," Ofulue observes, it is also true that the Clinton administration—like the Bush and Reagan administrations before it—left nary a trace on the civil religious landscape. To be sure, Clinton wore his religious predilections on his sleeve and that gave him an unusual ability to relate to the American underclass. Although Mr. Clinton's personal theology is still not known in detail, he liked the *feel* of religion and he communicated that feeling better than any recent president with the exception of Jimmy Carter.

As Ofulue reports, however, Clinton's instincts left him during the "failed apology" of August 17, 1998 when he whined and denied and whined some more. To undo that performance, Clinton turned to King David's psalm of repentance when addressing the national prayer breakfast one month later. For Ofulue, Clinton's speech that morning was a superior one, with Clinton making himself low in order to make himself high. In doing so, he turned to a rich rhetorical heritage that agrees on comparatively little but that believes very much in believing. Clinton became priest and sinner simultaneously. Only in America.

Michael Eidenmuller provides a fascinating addition to the story just told. He traces the rhetoric of Promise Keepers across two different terrains—stadium speeches, during which the PK leaders spoke to those of like mind in local settings, and rallies held in Washington, D.C. (which attracted considerably more secular attention). Eidemuller tests the contractual model by asking whether the PK rhetoric could avoid being "overtly political while yet remaining true to its religious calling." His answer is situational, with the stadium speeches being highly forceful—direct, passionate, confessional, personal. This was revivalism, to be sure, but revivalism in a distinctively modern way, an unusual blending of religious devotion and emotional openness.

When the PK show came to the nation's capital, however, the picture changed, perhaps because of the increased visibility the speeches generated and because of orchestrated opposition by the National Organization for Women. Unlike the local addresses, the national addresses were more "religious" in tone—less personal and activistic, more inspirational and inclusive. In the shadow of the Lincoln Memorial, that is, the Promise Keepers kept the *national* promise—to be as inclusive as an evangelical organization could be and to avoid the testosteronal rhetoric favored in more local settings. As Eidenmuller notes, this engendered "a paradox between rhetorical style and ideological substance," a paradox that religionists of every stripe have felt since the nation's beginnings. That even Promise Keepers found it necessary to trim their sails when visiting Washington is surely vindication of the contractual model.

Not according to Marty Medhurst. He argues that *The Political Pulpit* is now severely dated, that it no longer adequately explains what is heard in the religious realm. Noting that "1977 was a long time ago," Medhurst says that the model may even have been out of date the day it was proclaimed, that "several parts of the contract have long since been breached." The book's understandings of both "government" and "religion" are too static for Medhurst. In their place, he offers a stunningly textured mini-history of how Evangelicals and Fundamentalists, as well as blue-collar Catholics and Orthodox Jews, have changed the terms of debate during the last twenty-five years. Then he calls the roll: the Religious Roundtable, the Christian Voice, the Moral Majority, Concerned Women for America, the American Family Association, the Family Research Council, the Christian Coalition. These groups employ "a new, more personalized, more religion-specific language" and their boldness undercuts the genteel contract described thirty years earlier.

Balderdash . . . is perhaps too strong a response to Professor Medhurst's claims. No doubt he is correct that the Christian Right bought itself some television stations recently even though Jim Bakker and, more recently, Pat Robertson, have made a botch of their investments. Cable television and local talk radio have also become their métier, but this is a métier that consistently fails to make converts. As a result, the Right talks to the Right and the Left to the Left. Centrists, meanwhile, watch *Friends* and *The X Files*, throw Gingrich and his rascals out of office when they get too big for their britches, and become nervous when Joe Lieberman talks too much about God. Roger Ailles may have summoned Fox News into existence to combat Ted Turner's liberal depredations, but both share a miniscule audience compared to the more bankable fare served up by *Survivor* and the World Wrestling Federation. Americans stand in the middle of the road because that's where they get the best TV reception.

In the United States, TV reception best predicts political reception. As of this writing, for example, President George W. Bush has failed at almost every turn to appoint a batch of right-wing jurists. This is not because, as Medhurst says, the nation treats "religiously inclined people as second class citizens." It is because *the nation has never agreed on the proper set of religious inclinations.* It is not surprising that Bill Clinton occupied the Oval Office during the (conservative) nineties or that Richard Nixon did so during the (liberal) seventies. Both were seen as appropriate checks on the centrifugal tendencies of the American polity. Because of these same fears, Democrats get out the vote by distributing placards containing the visage of Jerry Falwell, and Ralph Reed is shunted to the hinterlands because Republican realists judge him too toxic a political property. Discrimination? I think not. In the U.S., politics is rarely about moralisms. It is about passing legislation.

The civil-religious contract continues to be honored because these truths still hold. Do religious issues scare American politicians? They do indeed. Will Kansans throw out their state textbook committee when it runs amuck? Indeed they will. Will school vouchers ever pass? Only if a centrist coalition can be forged. Political compromise, not sectarian screeds, is the dominant language of American politics. *The Political Pulpit* described, and celebrated, that language twenty-five years ago. Its author still finds it descriptive.

Is the Contractual Model of Church-State Relations Normatively Justified?

But even if the contractual model is accurate, is it right and good? The final two contributors disagree on the matter. Steve Goldzwig, blessed creature that he is, endorses the contract, finding that it both condones and promotes "a community of values important to a democratic state, important, in particular, to a uniquely American vision and set of values—liberty, freedom, equality, justice, and fair play." But Goldzwig is quick to add that these positive outcomes are sometimes offset by the inherent tensions between religion and politics and that the "silent agreement" between them can break down over particulars.

The great value of Goldzwig's essay is his catalogue of the forces now threatening the civil-religious contract. He notes, for example, that arguments over rights and virtues, over what one is due versus what one owes, can easily break out between church and state. Limits on religious expression, government aid to religious charities, preferential hiring practices by church entities, release time in the schools, the proper use of public facilities—all these issues continue to be debated in the nation's courts. While the rhetoric of civic piety has been used to superintend these discussions historically, there is no guarantee that the "amicable divorce" between church and state will stay amicable. The religious repression found in Spain, Malaysia, Chile, and China beckon as a constant, deplorable alternative. As worrisome as these alternatives are, however, Goldzwig is more concerned that a discourse of rights will trump "traditional republican virtues" and that religious sectarianism will eviscerate the communitarian obligations Americans owe one another. As originally described, the civil-religious contract was silent about these matters.

The contract was also silent about the forces of globalization that now call into question the very concept of a nation-state. *The Political Pulpit* was written during a time when global markets, interlocking directorates, multiculturalism, the Concorde, and the Internet were nascent. But they have grown up since then and the world has gotten smaller. Thus we must ask: Is the contract rendered quaint by its Judeo-Christian emphases in a nation now housing seven million Muslims? Is the contract rendered provincial in a world filled with jet-hopping internationalists who identify more with a hotel chain than a national flag? Is the contract rendered elitist in a nation still bedeviled by grinding poverty and class warfare? Is the contract rendered irrelevant in a country comprised of consumers rather than believers? Steve Goldzwig asks these questions and they are fine ones. I have no answers for them at present.

Mark Gring has answers, though. And he is manifestly unhappy with the reality described in *The Political Pulpit*. While "I do not deny the accuracy of [Hart's] description," says Gring, "I repudiate the presumption . . . that this rhetorical bridging between church and state is the best of the desired outcomes." "Hart refuses to recognize," Gring adds, "that every social order rests on a creed (or covenant—as per Althusius) that is the embodiment of its religion." Gring is unhappy with the contract because it lets a statist religion supercede an orthodoxy based on "the sovereignity of Christ and the supremacy of God's laws over all areas of life." It has made "Historic Christianity" an outlaw, resulting in a kind of low-level, but persistent, state of "sociopolitical warfare" between the sacred and the secular in the U.S.

Gring's essay is eminently thoughtful, well worth reading. It is also ambitious, laying out an alternative, "covenantal" model of church-state relations that, he hopes, will clarify what my book has muddied. Gring explains the history of the covenant, a history that includes animals and sacrifice, blessings and curses, oaths and meal-sharing, and, unsettlingly, bloodletting. He goes on to show how central this idea has been in U.S. history and how it helped justify the American war for independence (a "shining city on a hill" and all that). Since then, he laments, the nation has turned its back on the covenant, leaving the concept in the unsteady hands of Alabama Supreme Court Justice, Roy Moore, the once-sinful Chuck Colson and the rarely-sinful James Dobson, and a panoply of rightist groups like the National Reform Association. All this has thrust religion and government into a state of "mortal combat" that pits the acquiescent—a cadre that includes most Americans, slackards that they are—against "those who refuse to subjugate themselves to the statist religion."

The underlying idea here is that "left to themselves, humans will destroy each other and it is only by God's grace that we have life and order." I could not disagree more. It does not so much bother me that Gring wants the nation to "regain the thoughtfulness and depth of historic Christianity" or that he fears a state that "offers the appearance of unity but the absence of freedom." The former is a vaunted goal (although it is not my own) and the latter a legitimate fear (but not one I share). I am bothered more by Gring's dismissal of the political, a concept in which I place *all* my faith. I take delight in the wrangling and railing and excoriating of politics. I take even greater delight in its caucusing and lobbying and, most of all, in its compromises. I revere its deal-making, its give and take, its tireless flexibilities.

The political instinct is our noblest instinct. It is our safety-valve as a species, our way of overcoming our bestiality. They say that politics is warfare by other means. How wonderful—this other means. How wonderful that we can use our ingenuity to forge common ground between rival tribes, to imagine maps not yet drawn to ensure a new peace. How wonderful we can use words to keep Protestants and Catholics, Shiites and Sunnis, from repeating their sorrowful histories of enmity.

Personally, I want nothing to do with Gring's covenant. I want constitutions and courts and legislatures to solve our squabbles and I want laws to keep them solved. I want as much freedom of speech as we can afford and I want people to be able to fulminate from their rooftops until 11:00 p.m., after which all decent people should be asleep. I want religion respected in the United States because it keeps us on the right path more often than it throws us into the brambles. It does not bother me that Congress begins its day with a prayer or that presidents continue to speak of the Lord's bounties. Let them talk. It can't hurt. It might even help. Someone should write a book about it.

Notes

Chapter 1

1. Richard Morin, "Keeping the Faith," *Washington Post*, Monday, Jan. 12, 1998. Accessed on 30 December, 2003 at http://www.washingtonpost.com.

2. K.M. Kirk, et al., "Frequency of Church Attendance in Australia and the United States: Models of Family Resemblance," *Twin Research*, 2 (1999), 99–107.

3. Quoted in Aaron Latham, "How George W. Found God," *George Magazine*, September, 2000. Accessed on 29 December, 2003 at http://www.christianitytoday.com

4. Steven Thomma, "Religion, Politics Go Hand in Hand," *Austin American Statesman*, 14 December, 2003, pp. A21ff.

5. These titles (sometimes abbreviated here) can be found in the following issues of *Time*: 29 October, 1979; 17 December, 1979; 19 April, 1980; 9 July, 1984; 24 December, 1984; 2 September, 1985; 27 October, 1986; 1 May, 1989; 17 July, 1989; 19 February, 1990; 15 May, 1995; 6 October, 1997.

6. As quoted in Barry W. Lynn, "Preacher or President? Politicians, Pandering and Campaign 2000," 17 December 1999. Accessed at http://www.au.org/press/pr121799.htm on 29 December, 2003.

7. George W. Bush, Inaugural Address, 20 January, 2001. Accessed on 29 December, 2003 at http://www.washingtonpost.com.

8. George W. Bush, National Prayer Breakfast, Washington Hilton Hotel, 1 February, 2001. Excerpted in *Partners Newsletter* and accessed at http://www.catholic-men.org on 29 December 2003.

9. Quoted in Jonathan Lyons, "Bush Enters Mideast's Rhetorical Minefield," Reuters, 21 September, 2001. Accessed on 29 December 2003 at http://www.positiveatheism.org.

10. George W. Bush, ordering the National Day of Prayer and Remembrance for 14 September, 2001. As excerpted in Josh Karpf, "Atheism in the New Holy War." Accessed on 29 December 2003 at http://www.positiveatheism.org.

11. Address to Urban Leaders, Eisenhower Executive Office Building, 16 July 2003. Accessed on 29 December 2003 at http://www.positiveatheism.org.

12.   Bill Keller, "God and George W. Bush," *New York Times*, Opinion, 17 May 2003. Accessed on 29 December 2003 at http://query.nytimes.com.

13.   Jim Wallis, "Dangerous Religion: George W. Bush's Theology of Empire," *Sojourners Magazine*, September–October 2003. Accessed online at http://www.sojo.net on 29 December 2003.

14.   Robert Marus, "Amended Faith-Based Bill Approved by U.S. Senate," Associated Baptist Press. Accessed on 29 December 2003 at http://www.bjcpa.org.

Chapter 2

1.   Michael Novak, *Choosing Our King* (New York: Macmillan, 1974), pp. 303 ff.

2.   Conrad Cherry, "American Sacred Ceremonies," in *American Mosaic: Social Patterns of Religion in the United States,* ed. Phillip E. Hammond and Benton Johnson (New York: Random House, 1970), p. 304.

3.   George N. Gordon, *Persuasion: The Theory and Practice of Manipulative Communication* (New York: Hastings House, 1971), p. 198.

4.   Novak, *Choosing,* p. 127.

5.   Robert S. Alley, *So Help Me God* (Richmond, Va.: John Knox Press, 1972), pp. 78–79.

6.   Will Herberg, "Religion in a Secularized Society: The New Shape of Religion in America," in *The Sociology of Religion: An Anthology,* ed. Richard D. Knudten (New York: Meredith, 1967), p. 475.

7.   Quoted in Alley, p. 120.

8.   David W. Glockley, Executive vice president, Religion in American Life, Personal communication, 1 March 1974.

9.   God is Alive (and Working on Madison Avenue). Pamphlet issued by Religion in American Life. (n.d., not paginated).

10.   Quoted in Mary H. Weinberg, "The Flag Lady," *Indianapolis Star Magazine,* 6 February 1972, p. 11.

11.   Herbert Schneider, *Religion in Twentieth Century America* (Cambridge, Mass.: Harvard University Press, 1952), p. 58. With regard to the religious-military establishment, Schneider's remarks are especially apt. Harvey Cox, for example, has recounted the pervasive influence enjoyed by organized religion in the nation's military units: "Here are some statistics, however, supplied by the Defense Department, which give some indication of the number of persons involved: In July 1970 the Defense Department reported there were a total of 4,020 chaplains serving in the Army (1,792), Navy (1,068) and Air Force (1,160). The chaplain's average age is about 40 (a little younger in the Army, a little older in the Air Force). In the Army, 1,040 are Protestants, 600 are Catholics, 60 are Jews and 5 are Eastern Orthodox. The ratios among denominations are about the same in the other branches. It is interesting to note in glancing at the list of Protestant denominations represented, that although the 'mainline' de-

nominations understandably supply most chaplains, there are also chaplains from the Christian Missionary Alliance Church (6), Church of the Nazarene (31), Churches of God in North America (2), Free Will Baptists (2), Moravians (4), and the Salvation Army (3). The Defense Department lists no chaplains from the Society of Friends, Buddhists, International Society for Krishna Consciousness ('Hare Krishnas'), Amish, or Black Muslims. Over 80 percent of the chaplains are career officers as opposed to men serving only a limited term." *Military Chaplains: From a Religious Military to a Military Religion*, ed. Harvey G. Cox (New York: American Report Press, 1971), p. xii.

12.   Harry P. Kerr, "Politics and Religion in Colonial Fast and Thanksgiving Sermons, 1763–1783," *Quarterly Journal of Speech,* 46 (1960), 382.

13.   Howard H. Martin, "The Fourth of July Oration," *Quarterly Journal of Speech,* 44 (1958), 394.

14.   William Gribbin, *The Churches Militant* (New Haven: Yale University Press, 1973), p. 19.

15.   Will Herberg, *Protestant, Catholic, Jew* (Garden City, N. Y.: Doubleday & Co., 1955), p. 65. Alley, p. 91, reveals the civil-religious tones of the fifties most dramatically when he reports: "The White House religion, which so encouraged the nation in its piety and aided in the rise to prominence of Billy Graham as a political force, placed little emphasis on sect or faith commitment, only on a kind of divine feeling. It was the era of the 'Man Upstairs' and prayer before college football games. The people felt quite self-righteous, though the fear of Communism and the 'bomb' pervaded the fifties and Sputnik frightened the nation in 1957. For many, prayer was a substitute for thinking about problems. It was during the reign of Ike that the country came closer than ever before to establishing a civil religion. It would have been modified Puritanism divested of ethical and theological content. There was a totally uncritical approach to the Bible, a fact which is attested by the various motion pictures of the period. Modern biblical scholarship was rejected or ignored. It was a decade of simplistic faith when Hollywood could market 'Peter Marshall' and audiences would respond with tears and faith. It was a nostalgic effort to return to the old-time religion."

16.   Leo Pfeffer, *Church, State, and Freedom* (Boston: Beacon Press, 1953), p. 192.

17.   David L. Cohn, "Politics in a God-Fearin' Key," *Saturday Review,* 3 April 1954, p. 12.

18.   "The Child's Political World," *Midwest Journal of Political Science,* 6 (1962), 238–39.

19.   Willmoore Kendall and George W. Carey, *The Basic Symbols of the American Political Tradition* (Baton Rouge: Louisiana State University Press, 1970).

20.   See Kenneth Burke, *Attitudes Toward History,* vol. 1 (New York: New Republic, 1937.

21.   Gordon, *Persuasion,* p. 194.

22.   *Time,* 19 November 1973, p. 18.

23. Quoted in Norman Vincent Peale, *A New Birth of Freedom* (New York: Foundation for Christian Living, n.d.), p. 10.

24. *Newsweek,* 24 June 1974, p. 33.

25. Novak, *Choosing,* p. 302.

26. Quoted in *Indianapolis Star,* 30 January 1972.

27. (Van Nuys, Calif.: Bible Voice, Inc., 1970), p. 30. Robert Jewett, in a brilliant book entitled *The Captain America Complex* (Philadelphia: Westminster Press, 1973) refers to what he calls "hot zeal" and "cool zeal." The heat given off by unofficial civil religionists in their rhetoric contrasts sharply, as we shall see, with the ice-cold distancing rhetoric employed by their official counterparts.

28. Reprinted in Boone et al.

29. Martin E. Marty, "Sects and Cults," *The Annals of the American Academy of Political and Social Science,* 332 (1960), p. 128.

30. Lloyd F. Bitzer, "The Rhetorical Situation," *Philosophy and Rhetoric,* 1 (1968), 1–14.

31. Perhaps no better coverage of the wide scope of church-state interaction exists than that provided by Leo Pfeffer, *Church, State, and Freedom.*

32. Marty, "Sects and Cults," p. 129.

33. *The Christian Patriot,* 30:1 (January 1974), 6.

34. "Editorial: Senator Harold Hughes," *The N.A.C.P.A. Politikon,* 3 (February 1974), 2.

35. Robert N. Bellah, "Civil Religion in America," *Daedalus* (Winter 1967), p. 14.

36. Quoted in Duncan Howlett, "The Sleeper in the Prayer Amendment," Address delivered at the All Souls Unitarian Church, Washington, D.C., 24 May 1964. While Billington's remarks are admittedly singular, a penchant for active and practical involvement with the vicissitudes of this world does indeed earmark the rhetoric of the civil-religious Right. As John Birch leader Tom Anderson has implied, to cling exclusively to symbolic influence is to forsake one's commitment to God and country: "What irritates me is seeing Christians used to destroy their own faith and the faith of this once-Christian nation. All that is necessary to cause fifty million American Christians—real Christians—to be murdered by the Communists is for Christian Americans to devote themselves exclusively to prayer and let the Communists take over our country!" See "For Christians: Put on the Whole Armor of God," *American Opinion,* November 1972, p. 6.

37. *Christian Crusade Weekly,* 30 June 1974, p. 1.

38. What Is the Church League of America? (Wheaton, Ill.: Church league of America, n.d.), p. 3.

39. Frank Hughes, *The Church League of America Story* (pamphlet issued by the Church league of America, n.d.).

40. *Christian Crusade Weekly,* 14 April 1974, p. 4.

41. Peter L. Berger and Daniel Pinard, "Military Religion: An Analysis of Educational Materials Disseminated by Chaplains," in *Military Chaplains,* p. 91.

42. Sidney E. Mead, *The Lively Experiment* (New York: Harper & Row, 1963), p. 152.

43. Kenneth L. Sheek, "Letter to the Editor," *Indianapolis Star,* 23 December 1973.

44. Smith is, in my terminology, a decidedly unofficial civil religionist and editor of a journal (*The Cross and the Flag*) which "makes its way through the mails in a plain brown wrapper." See Barnett Baskerville, "The Cross and the Flag: Evangelists of the Far Right," in *The Rhetoric of Our Times,* ed. J. Jeffery Auer (New York: Meredith, 1969), p. 434.

Chapter 3

1. Sherwood Eddy, *The Kingdom of God and the American Dream* (New York: Harper & Row, 1941), p. 79.

2. Charles Smith, *Why Read the Bible in the Public Schools?* (New York: National Liberal League, Inc., 1949), not paginated.

3. "The Case for Separation," in *Religion in America,* ed. John Cogley (New York: Meridian, 1958), p. 59.

4. "Commentary," in *The Religious Situation: 1968,* ed. Donald R. Cutler (Boston: Beacon Press, 1968), p. 358. See also Andrew M. Greeley, *Unsecular Man* (New York: Schocken Books, 1972), p. 129.

5. For a more complete discussion of such matters, see Leo Pfeffer, *Church, State, and Freedom* (Boston: Beacon Press, 1953), p. 108.

6. Ernest S. Bates, *American Faith* (New York: Norton, 1940), pp. 83–84.

7. Don Higginbotham, "The Relevance of the American Revolution," *Anglican Theological Review,* no. 1 (July 1973): 29.

8. Edwin Gaustad, *A Religious History of America* (New York: Harper & Row, 1966), p. 257.

9. Loren Beth, *The American Theory of Church and State* (Gainesville: University of Florida Press, 1958), p. 72.

10. Bernard Bailyn, *The Ideological Origins of the American Revolution* (Cambridge, Mass.: Harvard University Press, 1967), p. 271.

11. See Annemarie de Waal Malefijt, *Religion and Culture* (New York: Macmillan Co., 1968), p. 235.

12. Billy Graham, "White House Sermon, March 15, 1970," in *White House Sermons,* ed. Ben Hibbs (New York: Harper and Row. Inc., 1972), p. 136. Anthropologist of religion, Annemarie de Waal Malefijt, remarks: "Diviners often wield a significant amount of political power. . . . The rules of augury were secret, and the signs were usually vague enough to allow alternate interpretations in order to please the rulers in power and to dispose of others." (See her *Religion and Culture,* p. 217). When Richard Nixon was the Grand Shaman of the American civil religion, at least, Billy Graham's divinations were found to be particularly valuable.

13.   Conrad Cherry, *God's New Israel* (Englewood Cliffs, N. J.: Prentice-Hall, 1971), p. 13.

14.   Peter Berger, *The Sacred Canopy* (Garden City, N.Y.: Doubleday & Co., 1967), p. 58.

15.   Michael C. Thomas and Charles C. Flippen, "American Civil Religion: An Empirical Study," *Social Forces,* 51 (December 1972): 218–25.

16.   Robert N. Bellah, "American Civil Religion in the 1970's," *Anglican Theological Review,* no. 1 (July 1973): 8.

17.   John F. Wilson, "The Status of 'Civil Religion' in America," in *The Religion of the Republic,* ed. Elwyn A. Smith (Philadelphia: Fortress Press, 1971), p. 15.

18.   Ibid., p. 14.

19.   Bellah, "Civil Religion in the1970's," p. 9. Robert Stauffer also feels that rigorous use of the term religion in this context is unnecessarily constraining. See his "Civil Religion, Technocracy, and the Private Sphere: Further Comments on Cultural Integration in Advanced Societies," *Journal for the Scientific Study of Religion,* 12, no. 4 (December 1973): 417.

20.   O'Dea delineates each of these functions more precisely in *Sociology and the Study of Religion* (New York: Basic Books, 1970), pp. 205–207, 262–267.

21.   Robert S. Alley, *So Help Me God* (Richmond, Va.: John Knox Press, 1972), p. 18.

22.   O'Dea, pp. 240–55.

23.   Alternative explanations for the American civil religion's having escaped O'Dea's problems would be that it is too "young" to have been institutionalized or that it has been hardy enough to foresee and to take steps to prevent such vicissitudes from arising. The first alternative seems unlikely when we consider that the "religion" has existed for almost two hundred years (according to Bellah), a time-span which is more than sufficient for producing the natural developmental problems O'Dea sees as common to most all religions. Also, the fact that the "hierarchy" of our national faith, as well as the attitudes and motivations of its "members," have changed so fundamentally and so rapidly since 1776 seems to indicate that scant attention could have been directed to heading off such naturally occurring difficulties.

24.   Wilson, "Status of Civil Religion," pp. 20–21.

25.   Robert N. Bellah, "Civil Religion in America," *Daedalus* (Winter 1967): 1.

26.   Dwight D. Eisenhower, "First Inaugural Address, January 20, 1953," in *Inaugural Addresses of the Presidents of the United States* (Washington, D.C.: U.S. Government Printing Office, 1969), p. 256.

27.   Bellah, "Civil Religion in the 1970's," p. 19.

28.   See, for example, Charles Henderson, *The Nixon Theology* (New York: Harper & Row, 1972).

29. "Feature Review," *Religious Education* (September–October 1975), p. 552.

30. "Two Kinds of Two Kinds of Civil Religion," in *American Civil Religion,* ed. Russell E. Richey and Donald G. Jones (New York: Harper, 1974), p. 141.

31. In Richey and Jones, p. 137.

32. Ibid., p. 135.

33. Alley, p. 17.

Chapter 4

1. Peter Berger, *The Noise of Solemn Assemblies* (Garden City, N.Y.: Doubleday & Co., 1961), p. 60.

2. "The Present Embarrassment of the Church," in *Religion in America,* ed. John Cogley (New York: Meridian, 1958), p. 23.

3. Benjamin Weiss, *God in American History* (Grand Rapids, Mich.: Zondervan, 1966), p. 36.

4. Reprinted in Weiss, pp. 37–38.

5. Weiss, p. 36.

6. Berger, *The Sacred Canopy* (Garden City, N.Y.: Doubleday & Co., 1967), p. 33.

7. Madlyn Murray O'Hair, *Freedom Under Siege* (Los Angeles: J. P. Tarcher, 1974).

8. "The King's Chapel and the King's Court," *Christianity and Crisis*, 4 August 1969, p. 211.

9. "Civil Religion in America," *Daedalus* (Winter 1967): 3.

10. Leo Pfeffer, *Church, State, and Freedom* (Boston: Beacon Press, 1953), p. 109.

11. Ibid.

12. Sidney Mead, *The Lively Experiment* (New York: Harper & Row, 1963), p. 65.

13. Quoted in Paul Blanshard, *God and Man in Washington* (Boston: Beacon Press, 1960), p. 100.

14. Ibid.

15. Ibid.

16. Mead, p. 97.

17. For more information on such matters, see Mead.

18. See William Gribbin, *The Churches Militant* (New Haven: Yale University Press, 1973).

19. Ray Abrams, *Preachers Present Arms* (New York: Round Table Press, 1933), p. 121.

20. Mead, p. 65.

21. Blanshard, p. 25.

22. Frederick Fox, "The National Day of Prayer," *Theology Today*, 26, no. 3 (October 1972): 273.

23. Franklin Littell, *From State Church to Pluralism* (Chicago: Aldine Publishing Company, 1962), pp. xi–xii.

24. O'Hair, pp. 3–5.

25. Oswald C. J. Hoffmann, "Faith and Force," *And Our Defense Is Sure*, ed. H. D. Moore, E. A. Ham, and C. E. Hobgood (New York: Abingdon, 1964), p. 77.

26. Bernard Bell, *Crowd Culture* (New York: Harper, 1952), p. 98.

27. Alan Heimert, *Religion and the American Mind* (Cambridge, Mass.: Harvard University Press, 1966), pp. 540–41.

28. Berger, *Solemn Assemblies* (Garden City, N.Y.: Doubleday & Co., 1961), p. 67. During times of conflict, members of the clergy have often leapt to the defense of the American nation. Harry Kerr reports that during the Revolution, for example, the election sermons played an important role in preparing the way for the Revolution and for the establishment of a democratic form of government in America. Also, in World War I, Roman Catholic prelate John Cardinal Farley reminded his congregation that "As Catholics we owe unswerving allegiance to the government of America, and it is our sacred duty to answer with alacrity every demand our country makes upon our loyalty and devotion." At approximately the same time, the pastor of the First Baptist Church of New London, Connecticut, "preached in his (chaplain's) uniform with a machine gun and an American flag on the platform beside him." In more recent times the American clergy was asked by a federal agency to be ready to launch the "spiritual mobilization of the country in case of war," while, at the same time, the agency was inquiring into the possibility of using church buildings as civil defense shelters! Besides rendering rhetorical assistance to the government when requested, it would seem that organized religion is required to share with its "partner" many of its non-rhetorical possessions as well. See Harry P. Kerr, "The Election Sermon: Primer for Revolutionaries," *Speech Monographs*, 29, no. 1 (March 1962): p. 18; Abrams, pp. 73 and 245–46; and Berger, *Solemn Assemblies*, p. 61.

29. Will Herberg, *Protestant, Catholic, Jew* (Garden City, N.Y.: Doubleday & Co., 1955), p. 286.

30. Ibid., p. 96.

31. Loren Beth, *The American Theory of Church and State* (Gainesville: University of Florida Press, 1958), p. 151.

32. For a fuller discussion, see ibid., pp. 124 ff.

33. *Time*, 17 December 1973, p. 78.

34. Quoted in ibid.

35. Harry P. Kerr, "Politics and Religion in Colonial Fast and Thanksgiving Sermons, 1763–1783," *Quarterly Journal of Speech*, 46 (1960), 376.

36. Heimert, p. 240.

37. For a more detailed discussion of such issues, see Abrams, p. 207.

38. Quoted in Fay Valentine, *Citizenship for Christians* (Nashville, Tenn.: Broadman Press, 1965), p. 17.

39.   Nick Thimmesch, "The Lord and Harold Hughes," *Saturday Evening Post*, June–July 1974, p. 45.

40.   Richard J. Neuhaus, "The War, the Churches, and Civil Religion," *The Annals*, 387 (January 1970), 134.

41.   Ibid.

42.   Robert S. Alley, *So Help Me God* (Richmond, Va.: John Knox Press, 1972), p. 95.

43.   Neuhaus, p. 130.

44.   See ibid., p. 131.

45.   Littell, p. 163.

Chapter 5

1.   Kathleen Jamieson, "Generic Calcification: An Undiagnosed Rhetorical Malady," Paper presented at the annual convention of the Speech Communication Association, New York City, December 1974.

2.   Kathleen Jamieson, "Generic Constraints and the Rhetorical Situation," *Philosophy and Rhetoric*, 6 (1973), 163.

3.   Frederick Fox, "The National Day of Prayer," *Theology Today*, 26 (1972), 269.

4.   Gabriel Fackre, "Of Hope and Judgment," in *Bicentennial Broadside* (New York: United Church Board for Homeland Ministries, 1975), p. 6.

5.   "In God We Trust," *Christian Century*, 27 May 1964, p. 719.

6.   Robert Alley, *So Help Me God* (Richmond, Va.: John Knox Press, 1972), p. 15.

7.   Ibid.

8.   Robert Bellah, "Civil Religion in America," *Daedalus* (Winter 1967), p. 7.

9.   *Inaugural Addresses of the Presidents of the United States* (Washington, D.C.: U.S. Government Printing Office, 1969). All subsequent quotations from the presidential inaugurals have been extracted from this source.

10.   A careful inspection of Richard Nixon's rhetoric reveals that the data reported here do not reflect inaugural rhetoric exclusively. After analyzing the twenty-eight speeches by Nixon mentioned earlier, speeches which contained references to the deity and speeches which were delivered in a wide variety of rhetorical settings, the following proportions were revealed: God the Inscrutable Potentate (37.7 percent of the references); God the Witnessing Author (19.6 percent); God the Wise and the Just (6.5 percent); God the Genial Philanthropist (28.0 percent); and God the Object of Affection (8.2 percent). Thus, except for Nixon's being a bit less taken with the wisdom and justice of the Lord, his overall rhetorical behavior is quite reminiscent of the inaugural remarks made by his predecessors in office.

11.   Robert Alley has suggested that each of America's presidents has embraced a particular God, implying that the "pantheon" I am describing here is made up of a variegated grouping of individually prized gods. Says Alley: "When

Americans determine to inject God into this political complexity in order to sim-
plify by divine decree, the question is raised as to who is this God. Is he the selec-
tive God of judgment that inspired Wilson? Is he the God of business who rewards
those who practice diligence as defined by Hoover? Is he the God of the universe
whose benevolent plan may inspire all men as it did Roosevelt? Is he the friendly
sovereign who has chosen America, blessed her, and given her a special mission as
seen by Truman and Eisenhower?" (Alley, p. 81). While Alley's argument may be
correct, it should be noted that the data presented above do not support his contention as regards presidential inaugurals. Rather, most American presidents sampled
liberally from the pantheon when framing their maiden remarks as chief executives.

12.   Will Herberg, *Protestant, Catholic, Jew* (Garden City, N.Y.: Doubleday & Co., 1955), p. 285.

13.   Annemarie de Waal Malefijt, *Religion and Culture* (New York: Macmillan Co., 1968), p. 215.

14.   Herberg, p. 285.

15.   "'Civil Religion' vs. 'Biblical Religion,'" reprinted in *The Christian
Patriot,* May 1973, pp. 6–7.

16.   "The Church of the Covenants: Plans for the Bicentennial," *Bicentennial Broadside* (New York: United Church Board for Homeland Ministries,
1975), p. 30.

17.   Ibid.

18.   Lynn E. May, *Baptists and the Bicentennial* (pamphlet prepared by the
Southern Baptist Council Historical Commission, 1975).

19.   *Forward* 1 (Spring 1974): p. 4. (*Forward* is a periodical issued by the
Interchurch Center in New York City.)

20.   Willmoore Kendall and George W. Carey, *The Basic Symbols of the
American Political Tradition* (Baton Rouge: Louisiana State University Press,
1970), p. 12.

21.   *The Word "Comrade," Should We Abandon It?* (A publication of the
Americanism Department, Veterans of Foreign War, n.d.), p. 2.

22.   *The Word "Comrade," Should We Abandon It?* p. 2.

23.   Joseph Costanzo, *This Nation Under God* (New York: Herder & Herder,
1964), p. 34.

24.   Leo Pfeffer, *Church, State, and Freedom* (Boston: Beacon Press, 1953),
p. 151.

25.   See J. L. Austin, *How to Do Things with Words* (New York: Oxford
University Press, 1965).

26.   *Time,* 13 November 1972.

27.   Conrad Cherry, "American Sacred Ceremonies," in *American Mosaic:
Social Patterns of Religion in the United States,* ed. Phillip E. Hammond and
Benton Johnson (New York: Random House, 1970), p. 313.

28.   Wallace Fisher, *Politics, Poker, and Piety* (Nashville, Tenn.: Abingdon
Press, 1972), p. 138.

29.   Fox, p. 276. Things get a bit more confusing, of course, when civil war

splits a nation (and its legitimizing God) apart. Rhetorically speaking, such an exigence requires that God take everybody's part. For an interesting discussion of such matters, see H. V. Taylor's study, "Preaching on Slavery, 1831–1861," in *Preaching in American History,* ed. D. Holland (New York: Abingdon Press, 1969), 168–83.

30. Andrew Greeley, *The Denominational Society* (Glenview, Ill.: Scott, Foresman & Co., 1972), p. 163.

31. Robert N. Bellah, "American Civil Religion in the 1970's," *Anglican Theological Review,* no. 1 (July 1973): 18–19.

32. Peter Berger, *The Sacred Canopy* (Garden City, N.Y.: Doubleday & Co., 1967), p. 32.

33. "Piety along the Potomac," *The Reporter,* 17 August 1954, p. 26.

34. (New York: The Christophers, 1964).

35. *To the Republic: One Nation under God* (South Bend, Ind.: Manion Forum, 1968), p. 4.

36. Malefijt, *Religion and Culture,* p. 162. Hart has suggested that placing a rhetorical emphasis on the past is characteristic of much "true believer" discourse. While civil-religious discourse does not qualify for "true believer" status, the parallels are dramatic and worth noting. See Roderick P. Hart, "The Rhetoric of the True Believer," *Speech Monographs,* 38 (1971), 249–61.

37. Vol. 46 (July–August 1973), 7.

38. "Religion and the 'Informing' of Culture," in *Religion's Influence in Contemporary Society,* ed. Joseph E. Faulkner (Columbus: Merrill, 1972), p. 282.

39. "This Nation Shall Endure," Address delivered at Brigham Young University, 4 December 1973, unpublished text, p. 8.

40. See M. Darroll Bryant, "America as God's Kingdom," in Jurgen Moltmann et al., eds., *Religion and Political Society* (New York: Harper, 1974), pp. 54–94.

41. Sidney Ahlstrom, *A Religious History of the American People* (New Haven: Yale University Press, 1972), p. 311.

42. J. F. Maclear, "The Republic and the Millenium," in *Religion of the Republic,* ed. Elwyn A. Smith (Philadelphia: Fortress Press, 1971), 183–216.

43. Mentioned in *The Light in the Steeple* (New York: National Council of Churches, 1975), p. 8.

44. Maclear, p. 204. See also William Gribbin, *The Churches Militant* (New Haven: Yale University Press, 1973), p. 130.

45. See Ray Abrams, *Preachers Present Arms* (New York: Round Table Press, 1933).

46. Quoted in Alley, p. 80.

47. "Resignation Address," *New York Times,* 16 October 1973, p. 34.

48. Personal communication, 22 January 1974. Rev. Litfin was then an assistant professor of practical theology at Dallas Theological Seminary, Dallas, Texas.

49. Thomas O'Dea, *Sociology and the Study of Religion* (New York: Basic Books, 1970), p. 242.

50. *The Catholic War Veteran,* July–August 1973, p. 5.

51. Ibid.

52. Conrad Cherry, "Two American Sacred Ceremonies: Their Implications for the Study of Religion in America," *American Quarterly,* 21 (1969), 754.

53. Paul Blanshard, *God and Man in Washington* (Boston: Beacon Press, 1960), p. 3.

54. Clarence DiChiara, "National 1st Vice Commander's Program for 1973–1974" (unpublished memorandum of the American Legion, October 1973), p. 3.

55. Fox, pp. 263–64.

56. Ibid., p. 263.

57. Costanzo, p. 35.

58. Michael Novak, *Choosing Our King* (New York: Macmillan Co., 1974), p. 3.

59. Ibid., p. 193.

60. For a more complete understanding of this particular service, see Ben Hibbs, ed., *White House Sermons* (New York: Harper, 1972), pp. 62–69.

61. Edward B. Fiske, "Controversy over Those White House Services," *New York Times,* 10 August 1969, p. 7.

62. Bellah, "Civil Religion in America," p. 15.

63. Bellah, "Civil Religion in America," p. 5.

64. If asked, Irving Kristol would probably agree with the position being taken here—that rhetorical conventions, not philosophical predilections, are the operant forces in much presidential discourse. Says Kristol: "Some time around the turn of the century, the impact of the Populist and Progressive movements combined to establish the vernacular utopian-prophetic rhetoric as the official rhetoric of American statesmen. It happened gradually, and it was not until the nineteen-thirties that the victory of the vernacular was complete and unchallengeable. But it also happened with a kind of irresistible momentum, as the egalitarian, 'democratic' temper of the American people remorselessly destroyed the last vestiges of the neo-Whiggish, 'republican' cast of mind. By now, we no longer find it in any way odd that American Presidents should sound like demagogic journalists of yesteryear. Indeed, we would take alarm and regard them as eccentric if they sounded like anything else." See *On the Democratic Idea in America* (New York: Harper & Row, 1972), p. 134.

65. Winthrop Hudson, *Religion in America* (New York: Charles Scribner's Sons, 1973), p. 112.

66. Bernard Bailyn, *The Ideological Origins of the American Revolution* (Cambridge, Mass.: Harvard University Press, 1967), p. 251.

67. Richard K. Fenn, "Toward a New Sociology of Religion," *Journal for the Scientific Study of Religion,* 11 (March 1972), p. 21.

68. *Service to God and Country Handbook* (Indianapolis: The American Legion, 1971), p. 3.

69. Murray Edelman, *The Symbolic Uses of Politics* (Champaign: University of Illinois Press, 1964), p. 125.

70. Cherry, "American Sacred Ceremonies," p. 311. Lloyd Warner views America's holidays as performing the same sort of unifying function we are noting here. See his *American Life* (Chicago: University of Chicago Press, 1953).

71. Martin E. Marty, Stuart E. Rosenberg and Andrew M. Greeley, *What Do We Believe?* (New York: Meredith, 1968), p. 28.

72. Quoted in Abrams, p. 121.

73. "How to Improve your Government: 19 Tips," *Christopher News Notes,* no. 138, October 1964, not paginated.

74. Cherry, "Two Sacred Ceremonies," p. 742.

75. "The Election Sermon: Primer for Revolutionaries," *Speech Monographs,* 29:1 (March 1962): 22.

76. "The Fact of Pluralism and the Persistence of Sectarianism," in *Religion of the Republic,* ed. Elwyn A. Smith (Philadelphia: Fortress Press, 1971), pp. 251–52.

77. Andrew M. Greeley, *Unsecular Man* (New York: Schocken Books, 1972), p. 93.

78. Conrad Cherry, *God's New Israel* (Englewood Cliffs, N.J.: Prentice-Hall, 1971), p. 18. Kenneth Burke, especially, sees mythification to be essential to all political orders. Such myths, implies Burke, allow governments to transcend the mundane and groveling imprecations of feckless nationalism in favor of a more majestic view of the collective's destiny. See his *A Rhetoric of Motives* (Berkeley: University of California Press, 1969), pp. 113–14.

79. Kristol, pp. 148–49.

80. Anecdotally, at least, Kristol's assumption seems to hold when the rhetoric of America's statesmen is compared to that of Great Britain's leaders: "'If you desire a purpose in life,' Prime Minister Heath told some of his idealistic constituents, 'don't come to me. Kindly call on your archbishop.'" Quoted in Novak, p. 108.

81. Abrams, pp. xvii–xviii.

82. Quoted in Peter L. Berger and Daniel Pinard, "Military Religion: An Analysis of Educational Materials Disseminated by Chaplains," in *Military Chaplains: From a Religious Military to a Military Religion,* ed. Harvey G. Cox (New York: American Report Press, 1971), p. 92.

83. David O. Moberg, *The Church as a Social Institution* (Englewood Cliffs, N.J.: Prentice-Hall, 1962), p. 161.

84. William L. Miller, *Piety Along the Potomac* (New York: Houghton, 1964), p. 41.

85. Robert D. Clark, "The Oratorical Career of Bishop Matthew Simpson," *Speech Monographs,* 16 (1949), 4.

86. *Protestant, Catholic and Jew,* p. 96.

87. William L. Miller, "American Religion and American Political Attitudes," in *Religious Perspectives in American Culture,* ed. James W. Smith and A. Leland Jamison (Princeton: Princeton University Press, 1961), p. 93.

88. Blanshard, p. 21.

89. Hudson, p. 114.

90. Quoted in the *National Catholic Reporter,* vol. 10, 23 November 1973, p. 4.

91. *Dwight D. Eisenhower: In Memoriam* (pamphlet issued by the Billy Graham Evangelistic Association, 1969), not paginated.

92. George H. Williams, "The Chaplaincy in the Armed Forces of the United States of America in Historical and Ecclesiastical Perspective," in *Military Chaplains: From a Religious Military to a Military Religion,* ed. Harvey G. Cox (New York: American Report Press, 1971), p. 14.

93. Mary Ruth Cavanaugh, "The Ladies' Auxiliary's National President's Message," *Catholic War Veteran,* January–February 1974, p. 7.

94. Herbert Schneider, *Religion in Twentieth Century America* (Cambridge, Mass.: Harvard University Press, 1952), p. 32.

95. John F. Wilson, "The Status of 'Civil Religion' in America," in *The Religion of the Republic,* ed. Elwyn A. Smith (Philadelphia: Fortress Press, 1971), p. 5. Felix Keesing has suggested that religion-in-general is possessed of special emotional resources during anxious times. See his *Cultural Anthropology* (New York: Holt, Rinehart, & Winston, 1965), pp. 328–29.

96. *Protestant, Catholic and Jew,* p. 97.

97. Sperry, p. 252.

98. "This Nation Shall Endure," an address delivered at Brigham Young University in Provo, Utah, on 4 December 1973.

99. Ibid.

100. "I Pledge Allegiance," in *Creative Help for Daily Living,* 25 (July 1974), p. 9.

101. Blanshard, p. 33.

102. Robert E. Fitch, "Piety and Politics in President Eisenhower," *The Antioch Review,* 15:2 (Summer 1955): 154.

103. Bellah, "Civil Religion in America," p. 18.

104. Robert M. Bellah, *The Broken Covenant* (New York: Seabury Press, 1975), p. 162.

105. "In God Let Us Trust," in H. D. Moore, E. A. Ham, and C. E. Hobgood (eds.), *And Our Defense Is Sure* (New York: Abingdon, 1964), p. 152.

Chapter 6

1. William Gribbin, *The Churches Militant* (New Haven: Yale University Press, 1973), p. 19.

2. Quoted in Paul Blanshard, *God and Man in Washington* (Boston: Beacon Press,1960), p. 32.

3. See Richard K. Fenn, "Toward a New Sociology of Religion," *Journal for the Scientific Study of Religion*, 11 (1972), 16–32.

4. Conrad Cherry, *God's New Israel: Religious Interpretations of American Destiny* (Englewood Cliffs, N. J.: Prentice-Hall, 1971), p. 19.

5. Ernest S. Bates, *American Faith* (New York: Norton, 1940), p. 86.

Chapter 7

1. Bellah, "Civil Religion in America," p. 4.

2. Hart, *The Political Pulpit,* p. 45 (this edition, p. 44).

3. Hart, *The Political Pulpit*, p. 40 (this edition, p. 39).

4. Hart, *The Political Pulpit*, p. 44 (this edition, p. 44).

5. Hart, *The Political Pulpit*, pp. 62–63 (this edition, pp. 57–58).

6. Hart, *The Political Pulpit*, p. 52 (this edition, p. 49).

7. Hart, *The Political Pulpit*, pp. 67–69 (this edition, pp. 61–63).

8. Hart, *The Political Pulpit*, p. 67 (this edition, p. 62). Fackre, *Bicentennial Broadside*, p. 6.

9. Hart, *The Political Pulpit*, pp. 81–82 (this edition, p. 73).

10. Hart, *The Political Pulpit*, pp. 81–82 (this edition, p. 73).

11. Hart, *The Political Pulpit*, p. 82 (this edition, p. 73).

12. Hart, *The Political Pulpit*, p. 82 (this edition, p. 73).

13. King, *Why We Can't Wait*, p. 89.

14. See R. Lee, "The Rhetorical Construction of Time in Martin Luther King, Jr.'s 'Letter from Birmingham Jail.'"

15. King, *Why We Can't Wait*, p. 86.

16. Quayle, *Prepared Remarks by the Vice President.*

17. Quayle, *Cultural Elites Speech.*

18. See L. Murfield, *The Rhetorical Renegotiation of the "Family": From the New Christian Right to the 1992 Presidential Campaign.*

19. See R. Lewis & R. Campbell, *Real Family Values: Keeping Faith in an Age of Cultural Chaos.* C. Swindoll, *Strong Family: Growing Wise in Family Life.*

20. See Lee & Murfield, "Christian Tradition, Jeffersonian Democracy, and the Myth of the Sentimental Family: An Exploration of the Premises of Social Conservative Argumentation."

21. S. Coontz, *The Way We Never Were: American Families and the Nostalgia Trap,* pp. 76–79.

22. See M. Barton, *Confession, Contrition, and Forgiveness: The Intersection of Religion and Politics in Bill Clinton's Explanation of the Monica Lewinsky Affair.*

23. R. Pierard & R. Linder, *Civil Religion and the Presidency,* p. 204.

24. Clinton, *Public Papers of the President of the United States,* p. 1565.

25. Clinton, *Public Papers of the President of the United States,* p. 1565.

26.   Clinton, *Public Papers of the President of the United States*, p. 1565.

27.   Clinton, *Public Papers of the President of the United States*, p. 1566.

28.   Clinton, *Public Papers of the President of the United States*, p. 1566.

29.   Bennett, "Testing of a President: Tearful Clinton Tells Group of Clerics, 'I Have Sinned,'" p. A1.

30.   Bennett, "Testing of a President: Tearful Clinton Tells Group of Clerics, 'I Have Sinned,'" p. A1

31.   Bennett, "Testing of a President: Tearful Clinton Tells Group of Clerics, 'I Have Sinned,'" p. A1.

32.   Niebuhr, "Testing of a President: The Religious Issues; King David Inspires Plea for Pardon," p. A12.

33.   Niebuhr, "Testing of a President: The Religious Issues; King David Inspires Plea for Pardon," p. A12.

34.   Niebuhr, "Testing of a President: The Religious Issues; King David Inspires Plea for Pardon," p. A12.

35.   Niebuhr, "Testing of a President: The Religious Issues; King David Inspires Plea for Pardon," p. A12.

36.   Goodstein, "Guidepost from Country's Pulpits: The Power to Judge Belongs to God," p. A25.

37.   Hart, *The Political Pulpit*, pp. 37–38, 63–64, 66–67, 94 (this edition, pp. 37–38, 58, 61–62, 81–82).

38.   Bush, "Inaugural Address," p. 209.

39.   Bush, "Inaugural Address," p. 209.

40.   Bush, "Inaugural Address," p. 211.

41.   Bush, "Inaugural Address," p. 211.

42.   See Lee & R. Patterson, "The Genealogy of Social Conservative Argumentation: Demonstrating the Family Resemblance among Three Influential discourses."

43.   Bush, "Inaugural Address," p. 210.

44.   Bush, "Inaugural Address," p. 211.

45.   Bush, "Inaugural Address," p. 210.

46.   See Bush, "Duty of Hope: Armies of Compassion"; M. Olasky, *The Tragedy of American Compassion*; Olasky, *Compassionate Conservatism: What It Is, What It Does, and How it Can Transform America*.

47.   See H. White, *Tropics of Discourse: Essays in Cultural Criticism.*

48.   K. Burke, "Ideology and Myth," p. 200.

49.   T. Pangle, *The Spirit of Modern Republicanism: The Moral Vision of the American Founders and the Philosophy of John Locke*, p. 131. A. Rapaczynski, *Nature and Politics: Liberalism in the Philosophies of Hobbes, Locke, and Rousseau.*

50.   See M. McGee, "In Search of 'The People': A Rhetorical Alternative." H. Roelofs, *Ideology and Myth in American Politics: A Critique of a National Political Mind.*

Chapter 8

1.   Robert Bellah, "Civil Religion in America," *Daedalus* (Winter, 1967), pp. 1–21.

2.   West Lafayette, Ind.: Purdue University Press, 1977.

3.   Carolyn Marvin and David W. Ingle, *Blood Sacrifice and the Nation: Totem Rituals and the American Flag* (New York: Cambridge University Press, 1999).

4.   See Marvin and Ingle, pp. 41–63, and Marvin, "The Body of the Text: Literacy's Corporeal Constant," *Quarterly Journal of Speech* 80 (1994).

5.   Rene Girard, *Violence and the Sacred*, trans. P. Gregory, Baltimore: Johns Hopkins University Press, 1977.

6.   Quoted in Hart, *The Political Pulpit*, pp. 100–101 (this edition, p. 86).

7.   Dwight D. Eisenhower, "The Day I Knew I Belonged to the Flag," *Reader's Digest* 94 (March, 1969), p. 93.

8.   Hart, *The Political Pulpit*, p. 5.

Chapter 9

1.   Hart, *The Political Pulpit*, pp. 43–65 (this edition, pp. 43–59).

2.   Hart, *The Political Pulpit*, p. 5.

3.   Hart, *The Political Pulpit*, p. 44 (this edition, p. 43).

4.   On the Jewish population and settlement of the colonies see any standard history of American Judaism. For example, Stanley Feldstein, *The Land That I Show You: Three Centuries of Jewish Life in America*, pp. 1–34.

5.   Hart, *The Political Pulpit*, p. 46 (this edition, p. 45).

6.   All quotations in this paragraph are drawn from George W. Bush, "The Commitment of Our Fathers Is Now the Calling of Our Time," address at the National Cathedral, September 14, 2001.

7.   See Kevin Eckstrom, "Poll: Religion Increasing in American Public Life."

8.   Hart, *The Political Pulpit*, p. 44 (this edition, p. 45).

9.   Robert Bellah, "Civil Religion in America," p. 5.

10.   Rhode Island's history of religious tolerance attracted approximately 50% of the Jewish population of the colonies and three of the five synagogues in the colonies at the time of the revolution. See Jacob Marcus, *The Colonial American Jew 1492–1776*, vol. 2., p. 860.

11.   For a brief overview of religious diversity in the colonies at the time of the revolution see Curtis P. Nettles, *The Roots of American Civilization: A History of American Colonial Life*, pp. 470–484.

12.   Hart, *The Political Pulpit*, p. 44 (this edition, p. 44).

13.   Robert V. Friedenberg, *Theodore Roosevelt and the Rhetoric of Militant Decency*, pp. 15–17.

14.   See Chapter 2 of Friedenberg, *Theodore Roosevelt and the Rhetoric of Militant Decency*.

15.   Friedenberg, *Theodore Roosevelt and the Rhetoric of Militant Decency*.

16.   For example, the 2000 convention acceptance addresses of both George W. Bush and Albert Gore include passages that treat all five of these topics; power, order, work, social responsibility and character.

17.   Jules Harlow, ed. *Siddur Sim Shalom: A Prayer Book for Shabbat, Festivals, and Weekdays,* p. 415. This is the standard prayer book used in most conservative synagogues in the United States. Similar prayers can be found in the prayer books of the other major Jewish denominations within the United States.

18.   Hart, *The Political Pulpit,* p. 44 (this edition, p. 44).

19.   Hart, *The Political Pulpit,* pp. 66–75 (this edition, pp. 61–68).

20.   Hart, *The Political Pulpit,* pp. 68–69 (this edition, pp. 62–63).

21.   George W. Bush, "Remarks at the Islamic Center of Washington."

22.   Hart, *The Political Pulpit,* pp. 70–73 (this edition, pp. 64–66).

23.   Hart, *The Political Pulpit,* p. 74 (this edition, p. 67).

24.   Hart, *The Political Pulpit,* pp. 81–82 (this edition, p. 73).

25.   For a brief sympathetic synopsis of Bush's proposals see Joseph Loconte, "Government and Religion: Have Faith."

26.   Gershom Seixas, "Religious Discourse—Thursday, 26 of November, 1789," pp. 13–14.

Chapter 10

1.   See Robert Bellah, "Civil Religion in America."

2.   See Novak, *Choosing Our King: Powerful Symbols in American Politics.*

3.   See Hart, *The Political Pulpit.*

4.   See W. Fisher, "Rhetorical Fiction and the Presidency."

5.   Bellah, "Civil Religion in America," p. 104.

6.   Hart, *The Political Pulpit*, p. 53 (this edition, p. 50).

7.   Fisher, "Rhetorical Fiction and the Presidency," p. 119.

8.   Hart, *The Political Pulpit*, p. 9 (this edition, p. 16).

9.   Hart, *The Political Pulpit*, pp. 9–10 (this edition, p. 17).

10.   K. Campbell & T. Burkholder, *Critiques of Contemporary Rhetoric*, p. 21.

11.   See J. Murphy, "Inventing Authority: Bill Clinton, Martin Luther King, Jr., and the Orchestration of Rhetorical Tradition"; P. Japp, "Esther or Isaiah? The Abolitionist-Feminist Rhetoric of Angelina Grimke."

12.   Fisher, "Rhetorical Fiction and the Presidency," p. 123.

13.   H. Rosin, "Clinton Faces Test at Annual Prayer Breakfast Today," p. A34. S. Page, "Clinton's 'Final Campaign': Survival Through Contrition," p. 1A. A. Miga, "Web of Deceit; Report Alleges Lies, Obstruction by Clinton; Starr's Report Could Be Made Public Today," p. 1. P. Reusse, "It's High Time for More Mea Culpas," p. 1C.

14.   See J. Morse, "Going Public With Prayer."

15.   New International Version, 1 Samuel 13:13.

16.   See Clinton, "Remarks by the President at Religious Leaders Breakfast."

17.   See Clinton, "Remarks by the President at Religious Leaders Breakfast."

18. See Clinton, "Remarks by the President at Religious Leaders Breakfast."
19. See Clinton, "Remarks by the President at Religious Leaders Breakfast."
20. See Clinton, "Remarks by the President at Religious Leaders Breakfast."
21. See Clinton, "Remarks by the President at Religious Leaders Breakfast."
22. See Clinton, "Remarks by the President at Religious Leaders Breakfast."
23. See Clinton, "Remarks by the President at Religious Leaders Breakfast."
24. See Clinton, "Remarks by the President at Religious Leaders Breakfast."
25. See Clinton, *Public Papers of the Presidents of the United States: William J. Clinton, 1999.*

Chapter 11

1. See A. Tocqueville, *Democracy in America.*
2. See Hart, *The Political Pulpit.*
3. Hart, *The Political Pulpit*, p. 49 (this edition, p. 47).
4. See Hart, *Campaign Talk* and "Redeveloping DICTION: Theoretical considerations."
5. The stadium event attendance figure was provided by PK spokesman and Director of Advance Planning, Steve Chavis (personal communication, February 1, 2002). No official attendance estimates of SITG were taken. Unofficial estimates vary widely between 480,000 and 1,500,000 (see, for example, Koch & Karl, Mattingly, Stodghill, and Wheeler). Two sociologists using police aerial photographs initially settled on a range of 480,000–720,000, but later revised it to a (conservative) point estimate of 600,000 ("Numbers Revised"). The PK-friendly Charles Colson, using similar techniques, arrived at an estimate of 1,400,000—give or take one hundred thousand. Additional SITG statistics: 700 individual cable systems televised SITG and more than 280 radio stations broadcast SITG live. Rally equipment included 24 generators to power screens, speakers, and lights. 250,000 watts of sound covered the entire Mall. 4,200 registered chartered busses were counted, and 50,000 total volunteers served the event. 1,098 credentialed passes were issued to representatives of some 20 countries. 1,000,000 Bibles requiring 21 tractor trailers were delivered onsite (S. Chavis, personal communication, February 14, 2002). The event's title was inspired by a Scripture verse found in the Old Testament book of Ezekiel (22:30): "I looked for a man among them who would build up the wall and stand before me in the gap on behalf of the land so I would not have to destroy it, but I found none" (New International Version).
6. See D. Bebbington, "Evangelicanism in its Settings: The British and American Movements Since 1940."
7. See Hatch, *The Democratization of American Christianity.*
8. See Hatch, "Evangelicanism as a Democratic Movement."
9. See Hatch, *The Democratization of American Christianity.*
10. See S. Kessler, *Tocqueville's Civil Religion.*
11. Scholarly accounts of the advent, development, and diffusion of American evangelicalism are legion. For a useful online reference to some of the more important contributions, see Eskridge.

12. See M. Eidenmuller, "A Rhetoric of Religious Order: The Case of the Promise Keepers," and "Promise Keepers and the Rhetoric of Recruitment: The Context, the Persona, and the Spectacle." R. Stewart, "Identification and Invitation as Competing Rhetorics in the Promise Keepers Movement."

13. See J. Ireland, "A Look at . . . Promise Keepers: Beware of 'Feel-Good Male Supremacy.'" See A. Ross & L. Cokorinos, "Promise Keepers: A Real Challenge From the Right."

14. See Minkowitz, "In the Name of the Father."

15. D. Hagopian & D. Wilson, *Beyond Promises: A Biblical Challenge to the Promise Keepers*, p. 55. See A. Dager, "Beyond Promises: Is What You See What You Get?"

16. See M. Bobgan & D. Bobgan, *Promise Keepers and Psychoheresy.* G. Rugh, *The Rising Tide of Ecumenicalism.*

17. Clinton, cited in C. Bierbauer & J. Karl, "Promise Keepers' Rally 'Unapologetically Christian': CNN interactive," Sixth section, para. 3.

18. Balmer, "Keep the Faith and Go the Distance: Promise Keepers, Feminism, and the World of Sports," p. 1. Compare with Hart, *Campaign Talk*, p. 237.

19. Simons, cited in Hart, *The Political Pulpit*, pp. 2–3.

20. See Hart, "DICTION."

21. A thorough explanation of DICTION's assumptions and procedures is beyond the scope of this essay. Interested readers should consult Hart.

22. See Hart, "DICTION."

23. See Hart, "DICTION."

24. See Hart, "DICTION."

25. See Hart, "DICTION."

26. Hart, *Campaign Talk*, p. 78.

27. See Hart, "DICTION."

28. See Hart, "DICTION."

29. The dictionaries were provided to the researcher by Hart, and used previously in his studies of political discourse. The *religious* dictionary contained 201 individual words; the *irreligious* dictionary contained 105 words.

30. Hart, *The Political Pulpit*, pp. 102–103 (this edition, p. 88).

31. See Hart, "DICTION."

32. At best this measure provides a single indicator of a multi-dimensional construct and must be interpreted with due caution. Hart's measure of *optimism* is considerably more sophisticated, and includes the "subtractive" variables *blame, hardship,* and *denial.* Interested readers should consult Hart. Also, there is an unavoidable redundancy in using the word lists *satisfaction* and *inspiration* as measures of both sermonic discourse *and* verbal *optimism.* This interpretive problem is partially ameliorated in the recognition that the individual words found in these dictionaries vary widely in their denotative sense, between those that have religious and non-religious senses. In the final analysis, I redress this redundancy, for better or worse, under a rubric of "religious optimism."

33. Hart, *The Political Pulpit*, pp. 69–75 (this edition, pp. 63–68).

34. Hart used a similar procedure in constructing the Gods of civic piety, the data for which were U.S. President inaugural addresses.

35. The nine speeches delivered in Honolulu (January 10–11) and the nine delivered in New York (September 19–20) were not provided. Only one of the nine speeches delivered in Irving, Texas (October 24–25) was provided. Of the remaining transcripts, three contained little or no information and so were not used. The population of discourse at SITG included numerous speeches of varying length, prayers, and the lyrics of religious hymns. Concerning the transcription process, all PK discourse in 1997 was transcribed from start-to-finish, live-to-tape broadcasts. The actual transcribing was done by a single PK employee and checked independently by a second employee. Errors were corrected under joint agreement by both employees.

36. Italicized terms within PK discourse quotations refer to words specific to a given lexical dictionary in DICTION. Moreover, the various quotations cited in this essay are designed to *illustrate* how certain lexical variables contribute to the rhetorical tonalities of PK discourse, as well as to provide a textual point of reference by which to understand the specific rhetorical functions served by those tonalities. The problem of "representativeness" does not arise in the present analysis with any clear force because the quotations do not serve this logical function. Illustration is *not* (inductive) inference. Various contextual features germane to the quotations, obviously helpful in other kinds of rhetorical/textual analyses, have been left out on similar grounds. The technique, as Hart has described it, is analogous to the difference between aerial and close-quarter views of a neighborhood. DICTION provides the general structural patterns of a rhetorical area from on high. It is in view of the difficulty that arises in making textual-tonal sense of the word list abstractions (e.g., *present concern*) from such a vantage that a "zoom in" feature is used on occasion to provide momentary, demonstrative relief.

37. See Graham, "Delivered at Promise Keepers Conference, Legion Field, Birmingham, Alabama."

38. Hart, *Campaign Talk*, p. 19.

39. See Smalley, "Delivered at Promise Keepers Conference, Cinergy Field, Cincinatti, OH."

40. The use of masculine pronouns is meant to preserve the rhetorical construction of "God" vis-à-vis the ideological paradigm of evangelicalism.

41. Evidence of God-types is merely suggestive, as no comparative analysis in kind was performed on the discourse of PK stadium events.

42. See Stand in the Gap, "Delivered at Promise Keepers Rally on the Washington Mall." The identities of individual speakers at SITG were difficult to discern.

43. Hart, *The Political Pulpit*, p. 71 (this edition, pp. 64–65).

44. Hart, *The Political Pulpit*, pp. 70–71 (this edition, p. 64).

45. See Stand in the Gap, "Delivered at Promise Keepers Rally on the Washington Mall."

46. Hart, *The Political Pulpit*, pp. 71–72 (this edition, p. 65).

47. See Stand in the Gap, "Delivered at Promise Keepers Rally on the Washington Mall."

48. See Stand in the Gap, "Delivered at Promise Keepers Rally on the Washington Mall."

49. Hart, The Political Pulpit, p. 72 (this edition, pp. 65–66).

50. See Stand in the Gap, "Delivered at Promise Keepers Rally on the Washington Mall."

51. See Stand in the Gap, "Delivered at Promise Keepers Rally on the Washington Mall."

52. See Stand in the Gap, "Delivered at Promise Keepers Rally on the Washington Mall."

53. See Stand in the Gap, "Delivered at Promise Keepers Rally on the Washington Mall."

54. This essay was a adapted from a larger project that used additional measures of political and religious verbal style. The conclusions of this essay are consistent with the findings of the larger project. PK's discursive style bears more in common with the language of political campaigns than with religious sermons. Further analyses along these lines should consider lexical patterns and pattern deviations within and across PK events according to speech topic and speaker, among other situational features. More sophisticated statistical analyses might chart the relationships among language variables at different moments within any given speech and across different speeches. Longitudinal analyses examining differential patterns across time for a single movement (e.g., PK 1993–2002) and across different movements should further enrich our understanding of the stylistic episodes of evangelical movement discourse. Perhaps most importantly, future studies would do well to employ other or additional discourse classes (e.g., social movement, public policy, corporate advertising, military, Islamic and other religious movements) to further determine whether and to what extent evangelical Christian movement discourse may be distinguishable stylistically in any generic sense.

55. Tocqueville, *Democracy in America*, p. 281.

56. See Stand in the Gap, "Delivered at Promise Keepers rally on the Washington Mall."

57. See Carter, *God's Name in Vain: The Wrongs and Rights of Religion in Politics.*

58. Hart, *The Political Pulpit*, p. 64 (this edition, p. 58).

59. See K. Burke, *A Rhetoric of Motives.*

60. Hart, *The Political Pulpit,* pp. 46–47, 54 (this edition, pp. 45–46, 51).

Chapter 12

1. See Medhurst, "American Cosmology and the Rhetoric of Inaugural Prayer."

2. See Medhurst, "'God Bless the President': The Rhetoric of Inaugural Prayer."

3.   Hart, *The Political Pulpit,* pp. 43–44 (this edition, pp. 43–44).

4.   Sandel, "Freedom of Conscience or Freedom of Choice?" p. 78.

5.   Sandel, "Freedom of Conscience or Freedom of Choice?" p. 79.

6.   Hart, *The Political Pulpit*, p. 29 (this edition, p. 31).

7.   Conrad Cherry, *God's New Israel: Religious Interpretations of American Destiny,* pp. 1–109.

8.   See Sacvan Bercovitch, *The Puritan Jeremiad.*

9.   Ritter, "Reagan's 1964 TV Speech for Goldwater: Millennial Themes in American Political Rhetoric," pp. 58–72.

10.   James Hunter, Culture Wars: The Struggle to Define America, pp. 68–69.

11.   Herberg, *Protestant, Catholic, Jew: An Essay in American Religious Sociology*, pp. 74–89.

12.   Hunter, *Culture Wars: The Struggle to Define America*, pp. 67–132.

13.   See Ralph Reed, *Active Faith: How Christians Are Changing the Soul of American Politics.*

14.   See Michael Schudson, *The Good Citizen: A History of American Civic Life.*

15.   Medhurst, "Postponing the Social Agenda: Reagan's Strategy and Tactics," pp. 266–68.

16.   See Medhurst, "Postponing the Social Agenda: Reagan's Strategy and Tactics"; Hunter, *Culture Wars: The Struggle to Define America*, p. 105.

17.   Richard Berke, "Religion Center Stage in Presidential Race," p. 20.

18.   "Hannity and Colmes Post-Debate Special Coverage," p. 2.

19.   B. Robinson, "Religion and the U.S. Presidential Primaries in the Year 2000," p. 1.

20.   B. Robinson, "Religion and the U.S. Presidential Primaries in the Year 2000," p. 2.

21.   Berke, "Religion Center Stage in Presidential Race," p. 20.

22.   Gore, "Vote 2000: Al Gore," p. 79.

23.   Kevin Sack, "In a Texas Church, Gore Campaigns for Morality, Values and 'Prosperity of the Spirit'," p. 1.

24.   Kevin Sack, "In a Texas Church, Gore Campaigns for Morality, Values and 'Prosperity of the Spirit'," p. 1.

25.   Kevin Sack, "Gore Urges Votes of Black and Labor Base," p. 1.

26.   Ken Woodward, "Faith Is Busting Out All Over," p. 56.

27.   Ceci Connolly, "Taking the Spirit to the Stump: Leiberman Urges 'Place for Faith in Our Publc Life'," p. A01.

28.   Robinson, "Religion and the U.S. Presidential Primaries in the Year 2000," p. 5.

29.   Matthew Vita & Susan Schmidt, "The Interest Groups; Religious Right Mutes Voice, Not Efforts," p. A20.

30.   Jake Tapper, "Bush Makes a Final Push in Florida," p. 2.

31.   See Neuhaus, *The Naked Public Square: Religion and Democracy in America;*. Berger and Neuhaus, *To Empower People: The Role of Mediating Structure in Public Policy;* Novak, *The Spirit of Democratic Capitalism.*

32.   Neuhaus, *The Naked Public Square: Religion and Democracy in America*, p. 9.

33.   Berman, "Religious Freedom and the Challenge of the Modern State," p. 43.

34.   Charles Taylor, "Religion in a Free Society," p. 93.

35.   Neuhaus, *The Naked Public Square: Religion and Democracy in America*, pp. 86–87.

36.   Neuhaus, *The Naked Public Square: Religion and Democracy in America*, p. 84.

37.   Neuhaus, *The Naked Public Square: Religion and Democracy in America*, p. 84.

38.   Carter, *The Culture of Disbelief: How American Law and Politics Trivialize Religious Devotion*, pp. 230–31.

39.   See Carter, *Civility: Manners, Morals, and the Etiquette of Democracy,* pp. 230–31.

Chapter 13

1.   Quoted in Bellah, *The Broken Covenant,* p. 38.

2.   See Hart, *The Political Pulpit.*

3.   Bellah's original article appeared in *Daedelus*. After numerous attacks on his discussion of civil religion, Bellah published a vigorous defense in *Society*. This article was reprinted in Bellah's *The Broken Covenant.*

4.   In this regard, I would like to publicly thank Rod Hart for inspiring me to investigate the more sectarian, partisan, and ideological forms of civil religious discourse. Some ten years after his book appeared, I was able to identify a rhetoric of "public theology," which I argued was different from (and perhaps almost an inversion of) what Hart would call "official" civic piety. I defined public theology as "theologically-based discourse intentionally targeted for mass audiences in an attempt to influence the attitudes, beliefs, and values of both religious and secular publics on public policy" (p. 130). Overtly partisan in scope, I argued that public theology revealed three distinct rhetorical characteristics: expedient simplicity, existential content, and action rituals. I encountered these rhetorical characteristics in the "conservative" religious rhetoric of the Reverend Jerry Falwell and the "liberal" religious rhetoric of Archbishop Oscar Romero of El Salvador. This article would have been impossible without Hart's pioneering work. Any mistakes in my 1987 piece are uniquely my own.

5.   Hart, *The Political Pulpit*, p. 45 (this edition, p. 44).

6.   Hart, *The Political Pulpit*, pp. 43–44 (this edition, pp. 43–44).

7.   Hart, *The Political Pulpit*, p. 53 (this edition, p. 50).

8.   Hart, *The Political Pulpit*, p. 53 (this edition, p. 50).

9.   Hart, *The Political Pulpit*, p. 54 (this edition, p. 51).

10. Hart, *The Political Pulpit*, pp. 106–107 (this edition, pp. 90–91).

11. Pierard and Linder, *Civil Religion and the Presidency,* p. 19.

12. Pierard and Linder, *Civil Religion and the Presidency,* p. 25.

13. Pierard and Linder, *Civil Religion and the Presidency,* p. 25.

14. Qtd. in Pierard and Linder, *Civil Religion and the Presidency*, p. ix.

15. See Bush, "Inaugural Address."

16. See Bush, "President's Remarks at National Day of Prayer and Remembrance," National Cathedral, September 14, Washington, DC.

17. Pierard and Linder, *Civil Religion and the Presidency*, p. 28.

18. Qtd. In M. McConnell, "Believers as Equal Citizens," p. 96.

19. See, e.g., Cristi and L. Dawson, "Civil Religion in Comparative Perspective: Chile under Pinochet"; D. Regan, "Islam, Intellectuals, and Civil Religion in Malaysia"; E. Stevens, "Protest Movement in an Authoritarian Regime"; J. Zuo, "Political Religion: The Case of the Cultural Revolution in China."

20. See Sandel, *Democracy's Discontent: America in Search of a Public Philosophy.*

21. See Okin, "Review of Michael Sandel's *Democracy's Discontent: America in Search of a Public Philosophy.*"

22. Sandel, *Democracy's Discontent*, p. 12

23. Sandel, *Democracy's Discontent*, p. 6

24. Okin, "Review of Michael Sandel's *Democracy's Discontent*," p. 442.

25. Okin, "Review of Michael Sandel's *Democracy's Discontent*," p. 442.

26. See Herberg, *Protestant, Catholic, Jew: An Essay in American Religious Sociology.*

27. Cristi, *From Civil to Political Religion: The Intersection of Culture, Religion and Politics*, p. 70.

28. See Fenn, "Toward a New Sociology of Religion."

29. Cristi, *From Civil to Political Religion,* p. 75.

30. Cristi, *From Civil to Political Religion,* p. 75.

31. Thiemann, "Public Religion: Bane or Blessing for Democracy?" p. 83.

Chapter 14

1. Rousas Rushdoony, *The Foundations of Social Order: Studies in the Creeds and Councils of the Early Church,* p. 219.

2. Althusias, p. 27.

3. See Loffler, "Tiberius" in the *Catholic Encyclopedia,* vol. 14, as found at <http://www.newadvent.org/cathen/1417b.htm>.

4. Justin Martyr as found in Dale Sullivan's "Francis Scheaffer's Apparent Apology in Pollution and the Death of Man," p. 207.

5. Annales as quoted in Robert Wilken's *The Christians As the Romans Saw Them,* p. 49.

6. See Hart, *The Political Pulpit.*

7. This should not be mischaracterized as a disagreement between believers and nonbelievers. There are several self-defined "evangelical Christians" who are in hearty agreement with the American civic religion. Those in agreement

with the statist religion are enthused that the words "God" and "evil" are acknowledged in the public sphere but oppose policy decisions based upon Christian or theistic assumptions and oppose an acknowledgment of the Decalogue as
a legal, rather than merely religious, code.

8. Hart, *The Political Pulpit,* chapter 4 (this edition, chapter 5).

9. Hart, *The Political Pulpit,* p. 83 (this edition, p. 73).

10. Niebuhr, *Christ and Culture,* pp. 190–229.

11. Hart, *The Political Pulpit,* p. 21 (this edition, pp. 25–26).

12. See Douglas Kelly, *The Emergence of Liberty in the Modern World:
The Influence of Calvinism on Five Governments from the 16th Through 18th
Centuries;* and Abraham Kuyper, *Lectures on Calvinism.*

13. Tukey, "The Rhetorical Exigence of Covenant," p. 8.

14. George Mendenhall, *The Tenth Generation: The Origins of Biblical
Tradition,* p. 16.

15. See Meredith Kline, *Treaty of the Great King* and *By Oath Consigned;*
Gary Knoppers, "Ancient Near Eastern Royal Grants and the Davidic Cove-
nant: A Parallel?"; Dennis McCarthy, "Treaty and Covenant: A Study in Form in
the Ancient Oriental Documents and in the Old Testament"; George Mendenhall,
The Tenth Generation: The Origins of the Biblical Tradition; Ernest Nicholson,
God and His People: Covenant Theology in the Old Testament; Martin Noth,
The Laws in the Pentateuch; O. Robertson, *The Christ of the Covenants;* Geer-
hardus Vos, *Biblical Theology: Old and New Testaments;* and Andrea Weiss,
"Creative Readings of the Covenant: A Jewish-Christian Approach," among
many others.

16. Mark Noll describes this transition and equates it with anti-intellectualism
and an emphasis on individualism, revivalism, moral activism, populism, intuition,
and biblicism (especially chapters 3 and 6).

17. Gring, "Communication As Covenantal: Ritual, Ethical, and Interpersonal Dimensions," p. 5.

18. See Meredith Kline, *Treaty of the Great King* and *By Oath Con-
signed;* Dennis McCarthy, "Treaty and Covenant: A Study in Form in the
Ancient Oriental Documents and in the Old Testament"; George Mendenhall,
The Tenth Generation: The Origins of the Biblical Tradition; Ernest Nichol-
son, *God and his People: Covenant Theology in the Old Testament;* and O.
Robertson, *The Christ of the Covenants.*

19. O. Robertson, *The Christ of the Covenants,* pp. 5–6.

20. Ernest Nicholson, *God and His People: Covenant Theology in the
Old Testament,* p. 19.

21. Ernest Nicholson, *God and His People: Covenant Theology in the
Old Testament,* p. 33, emphasis added.

22. Arnett, "Interpersonal Praxis: The Interplay of Religious Narrative, Historicality, and Metaphor," p. 155.

23. See O. Robertson, *The Christ of the Covenants.* Eric Rothenbuhler,
*Ritual Communication: From Everyday Conversation to Mediated Cere-
mony.*

24. Mendenhall, *The Tenth Generation: The Origins of the Biblical
Tradition,* p. 14, n. 62.

25. Kline, *Treaty of the Great King,* p. 36.

26. Kuyper, p. 85. Others have misinterpreted the American Puritans' form of government as a theocracy but it was, in fact, a biblical federalism based on Calvin and his successors' arguments about the covenantal spheres.

27. See Rushdoony, *The Foundations of Social Order: Studies in the Creeds and Councils of the Early Church.*

28. Wilder, "The Covenantal Tradition in Political Theory: A Symposium," p. 5.

29. Here we see the emphasis of writers such as Heinrich Bullinger, Philippe Duplessis-Mornay, and Johannes Althusius (Samson, p. 29) and the influence of Calvinism on the governmental systems in Geneva, French Hugenots, England, Scotland, and the United States (Kelly). Especially influential in the United States at the time of the American Revolution was Samuel Rutherford's *Lex Rex.*

30. Rushdoony, *The Foundations of Social Order: Studies in the Creeds and Councils of the Early Church,* p. 124.

31. Calvin, *Institutes of the Christian Religion,* Book IV, chapter xx. See also R. Dabney, *The Practical Philosophy,* p. 395. Kuyper, *Lectures on Calvinism,* p. 78.

32. It is interesting to note that even the term "federal" denotes a covenantal understanding. Though the etymological argument is not conclusive in and of itself, the term "federal" is derived from the Latin term "foedus," which can be translated "covenant." In the Federalist Papers, especially No. 39, Madison takes great pains to argue that the proposed Constitution was a blend of the nationalist and federalist perspectives on government, pp. 240–246.

33. Wilder, "Federalism," p. 1.

34. Wilder, "Federalism," p. 2.

35. Eugene White, *Puritan Rhetoric: The Issue of Emotion in Religion,* p. 9.

36. John Murphy, "Comic Strategies and the American Covenant," p. 267.

37. Douglas Kelly, *The Emergence of Liberty in the Modern World: The Influence of Calvinism on Five Governments from the 16th through 18th Centuries,* pp. 54–55.

38. See Mark Noll, *The Scandal of the Evangelical Mind.*

39. Johannesen, "The Jeremiad and Lincoln Lloyd Jones," p. 160.

40. Murphy, "Comic Strategies and the American Covenant," p. 268.

41. David Carson, "A History of the Reformed Presbyterian Church in America to 1871," pp. 59–62.

42. W. Glasgow, *History of the Reformed Presbyterian Church in America,* p. 55.

43. David Carson, "A History of the Reformed Presbyterian Church in America to 1871," p. 63, emphasis in text.

44. RPCNA, "Testimony," section 16, p. A-80.

45. Hart, *The Political Pulpit,* p. 83 (this edition, p. 73).

46. See Noll, *The Scandal of the Evangelical Mind.*

47. Hart, *The Political Pulpit,* pp. 70–72 (this edition, pp. 64–66).

48. Hart, *The Political Pulpit,* p. 107 (this edition, p. 91).

49. "National Prayer Service," p. 24.

50. "National Prayer Service," p. 24.

51. "National Prayer Service," p. 24.

52. "National Prayer Service," p. 22.

53. See Niebuhr, *Christ and Culture,* especially chapter 6.

54. Roy Moore placed a monument of the Ten Commandments in the rotunda of the Alabama Supreme Court in August 2001 and was sued in 1995 by the ACLU for placing a plaque of the Ten Commandments on his courtroom wall while serving as an Alabama district court judge. (*Impact,* September 2001, p. 1.)

55. See Douglas Wilson, *Recovering the Lost Tools of Learning: An Approach to Distinctively Christian Education.*

56. See Olasky, *The Tragedy of American Compasion.*

57. See Olasky, *Compassionate Conservatism: What It Is, What It Does, and How It Can Transform America.*

58. See Olasky, *Prodigal Press: The Anti-Christian Bias of American News Media* and *Telling the Truth: How to Revitalize Christian Journalism.*

59. Dabney, *The Practical Philosophy,* p. 394.

References

Chapter 7

Barton, M. H. "Confession, Contrition, and Forgiveness: The Intersection of Religion and Politics in Bill Clinton's Explanation of the Monica Lewinsky Affair." Ph.D. diss., University of Nebraska, Lincoln, 2002.

Bellah, R. N. "Civil Religion in America." *Daedalus* 96 (1967): 1–21.

Bennett, J. "Testing of a President: Tearful Clinton Tells Group of Clerics, 'I Have Sinned.'" *New York Times*, Sept. 12, 1998, p. A1.

Burke, K. "Ideology and Myth." *Accent* 7 (1947): 195–205.

Bush, G. W. "Duty of Hope: Armies of Compassion." In *Renewing America's Purpose: Policy Addresses of George W. Bush July 1999, July 2000* (pp. 110–118) Washington, DC: Republic National Committee, 2000.

Bush, G. W. "Inaugural Address." *Weekly Compilation of Presidential Documents* 37 (2001) 209–211.

Clinton, W. J. "Remarks at a Breakfast with Religious Leaders, September 11, 1998." *Public Papers of the President of the United States, 1998* (vol. 2, pp. 1565–1566). Washington, DC: U.S. Government Printing Office, 2000.

Coontz, S. *The Way We Never Were: American Families and the Nostalgia Trap.* New York: Basic Books, 1992.

Fackre, G. "Of Hope and Judgment." In *Bicentennial Broadside.* New York: United Church Board for Homeland Ministries, 1975.

Goodstein, L. "Guidepost from Country's Pulpits: The Power to Judge Belongs to God." *New York Times*, Sept. 14, 1998, p. A25.

Hart, R. P. *The Political Pulpit.* West Lafayette, IN: Purdue University Press, 1977.

King, M. L., Jr. *Why We Can't Wait.* New York: Harper and Row, 1964.

Lee, R. "The Rhetorical Construction of Time in Martin Luther King, Jr.'s 'Letter from Birmingham Jail.'" *Southern Communication Journal* 56 (1991): 279–288.

Lee, R., and M. H. Barton. "Clinton's Rhetoric of Contrition." In R. E. Denton (ed.), *The Clinton Presidency: Images, Issues, and Communication Strategies*. Westport, CT: Praeger, 1996.

Lee, R., and L. O. Murfield. "Christian Tradition, Jeffersonian Democracy, and the Myth of the Sentimental Family: An Exploration of the Premises of Social-Conservative Argumentation." In S. Jackson (ed.), *Argumentation and Values* (pp. 36–42). Annadale, VA: Speech Communication Association, 1995.

Lee, R., and R. Patterson. "The Genealogy of Social Conservative Argumentation: Demonstrating the Family Resemblance among Three Influential Discourses." In G. T. Goodnight (ed.), *Arguing Communication and Culture* (vol. 2, pp. 487–495). Washington, DC: National Communication Association, 2002.

Lewis, R., and R. Campbell. *Real Family Values: Keeping Faith in an Age of Cultural Chaos*. Gresham, OR: Vision House, 1995.

McGee, M. C. "In Search of 'The People': A Rhetorical Alternative." *Quarterly Journal of Speech* 61 (1975): 235–249.

Murfield, L. O. "The Rhetorical Renegotiation of the 'Family': From the New Christian Right to the 1992 Presidential Campaign." Ph.D. diss., University of Nebraska, Lincoln, 1994.

Niebuhr, G. "Testing of a President: The Religious Issues; King David Inspires Plea for Pardon." *New York Times*, Sept. 12, 1998, p. A12.

Olasky, M. N. *The Tragedy of American Compassion*. Wheaton, IL: Crossway, 1992.

———. *Compassionate Conservatism: What It Is, What It Does, and How It Can Transform America*. New York: Free Press, 2000.

Pangle, T. L. *The Spirit of Modern Republicanism: The Moral Vision of the American Founders and the Philosophy of John Locke*. Chicago: University of Chicago Press, 1988.

Pierard, R. V., and R. D. Linder. *Civil Religion and the Presidency*. Grand Rapids, MI: Academie Books, 1988.

Quayle, D. "Prepared Remarks by the Vice President." Presented to the Commonwealth Club of California, San Francisco, CA, May 19, 1992.

———. "Cultural Elites Speech." Presented to the Southern Baptists' Convention, Indianapolis, IN, June 9, 1992.

Rapaczynski, A. *Nature and Politics: Liberalism in the Philosophies of Hobbes, Locke, and Rousseau*. Ithaca, NY: Cornell University Press, 1987.

Roelofs, H. M. *Ideology and Myth in American Politics: A Critique of a National Political Mind*. Boston: Little, Brown, 1976.

Swindoll, C. R. *Strong Family: Growing Wise in Family Life*. Portland, OR: Multnomah, 1991.

White, H. *Tropics of Discourse: Essays in Cultural Criticism*. Baltimore: Johns Hopkins University Press, 1978.

Chapter 8

Bellah, R. "Civil Religion in America." *Daedalus* 96 (1967): 1–21.

Eisenhower, D. "The Day I Knew I Belonged to the Flag." *Reader's Digest* 94 (March 1969): 91–94.

Girard, R. *Violence and the Sacred.* Trans. P. Gregory. Baltimore: Johns Hopkins University Press, 1977.

Hart, R. P. *The Political Pulpit.* West Lafayette, IN: Purdue University Press, 1977.

Marvin, C., and D. Ingle. *Blood Sacrifice and the Nation.* Cambridge: Cambridge University Press, 1999.

Marvin, C. (1994). "The Body of the Text: Literacy's Corporeal Constant." *Quarterly Journal of Speech*, 80, 129–149.

Minersville School District v. Board of Education, 310 U.S. 586 (1940).

"Terrorist Attacks on the United States," Congressional Record, vol. 147 (2001), p.S9303.

Texas v. Johnson, 491 U.S. 397 (1989).

United States v. Eichmann, 496 U.S. 310 (1990).

West Virginia State Board of Education v. Barnette, 319 U.S. 624 (1943).

Chapter 9

Bellah, Robert N. "Civil Religion in America." *Daedalus* 96: 1–21.

Bush, George W. "The Commitment of Our Fathers Is Now the Calling of Our Time." Address at the National Cathedral. September 14, 2001. <http:/www.georgewbush.com/newsroom/releases/September01presidentBushremarks 091401.htm>.

———. "Remarks at the Islamic Center of Washington," September 17, 2001. <http:frwebgate.access.gpo.gov/cgi../getdoc.cgi?dbname=2001-presidential-documents&docid=pd24se01-txt11/05/2001>.

———. "Acceptance Address to the 2000 Republic National Convention." <http://www.3.cnn.com/ELECTION/2000 Conventions/republican/transcripts/bush.html>.

Eckstrom, Kevin. "Poll: Religion Increasing in American Public Life." <http://pewforum.org/news/index.php3?NewsID=887>.

Feldstein, Stanley. *The Land That I Show You: Three Centuries of Jewish Life in America.* New York: Anchor Press, 1978.

Friedenberg, Robert. *Theodore Roosevelt and the Rhetoric of Militant Decency.* Westport, CT: Greenwood Press, 1990.

Gore, Albert, "Acceptance Address to the 2000 Democratic National Convention." <http://www3.cnn.com/ELECTION/2000Conventions/democratic/transcripts/gore.html>.

Harlow, Jules. ed. *Siddur Sim Shalom: A Prayer Book for Shabbat, Festivals, and Weekdays.* New York: United Synagogue of Conservative Judaism, 1985.

Hart, Roderick P. *The Political Pulpit*. West Lafayette, IN: Purdue University Press, 1977.

Loconte, Joseph. "Government and Religion: Have Faith." <http://www.heritage.org/views2001/ed01310b.html>.

Marcus, Jacob. *The Colonial American Jew 1492–1776*. Vol. 2. Detroit, MI: Wayne State University Press, 1970.

Nettles, Curtis P. *The Roots of American Civilization: A History of American Colonial Life*. New York: Appleton-Century-Crofts, 1963.

Seixas, Gershom. "Religious Discourse – Thursday 26 of November, 1789." New York, NY: Archibald McClean, 1789. Photocopy of original, Seixas Manuscript Collection, American Jewish Archives, Cincinnati, Ohio, Box 1. Original in the Lyons Collection, American Jewish Historical Society, New York, NY.

Chapter 10

Bellah, R. N. "Religion and Legitimation in the American Republic." *Society* 35 (1998): 193–201.

———. "Civil Religion in America." *Daedalus* 117 (1998): 97–118.

Campbell, K. K., and Burkholder, T. R. *Critiques of Contemporary Rhetoric*. 2nd ed. Belmont, CA: Wadsworth Publishing Company, 1997.

Clinton, W. J. "Nominee Clinton Describes Vision of 'New Covenant'." *Congressional Quarterly Weekly Report,* 18 July 1992, 2128–2130.

———. "Remarks by the President at Religious Leaders Breakfast. http://clinton5.nara.gov/textonly/WH/New/html/19980911-3640.html>

Fisher, W. R. "Rhetorical Fiction and the Presidency." *Quarterly Journal of Speech* 66 (1980): 119–126.

Hart, R. P. *The Political Pulpit*. West Lafayette, IN: Purdue University Press, 1977.

Japp, P. M. "Esther or Isaiah?: The Abolitionist-Feminist Rhetoric of Angelina Grimké." *Quarterly Journal of Speech* 71 (1985): 335–348.

Kennedy, G. A. *Aristotle On Rhetoric: A Theory of Civic Discourse*. New York: Oxford University Press, 1991.

Miga, A. "Web of Deceit; Report Alleges Lies, Obstruction by Clinton; Starr's Report Could Be Made Public Today." *The Boston Herald,* 11 September 1998, p. 1.

Morse, J. "Going Public with Prayer." *Time,* 28 September 1998, vol. 152, no. 13.

Murphy, J. M. "Inventing Authority: Bill Clinton, Martin Luther King, Jr., and the Orchestration of Rhetorical Tradition." *Quarterly Journal of Speech* 83 (1997): 71–89.

Novak, M. *Choosing Our King: Powerful Symbols in American Politics*. New York: Macmillan, 1974.

Page, S. "Clinton's 'Final Campaign': Survival through Contrition." *USA Today,* 11 September 1998, p. 1A.

Public Papers of the Presidents of the United States: William J. Clinton. 1999. Washington D.C: Government Printing Office, 2000. Vol. 2.

Reusse, P. "It's High Time for More Mea Culpas." *Star Tribune* (Minneapolis, MN), 12 September 1998, 1C.

Rosin, H. "Clinton Faces Test at Annual Prayer Breakfast Today." *The Washington Post,* 11 September 1998: A34.

Van der Silk, J. R., and S. J. Schwark. "Clinton and the New Covenant: Theology Shaping New Politics or Old Politics in Religious Garb?" *Journal of Church & State* 40 (1998): 873–890.

Chapter 11

Balmer, R. Keep the Faith and Go the Distance: Promise Keepers, Feminism, and the World of Sports. In D. S. Claussen (ed.), *The Promise Keepers: Essays on Masculinity and Christianity* (pp. 194–203). Jefferson, NC: McFarland & Company, Inc., 2000.

Bebbington, D. "Evangelicalism in Its Settings: The British and American Movements Since 1940." In Mark A. Noll, David W. Bebbington, & George A. Rawlyk (eds.), *Evangelicalism* (pp. 365–388). New York: Oxford University Press, 1994.

Bierbauer, C., and J. Karl (1997). "Promise Keepers' Rally 'Unapologetically Christian.'" CNN Interactive. <http://www.cnn.com/US/9710/04/promise. keepers/#clinton>

Bobgan, M., and D. Bobgan. *Promise Keepers & Psychoheresy.* Santa Barbara, CA: Psychoheresy Awareness Ministries, 1994.

Burke, K. *A Rhetoric of Motives.* Berkeley, CA: University of California Press, 1969.

Carter, S. L. *God's Name in Vain: The Wrongs and Rights of Religion in Politics.* New York: Basic Books, 2000.

Clinton, W. J. President's Weekly Radio Address to the Nation [Radio Broadcast], 4 October 1997.

Dager, A. J. Promise Keepers: Is What You See What You Get? *Media Spotlight* (pp. 1–24). Redmond, WA: Media Spotlight, July 1995.

Eidenmuller, M. E. "A Rhetoric of Religious Order: The Case of the Promise Keepers." PhD diss., Louisiana State University, 1998. *Dissertation Abstracts International,* 59, 0107.

———. "Promise Keepers and the Rhetoric of Recruitment: The Context, the Persona, and the Spectacle." In D. S. Claussen (ed.), *The Promise Keepers: Essays on Masculinity and Christianity* (pp. 91–101). Jefferson, NC: McFarland & Company, Inc., 2000.

Eskridge, L. (2001). Further Reading and Research on Evangelicalism. Institute for the Study of American Evangelicalism. <http://www.wheaton. edu/isae/further_reading.html>

Graham, F. (May 30, 1997). Delivered at Promise Keepers Conference, Legion Field, Birmingham, Alabama. [Speech].

Hagopian, D., and D. Wilson. *Beyond Promises: A Biblical Challenge to the Promise Keepers.* Moscow, ID: Canon Press, 1996.

Hart, R. P. *The Political Pulpit.* West Lafayette, IN: Purdue University Press, 1977.

————. DICTION (Version 5.0). [Computer software]. Thousand Oaks, CA: Sage Press, 1999.

————. DICTION (Version 5.0). [Manual]. Thousand Oaks, CA: Sage Press, 1999.

————. *Campaign Talk.* Princeton, NJ: Princeton University Press, 2000.

————. Redeveloping DICTION: Theoretical considerations. In. M. West (ed.), *Theory, Method, and Practice of Computer Content Analysis* (pp. 43–60). New York: Ablex, 2001.

Hatch, N.O. "Evangelicalism as a Democratic Movement." In G. E. Marsden (ed.), *Evangelicalism and Modern America* (pp. 71–82). New Haven, CT: Yale University Press, 1984.

————. *The Democratization of American Christianity.* New Haven, CT: Yale University Press, 1989.

Ireland, J. "A Look at . . . Promise Keepers: Beware of 'Feel-Good Male Supremacy.'" *The Washington Post*, 7 Sept. 1997, p. C03.

Kessler, S. *Tocqueville's Civil Religion.* Albany, NY: State University of New York Press, 1994.

Koch, K.., and J. Karl, (4 October, 1997). Promise Keepers Fill Washington's Mall with Prayer. CNN Interactive. <http://www.cnn.com/US/9710/04/promise.keepers.pm/>.

Mattingly, T. (25 February, 1998). What's Next for the Promise Keepers? Gospel Communications Network. <http://www.gospelcom.net/tmattingly/col.02.25.98.html>.

Minkowitz, D. "In the Name of the Father." *Ms*, November–December 1995, 64–71.

Morrison, G. Delivered at Promise Keepers Conference, Rich Stadium, Buffalo, New York, 14 June 1997. [Speech].

Numbers for the Promise Keepers Rally Revised. *The Washington Post*, 15 October 1997, p. B03.

Ross, A., & Cokorinos, L. Promise Keepers: A Real Challenge From the Right. National NOW Times, May 1997. <http://www.now.org/nnt/05-97/pk.html>

Rugh, G. (Speaker). *The Rising Tide of Ecumenicalism* [Cassette Recording No. GRM 410]. Lincoln, NE: Sound Words, 1994.

Smalley, G. Delivered at Promise Keepers conference, Cinergy Field, Cincinnati, OH, 10 May 1997. [Speech].

Stand in the Gap. Delivered at Promise Keepers Rally on the Washington Mall, 4 October 1997. [Speeches].

Stewart, R. A. Identification and Invitation as Competing Rhetorics in the Promise Keepers Movement. In D. S. Claussen (ed.), *The Promise Keepers: Essays on Masculinity and Christianity* (pp. 102–112*)*. Jefferson, NC: McFarland & Company, Inc, 2000.

Stodghill, R. God of our Fathers. *Time,* 6 October 1997, 150, 34–40.

Tocqueville, A. de. *Democracy in America.* New York: Alfred A. Knopf, Inc., 1966.

———. *Democracy in America.* Chicago: University of Chicago Press, 2000.

Wheeler, L. Unofficial Estimates Point to Crowded Day on the Mall. *The Washington Post*, 5 October 1997, p. A17.

Chapter 12

Bercovitch, Sacvan. *The Puritan Jeremiad.* Madison: University of Wisconsin Press, 1975.

Berger, Peter L., and Richard John Neuhaus. *To Empower People: The Role of Mediating Structures in Public Policy.* Washington, D.C.: American Enterprise Institute for Public Policy Research, 1977.

Berke, Richard L. "Religion Center Stage in Presidential Race."*New York Times*, 15 December 1999, section A, 20.

Berman, Harold J. "Religious Freedom and the Challenge of the Modern State."*Articles of Faith, Articles of Peace: The Religious Liberty Clauses and the American Public Philosophy.* Ed. James Davison Hunter and Os Guiness. Washington, D.C.: The Brookings Institution, 1990, 40–53.

Carter, Stephen L. *Civility: Manners, Morals, and the Etiquette of Democracy.* New York: BasicBooks, 1998.

———. *The Culture of Disbelief: How American Law and Politics Trivialize Religious Devotion.* New York: BasicBooks, 1993.

Cherry, Conrad, ed. *God's New Israel: Religious Interpretations of American Destiny.* Englewood Cliffs: Prentice-Hall, 1971.

Connolly, Ceci. "Taking the Spirit to the Stump: Lieberman Urges 'Place for Faith in Our Public Life'." *Washington Post*, 28 August 2000, p. A01.

Gore, Al. "Vote 2000: Al Gore."*Catholic Digest* (November 2000): 70–79.

"Hannity and Colmes Post-Debate Special Coverage." 13 December 13 1999. <http://www.keyes2000.org/issues_and_speeches/transcripts/han_colmes_p ost_debates.html>.

Hart, Roderick P. *The Political Pulpit.* West Lafayette: Purdue UP, 1977.

Herberg, Will. *Protestant-Catholic-Jew: An Essay in American Religious Sociology.* Garden City: Doubleday, 1955.

Hunter, James Davison. *Culture Wars: The Struggle to Define America.* New York: BasicBooks, 1991.

Hunter, James Davison, and Os Guiness, eds., *Articles of Faith, Articles of Peace: The Religious Liberty Clauses and the American Public Philosophy* (Washington, D.C.: Brookings Institution, 1990).

Medhurst, Martin J. "American Cosmology and the Rhetoric of Inaugural Prayer." *Central States Speech Journal* 28 (1977): 272–82.

————. "'God Bless the President': The Rhetoric of Inaugural Prayer." Ph.D. diss., Pennsylvania State University, 1980.

————. "Postponing the Social Agenda: Reagan's Strategy and Tactics." *Western Journal of Speech Communication* 48 (1984): 262–276.

Neuhaus, Richard John. *The Naked Public Square: Religion and Democracy in America.* Grand Rapids: William. B. Eerdmans, 1984.

Novak, Michael. *The Spirit of Democratic Capitalism.* New York: Simon and Schuster, 1982.

Reed, Ralph. *Active Faith: How Christians Are Changing the Soul of American Politics.* New York: Free Press, 1996.

Ritter, Kurt. "Reagan's 1964 TV Speech for Goldwater: Millennial Themes in American Political Rhetoric." *Rhetorical Dimensions in Media: A Critical Casebook*, 2nd ed. Ed. Martin J. Medhurst and Thomas W. Benson. Dubuque: Kendall/Hunt, 1991, pp. 58–72.

Robinson, B.A. "Religion and the U.S. Presidential Primaries in the Year 2000." ReligiousTolerance.org <http://www.religioustolerance.org/poli_rel. htm>.

Sack, Kevin. "In a Texas Church, Gore Campaigns for Morality, Values and 'Prosperity of the Spirit.'" *New York Times*, 23 October 232000. <http://www. nytimes.com/2000/10/23/politics/23GORE.html>.

————. "Gore Urges Votes of Black and Labor Base." *New York Times.* November 5, 2000. <http://www.nytimes.com/2000/11/05/politics/05GORE.html>.

Sandel, Michael J. "Freedom of Conscience or Freedom of Choice?"*Articles of Faith, Articles of Peace: The Religious Liberty Clauses and the American Public Philosophy.* Ed. James Davison. Hunter and Os Guiness. Washington, DC.: The Brookings Institution, 1990, pp. 74–92.

Schudson, Michael. *The Good Citizen: A History of American Civic Life.* New York: Free Press, 1998.

Tapper, Jake. "Bush Makes a Final Push in Florida." Salon.com. http://www. salon.com/politics/feature/2000/11/05/florida/.

Taylor, Charles. "Religion in a Free Society."*Articles of Faith, Articles of Peace: The Religious Liberty Clauses and the American Public Philosophy.* Ed. James Davison Hunter and Os Guiness. Washington, D.C.: The Brookings Institution, 1990, 93–113.

Vita, Matthew and Susan Schmidt. "The Interest Groups; Religious Right Mutes Voice, Not Efforts." *Washington Post.* November 2, 2000, p. A20.

Woodward, Ken. "Faith Is Busting Out All Over."*Newsweek*, 11 September 2000, 56.

Chapter 13

Bellah, R. N. "Civil Religion in America." *Daedelus: Journal of the American Academy of Arts and Sciences* 96 (1967): 1–21.

———. "Religion and Legitimation in the American Republic." *Society* 15/4 (1978): 16–23.

———. *The Broken Covenant: American Civil Religion in Times of Trial.* 2nd ed. Chicago: University of Chicago Press, 1992.

———. Inaugural Address. 20 January 20 2001 Washington, D.C. Cited at <http://www.whitehouse.gov/news/print/inaugural-address.html>.

———. President's Remarks at National Day of Prayer and Remembrance, National Cathedral, 14 September 14 2001, Washington, DC. Cited at <http://www.whitehouse.gov/news/releases/20010914-2.html>.

Cristi, M. *From Civil to Political Religion: The Intersection of Culture, Religion and Politics.* Waterloo, Ontario: Wilfred Laurier University Press, 2001.

Cristi, M., and L. Dawson. "Civil Religion in Comparative Perspective: Chile under Pinochet (1973–1989)." *Social Compass* 43/3 (1996): 319–338.

Fenn, R. K. "Toward a New Sociology of Religion." *Journal for the Scientific Study of Religion* 11 (1972): 16–32.

Goldzwig, S. "A Rhetoric of Public Theology: The Religious Rhetor and Public Policy." *Southern Speech Communication Journal* 52 (1987): 128–150.

Hart, R. P. *The Political Pulpit.* West Lafayette, IN: Purdue University Press, 1977.

Herberg, W. *Protestant-Catholic-Jew: An Essay in American Religious Sociology.* New York: Doubleday, 1955.

McConnell, M. W. "Believers as Equal Citizens." In Nancy L. Rosenblum (ed.), *Obligations of Citizenship and Demands of Faith: Religious Accommodation in Pluralist Democracies* (pp. 90–110). Princeton, NJ: Princeton University Press, 2000.

Okin, S. Review of Michael Sandel's *Democracy's Discontent: America in Search of a Public Philosophy. American Political Science Review* 91/2 (1997): 441–442.

Pierard, R. V., & R. D. Linder. *Civil Religion & the Presidency.* Grand Rapids: MI: Academie Books, 1988.

Regan, D. "Islam, Intellectuals, and Civil Religion in Malaysia." *Sociological Analysis* 37/2 (1976): 95–110.

Sandel, M. *Democracy's Discontent: America in Search of a Public Philosophy.* Cambridge, MA: Harvard University Press, 1996.

Stevens, E. P. "Protest Movement in an Authoritarian Regime." *Comparative Politics* 7/3 (1975): 361–382.

Theimann, R. F. "Public Religion: Bane or Blessing for Democracy?" In N. L. Rosenblum (ed.), *Obligations of Citizenship and Demands of Faith:*

Religious Accommodation in Pluralist Democracies (pp. 73–89). Princeton, NJ: Princeton University Press, 2000.

Zuo, J. "Political Religion: The Case of the Cultural Revolution in China." *Sociological Analysis* 52/1 (1991): 99–110.

Chapter 14

Arnett, Ronald C. "Interpersonal Praxis: The Interplay of Religious Narrative, Historicality, and Metaphor." *Journal of Communication and Religion* 21.2 (1998): 141–63.

Calvin, John. *Institutes of the Christian Religion.* Translated by Henry Beveridge. Grand Rapids, MI: William B. Eerdmans Publishing Co., 1989.

Carson, David Melville. "A History of the Reformed Presbyterian Church in America to 1871." A Dissertation in History. University of Pennsylvania, 1964.

Dabney, R. L. *The Practical Philosophy. Being the Philosophy of the Feelings, of the Will, and of the Conscience, With the Ascertainment of Particular Rights and Duties.* Harrisonburg, VA: Sprinkle Publications, 1897/1984.

Glasgow, W. Melncthon. *History of the Reformed Presbyterian Church in America.* Baltimore: Hill & Harvey Publishers, 1888.

Gring, Mark A. "Communication As Covenantal: Ritual, Ethical, and Interpersonal Dimensions." Chicago, IL: Unpublished manuscript presented at the National Communication Association's annual convention, November, 1999.

Hart, Roderick P. *The Political Pulpit.* West Lafayette, IN: Purdue University Press, 1977.

Johannesen, R. "The Jeremiad and Jenkin Lloyd Jones." *Communication Monographs* 52. (1985): 156–172.

Jones, Archie P. "Christianity, Our Early State Constitutions, and American Federalism." *Contra Mundum* 10. Winter (1994): 39–47.

Kelly, Douglas F. *The Emergence of Liberty in the Modern World: The Influence of Calvinism on Five Governments From the 16th Through 18th Centuries.* Phillipsburg, NY: Presbyterian & Reformed Publishing, 1992.

Kline, Meredith G. *Treaty of the Great King.* Grand Rapids, MI: William B. Erdmans Publishing Company, 1963.

———. *By Oath Consigned.* Grand Rapids, MI: William B. Eerdmans Publishing Company, 1968.

Knoppers, Gary N. "Ancient Near Eastern Royal Grants and the Davidic Covenant: A Parallel?" *Journal of the American Oriental Society.* 116 .4 (October) (1996): 670–97.

Kuyper, Abraham. *Lectures on Calvinism.* Grand Rapids, MI: Wm. B. Eerdmans Publishing Company, 1898–1931.

Loffler, Klemens, "Tiberius." *The Catholic Encyclopedia*, Vol. XIV. 1912–1999. <http://www.newadvent.org/cathen/1417b.htm>. February 2002.

Madison, James. "No 39: Madison." *The Federalist Papers.* Alexander Hamilton, James Madison, and John Jay. New York: Mentor—Published by Penguin Books, 1961. 240–46.

McCarthy, Dennis J. S. J. *Treaty and Covenant: A Study in Form in the Ancient Oriental Documents and in the Old Testament.* Rome: Pontifical Biblical Institute, 1963.

Mendenhall, George E. *The Tenth Generation: The Origins of the Biblical Tradition.* Baltimore, MD: The Johns Hopkins University Press, 1974.

"Moore Puts God's Law in Alabama Supreme Court." *Impact.* Vol. 13. Fort Lauderdale, FL: Coral Ridge Ministries Media, Inc., 2001. 1 & 4.

Murphy, John M. "Comic Strategies and the American Covenant." *Communication Studies* 40.4 (1989): 266–79.

"National Prayer Service: Order of Worship." *Credenda/Agenda.*Vol. 13. Moscow, ID: Christ Church, 2001. 22–25.

Nicholson, Ernest W. *God and His People: Covenant Theology in the Old Testament.* New York: Oxford University Press, 1986. Reprint: Reissued in paperback (1988).

Niebuhr, H. Richard. *Christ and Culture.* New York: Harper Torchbooks, 1951.

Noll, Mark A. *The Scandal of the Evangelical Mind.* Grand Rapids, MI: William B. Eerdmans Publishing Company, 1994.

Olasky, Marvin. *Compassionate Conservatism: What It Is, What It Does, and How It Can Transform America.* New York: The Free Press, 2000.

——. *Telling the Truth: How to Revitalize Christian Journalism.* Wheaton, IL: Crossway Books, 1996.

——. *The Tragedy of American Compassion.* Washington, D.C.: Regnery Gateway, 1992.

——. *Prodigal Press: The Anti-Christian Bias of American News Media.* Wheaton, IL: Crossway Books, 1988.

Robertson, O. Palmer. *The Christ of the Covenants.* Phillipsburg, NJ: Presbyterian and Reformed Publishing Co., 1980.

Rothenbuhler, Eric W. *Ritual Communication: From Everyday Conversation to Mediated Ceremony.* Thousand Oaks, CA: Sage Publications, 1998.

Rushdoony, Rousas John. *The Foundations of Social Order: Studies in the Creeds and Councils of the Early Church.* Fairfax, VA: Thoburn Press, 1968.

——. *The One and the Many: Studies in the Philosophy of Order and Ultimacy.* Fairfax, VA: Thoburn Press, 1978.

Samson, Steven Alan. "The Covenant Origins of the American Polity." *Contra Mundum* 10.Winter (1994): 26–38.

Stokes, Anson Phelps. *Church and State in the United States.* New York: Harpers, 1950.

Sullivan, Dale L. "Francis Scheaffer's Apparent Apology in Pollution and the Death of Man." *Journal of Communication and Religion* 21.2 (September) (1998): 200–29.

Tertullian, Trans. by the Reverend S. Thelwall. *Apology.* <http://www.newadvent. org/fathers/0301.htm>. February 2002.

Tukey, David D. "The Rhetorical Exigence of Covenant." *Journal of Communication and Religion* 19.2 (September) (1996): 5–27.

Vos, Geerhardus. *Biblical Theology: Old and New Testaments.* Carlisle, PA: Banner of Truth Trust, 1948.

White, Eugene E. *Puritan Rhetoric: The Issue of Emotion in Religion.* Carbondale, IL: Southern Illinois University Press, 1972.

Wilder, T. E. "The Covenantal Tradition in Political Theory: A Symposium." *Contra Mundum* 10.Winter (1994): 2–14.

———. "Federalism." *Contra Mundum* 10.Winter (1994): 1.

Wilken, Robert L. *The Christians As the Romans Saw Them.* New Haven: Yale University Press, 1984.

Wilson, Douglas. *Recovering the Lost Tools of Learning: An Approach to Distinctively Christian Education.* Turning Point Christian Worldview Series, Marvin Olasky, General Editor. Wheaton, IL: Crossway Books, 1991.

Index